The First World War
in Irish Poetry

The First World War
in Irish Poetry

Jim Haughey

Lewisburg
Bucknell University Press
London: Associated University Presses

Associated University Presses
440 Forsgate Drive
Cranbury, NJ 08512

Associated University Presses
16 Barter Street
London WC1A 2AH, England

Associated University Presses
P.O. Box 338, Port Credit
Mississauga, Ontario
Canada L5G 4L8

The paper used in this publication meets the requirements
of the American National Standard for Permanence
of Paper for Printed Library Materials Z39.48-1984.

Library of Congress Cataloging-in-Publication Data

Haughey, Jim, 1960–
    The First World War in Irish poetry / Jim Haughey.
        p. cm.
    Includes bibliographical references and index.
    ISBN 0-8387-5496-1 (alk. paper)
    1. English poetry—Irish authors—History and criticism.
2. World War, 1914–1918—Ireland—Literature and
the war.   3. English poetry—20th century—History
and criticism.   4. War poetry, English—History
and criticism.   5. Ireland—In literature.   I. Title.
PR8781.W68 H38 2002
821'.91209358—dc21   2001043737

PRINTED IN THE UNITED STATES OF AMERICA

In memory of my great-grandfather
Rifleman David McGrann MM
9th Battalion Royal Irish Fusiliers
killed at Ypres, 16 August 1917

Contents

Acknowledgments

Without the help of quite a number of people this book would never have been finished. Let me begin by thanking Patrick Scott of the University of South Carolina whose insights on the war and wealth of knowledge about putting a book together were indispensable. I would also like to thank my dissertation committee, Ed Madden, Ashley Brown, Jeremiah Hackett, and Thomas J. Rice, for reading the first semi-intelligible draft of the manuscript and the anonymous reader for Bucknell University Press whose cogent comments were extremely helpful. A debt is owed to Susan Schreibman of University College Dublin, who graciously responded to my naïve inquiries concerning the life and work of Thomas MacGreevy, and Patrick Quinn of University College Northampton who made suggestions about where to look for materials on some of the more minor war poets.

On the other side of the *shugh*, I am indebted to the reference staff at the Linen Hall Library, Belfast, Queen's University, the National Library of Ireland, and Trinity College, who graciously responded to my requests and suggested alternative routes through the research labyrinth. Special thanks also go to Amanda Moreno, curator of the Royal Irish Fusiliers Regimental Museum in Armagh, for permission to use photographs and materials from the regimental archive, while fellow Lurgan men Dr. Frank McCorry and Kieran Clendinning provided a wealth of local materials about the Great War. Kieran deserves special acknowledgment for sharing with me his research and knowledge of the ordinary Irish soldier.

Other debts are owed to the reference librarians at Southern Wesleyan University and Anderson College who helped procure almost all of my interlibrary loan requests and to my former colleagues at Southern Wesleyan University who generously provided funding for travel expenses. A special thanks goes to Chris

Retz at Associated University Presses for her expert guidance through the editing process.

While I was at "home," my sisters Nuala, Sinéad, and Carol served as chauffeurs and tour guides and certainly enlivened an otherwise uneventful round of note taking and docket signing on the library and museum circuit. I also want to thank my parents and parents-in-law for their love and support, and, most importantly, my wife Laurie and children, Sinéad and Gabriel, for reminding me of the things that really matter in life. Finally I wish to thank the Big Man above and to one in His company whose memory started this whole enterprise. Time and history have not been kind to my great grandfather and his comrades, and this tribute, in its own humble way, is an attempt to reclaim the memory of one of so many lost lives.

Grateful acknowledgment is due to the following for permission to borrow copyright material: Curtis Brown Ltd. and the Estate of Lord Dunsany for excerpts from *Fifty Poems* and *War Poems*, copyright 1941, copyright Lord Dunsany; Frank Ormsby's *A Northern Spring* © 1986 by kind permission of the author and The Gallery Press; Seumas O'Sullivan's *Collected Poems*, copyright 1941, by kind permission of Mrs. Frances Sommerville; Eiléan Ní Chuilleanáin's *Site of Ambush*, copyright 1975, and *The Second Voyage*, copyright 1986, by kind permission of the author and The Gallery Press; Thomas Carnduff's *Poverty Street and Other Belfast Poems*, copyright 1993, by kind permission of Lapwing Publications; Michael Hall's *Sacrifice on the Somme*, copyright 1993, by kind permission of the author and Island Publications; John Montague's *Collected Poems*, copyright 1995, by kind permission of the author, The Gallery Press, and Wake Forest University Press; Patrick MacGill's *Soldier Songs* © 1917, by kind permission of Knight Features and Caliban Books; excerpts from Seamus Heaney's "In Memoriam Francis Ledwidge" from *Opened Ground: Selected Poems 1966–1996*, copyright 1996, reprinted by kind permission of Farrar, Straus, & Giroux, LLC and Faber and Faber Ltd.; for excerpts from Seamus Heaney's "Veteran's Dream" from *Poems 1965–1975*, copyright 1980 by Seamus Heaney, reprinted by kind permission of Farrar, Straus, and Giroux and Faber and Faber Ltd.; excerpts from Thomas MacGreevy's *Collected Poems* © 1991 by kind permission of The Catholic University of America Press; excerpt from Francis Ledwidge's "In France" from *The Complete Poems of Francis Ledwidge*, edited by Liam O'Meara © 1997, reprinted by permission of The Goldsmith Press; excerpts from Francis Ledwidge's

Collected Poems © 1974 and from Alice Curtayne's *Francis Ledwidge: The Life of the Poet* by kind permission of Martin, Brian and O'Keeffe; excerpt from Francis Ledwidge's "To One Who Comes Now and Then" by kind permission of New Island Books; excerpts from Michael Longley's *The Ghost Orchid* by kind permission of the author and Jonathan Cape; excerpts from Michael Longley's *Poems 1963–1983, Selected Poems* © 1999, and *The Weather in Japan*, © 2000, by kind permission of the author, Wake Forest University Press and Jonathan Cape; excerpts from Derek Mahon's "The Kensington Notebook" from *Collected Poems*, copyright 1999, by kind permission of the author and The Gallery Press; excerpts from James Joyce's "Dooleysprudence" from *The Critical Writing of James Joyce* by James Joyce, E. Mason, and R. Ellmann, editors, copyright © 1959 by Harriet Weaver and F. Lionel Munro, as administrators of the Estate of James Joyce, renewed © 1987 by C. Lionel Munro, used by permission of Viking Penguin, a division of Penguin Putnam, Inc. and the Estate of James Joyce ©, Estate of James Joyce; excerpts from *Ireland and the First World War* © 1988, edited by David Fitzpatrick, by kind permission of the Lilliput Press, Dublin, Ireland; excerpts from James Simmons' *Poems 1956–1986* © 1986, by kind permission of the author and The Gallery Press; excerpts from *The Collected Poems of W.B. Yeats* (revised 2nd edition), edited by Richard J. Finneran (New York: Scribner, 1996), by kind permission of A. P. Watt Ltd. on behalf of Michael B. Yeats. Used with the permission of Scribner, a Division of Simon & Schuster, Inc.; excerpts from *The Variorum Edition of the Poems of W. B. Yeats*, edited by Peter Allt and Russell K. Alspach (New York: Macmillan, 1957). Used with the permission of Scribner, a Division of Simon & Schuster, Inc.; excerpts from "Pat and Fritz" from *Seventy Years: Being the Autobiography of Lady Gregory* by Lady Gregory by kind permission of Colin Smythe Ltd., on behalf of Anne de Winton and the heirs of Catherine Kennedy; excerpts from Eavan Boland's *The War Horse* © 1975 and *An Origin like Water: Collected Poems 1967–1987* ©1996 by Eavan Boland, used by permission of W. W. Norton and Company, Inc. and Carcanet Press Limited; excerpts from Winifred Letts' *The Spires of Oxford* and *Hallowe'en* by kind permission of John Murray (publishers) Ltd.; excerpts from Katharine Tynan's *Flower of Youth: Poems in War Time* and *Collected Poems* © 1930, by kind permission of the executors of the Katharine Tynan Literary Estate; excerpts from Eva Gore-Booth's *Collected Poems* © 1929, by kind permission of Sir Josslyn Gore-Booth, BT; excerpts

The First World War
in Irish Poetry

1

Introduction

M ODERN MEMORY OF THE GREAT WAR HAS BEEN LARGELY SHAPED BY THE countless books written about England's celebrated soldier poets. Across the Irish Sea, however, Irish poetry about the Great War has elicited such scant critical attention that compiling a list of studies exclusively related to the subject results in an embarrassingly slim bibliography. This is particularly odd since Irish poets have hardly been silent about the subject. If Irish war poetry was uniformly bad, then one could understand why so little has been written about it, but this is far from the case.

One reason to explain this apparent lack of interest in Irish poetry about the Great War is that it is only within the last fifteen years or so that an effort has been made by some Irish historians to reexamine the island's overall role in the First World War. Prior to the 1980s, the general consensus was that Ireland played a minor part in the war. Furthermore, besides a slew of perfunctorily written wartime propaganda pieces, some postwar regimental histories and the occasional chapters buried in a survivor's memoir, to the casual reader, there was little evidence that Ireland had produced a significant body of Great War literature. As we shall see later, this general lack of interest in the war is chiefly due to the politics of Irish memory. Up until very recently, most people in the Irish Republic were infinitely more acquainted with the circumstances (and myths) of the 1916 Easter Rebellion in Dublin than they were with even the slightest detail about a global cataclysm that claimed the lives of thousands of Irish men and women. Certainly general historical ignorance, unionist triumphalism and nationalist irredentism explain, for the most part, why a climate of indifference toward the war prevailed in the Irish Republic for many years. It is hardly surprising, then, that Irish poetry about the Great War has garnered little interest either.

This general indifference to Irish war poetry can also be attributed to the perceived Anglocentric nature of First World War poetry. Judging by the content of most British school texts and war anthologies, the canonical war poets are still invariably of English public school and officer pedigree. The merit of the poetry written by Wilfred Owen, Siegfried Sassoon, and Rupert Brooke has been widely broadcast, but their confirmation as war poets of significance has also been accomplished by stressing their Englishness. In English memory, they represent a prewar world braced by pastoral sureties, Edwardian complacency and innocence. When we think of the poetry of the First World War, the enduring lines we half-recall speak of a place that is "forever England." In the popular English imagination, the war survives, veiled by mists of nostalgia, demarcated from the "filthy tide" of modernism by a pre-1914 world of absolutes. On the other hand, Irish memory of the war cannot easily accommodate such post-Edenic reflections. Memory of prewar Ireland is muddied too much by political dispute and tribal contention for such wistful nostalgias to flourish.

Consequently, Great War poetry has largely become the property of a particularly English mindset, its poets and themes defined by an Anglo ethnocentrism that overshadows the rest of the British archipelago's literary response to the war. The lack of attention given to Irish war poetry can also be traced to the general trend in twentieth-century Irish studies, which privileges Irish writers' contributions to the high modernist mode. (The Yeats and Joyce industries bear this out.) Edna Longley's (1987, 12) claim that "Modernist-based or -biased criticism" is partly responsible for the neglect of "War Poetry" explains, to some degree, why Great War verse is usually closeted with the Georgians and their supposed obsessions with romanticism and rural escapism. Not surprisingly, then, war poetry written by Irish soldier poets came to be regarded as a minor tributary of Georgian poetry as "traditionalists" and "disjunctive Modernists" went their separate ways, thus dividing the "old soldiers from their civilian contemporaries" (Hynes 1990, 339).

Besides the modernist bias that characterizes twentieth-century Irish studies, the idea that minor verse like Irish war poetry is significant only for its political or cultural value is partly due to the notion that excavating literary texts for their "ideological discourse" tends to negate their aesthetic importance (Cheng 1995, 2), especially those features associated with high modernism. Such a view explains why modernist and postmod-

ernist dialogues continue to dominate the study of Irish literature. Early Irish Great War verse, with its Edwardian and Georgian preciosities and sometimes overt political content, holds
little appeal for those preoccupied with Irish modernism's theoretical and aesthetic potentialities.

Finally, Yeats's well-known prejudices against war poetry and
his exclusion of the more celebrated English war poets (Owen,
Sassoon et al.) from his *Oxford Book of Modern Verse* (1936) appear to have had a trickle-down effect on contemporary Irish attitudes about war verse in general. Most Irish Studies programs do
little to remediate this neglect as the majority of them continue
to focus almost exclusively on the canonical figures like Yeats,
with most of his contemporaries (the poets anyway) consigned to
the collective anonymity of such abstractions as the Irish Literary Revival. Yeats's alleged distaste for war poetry is particularly
ironic considering the range of poems he himself wrote about
the Great War, the Anglo-Irish War and the Irish Civil War. Also
ironic is the extent to which his famous injunction against war
poetry ("I think it better in times like these / A poet's mouth be
silent.") has been ignored, as the two public events in twentieth-
century Irish history that have elicited the most response from
Irish poets are the First World War and the ongoing conflict in
Northern Ireland. Yet while this subgenre of poetry about the
so-called Troubles has its own anthology, no such volume of Irish
Great War verse exists.[1] These possible explanations for the general critical neglect of Irish war poetry are closely linked to the
fact that for many years the memory of the thousands of Irish
soldiers with nationalist sympathies who fought and died during the Great War was also poorly served by Irish historians. In
fact, historical studies of the war from an Irish perspective have
been up until quite recently rather patchy. This is not surprising
as even today many ordinary Irish people still generally believe
that Ireland was largely unaffected by the war. Some contemporary Irish writers like Maeve Binchy share this common misper-
ception. In an article she wrote for the *New York Times*, Binchy
noted that "while Britain was torn apart by World War 1 . . . Ireland was relatively untouched."[2] The death of anywhere from 27–
50,000 Irish soldiers (there seems to be no consensus about the
total number of Irish casualties), the maiming of thousands of
others, and the impact such losses had on communities on both
sides of the Irish border hardly leads one to conclude that the
island was left "relatively untouched" by the war.[3] If my own
secondary education in the Northern Ireland school system is

anything to go by, though, misinformed notions like Binchy's can be attributed to the fact that in the Irish Republic, the Great War from an Irish perspective was usually glossed over while in Northern Ireland, Irish history in general received little attention in the primary and secondary class curricula. Recollecting his and his fellow students' early education in his memoir *Tuppenny Stung*, Michael Longley recalls that "there was little on the curriculum to suggest that we were living in Ireland; no Irish history except when it impinged on the grand parade of English monarchs; no Irish literature; no Irish art; no Irish music" (1994, 27). The only book about the war that I read in high school was Robert Graves's *Good-bye to All That* (1929), while the period between 1914 and 1918 was largely reviewed as a minicourse in Easter Rebellion studies.

Such a lack of interest in Ireland's role in the war was not always the case, though, as quite a few "war books" were published during the conflict, but most of these were hastily written journalistic pieces glorifying the exploits of the Irish regiments in the Balkans, the Dardenelles, and on the Western Front. With their false optimism, these so-called histories demonstrate how "misreadings and (re-) constructions are themselves seen to be powerful agents of influence" (Lysaght 1996, 33). Among the most popular accounts of Irish soldiery was Irish journalist Michael MacDonagh's recruiting tome *The Irish at the Front* (1916), a heady cocktail of religious piety and racial hubris. Aimed largely at boosting enlistment figures in the south of Ireland during the war, MacDonagh's book portrays Irish troops as ever gallant and dutiful, buoyed as much by lashings of holy water as they are by warrior esprit. The stereotypical natural phlegm of the Irish character was also exploited by some in the military top brass who regarded the Irish as excellent "missile troops" whose reckless bravado and passion could be counted on for risky offensive operations (Denman 1991, 355). As MacDonagh's book indicates, though, the Irish were quite good themselves at perpetuating some of these ethnic stereotypes. In his memoir, *A Padre in France*, Belfast-born Canon James Owen Hannay (who published under the pen name of George A. Birmingham) became quite effusive about his countrymen's singular contributions to the empire: "Only an Irishman will venture lightheartedly to take short cuts through regulations. It is our capacity for doing things the wrong way which makes us valuable to the Empire, and they ought to decorate us oftener than they do for our insubordination" (1919, 135).

Some of the earliest histories of the war from an Irish perspective were written by Donegal-born Charles James O'Donnell (1849–1934), a former Liberal M.P. and veteran of the Indian Civil Service. In *The Lordship of the World: The British Empire, the United States and Germany* (1924) and *The Irish Future and the Lordship of the World* (1929), which is largely a reworking of the 1924 text, O'Donnell argues that the war and its disastrous consequences were chiefly due to Britain's supremacist imperial ideology rather than German aggression. Not all of the chapters in both books are devoted to the war, and those that are seem more preoccupied with countering British prowar propaganda and arguing the case that the promise of Home Rule was only offered so as to boost Irish enlistment. At no time is O'Donnell interested in the Irish soldier's experiences in the war itself; in those chapters where he does address the conflict, his chief aim is to exculpate Germany's part in the global disaster.

Unlike MacDonagh and Birmingham who depict Irish soldiers as latter-day Christian crusaders, defenders of empire, and resourceful adventurers, or O'Donnell who demonizes British imperialist expansionism, there were other early histories of Ireland's (and particularly Ulster's) part in the war that were written from a unionist point of view. In a 1991 reissue of *The Great War 1914–1918*, first published by the Citizens Committee, City Hall, Belfast in 1919, the exploits of the Thirty-sixth Ulster Division are recounted with imperial gusto. In the introduction and first chapter of this reissue, editors Frank Millar and Dr. Ian Adamson, both unionist politicians themselves, commemorate Ulster's sacrifice for "King and country" (1991, v–viii) while also noting that Ulster has a long history of serving "everywhere the Union Jack is raised aloft" (14). Great effort is made to emphasize Ulster's sense of colonial duty, while the fact that many Irish nationalists served with the Tenth and Sixteenth Irish divisions is noted almost as an afterthought. Similar to Millar and Adamson's imperialist encomiums is Cyril Falls's *The History of the Thirty-sixth (Ulster) Division* (1922), which, while providing an accurate and thorough account of the division's formation and war service, reads in places like Ulster's version of Foxe's *Actes and Monuments*. By highlighting the covenanting ethos of the division's predominantly Protestant membership (until heavy casualties reduced their numbers), Falls, himself a Thirty-sixth Division veteran, commemorates Ulster's imperial sacrifice and enshrines the Somme as another sacred river in unionist mythology. As Alvin Jackson notes, Falls's book forms part of a general trend in unionist historiography during the 1920s when "celebratory accounts of the Irish struggle against Kaiser Wilhelm" were all the rage (1994, 257).

Divisional histories were popular, too: Bryan Cooper, former unionist M.P. for South Dublin (1910), wrote a "eulogistic" history for the Irish dead at Gallipoli (Jackson 1994, 258). Reading his account of the Irish experiences in the Dardenelles is like thumbing through the pages of a medieval romance as in his description of the Tenth Irish Division's bloody assault on Kiretch Tepe Sirt in August, 1915: "In a few hours they were to plunge into a hand-to-hand struggle with the old enemy of Christendom, and their pulses throbbed with the spirit of Tancred and Godfrey de Bouillon, as they fitted themselves to take their places in the last of the crusades" (1993, 107). Cooper's high-flown language and self-conscious literary flourishes reflect the general style of historical narratives of that time. Nevertheless, histories like those written by O'Donnell, Falls and Cooper reveal the tensions within the Irish political scene, and Irish historians, "divided both politically and now by their choice of subject matter, compounded these tensions" (Jackson 1994, 258). The result was that Irish "historians supplied two distinctive devotional literatures to the two Irish states, and helped to fashion two distinctive iconographical traditions" (258). Inevitably, Irish war memory was doomed to reflect the partitioned politics of a divided island.

Despite its rather spotty documentation and occasional hyperboles, later histories like Henry Harris's *The Irish Regiments in the First World War* (1968) take a more comprehensive look at Irish military contributions to the war effort. Then, with the most recent bout of hostilities in Northern Ireland serving as an ironic backdrop, Philip Orr published perhaps the best book written to date about the war from an Ulster perspective. In *The Road to the Somme* (1987), Orr retraces the events leading up to the Thirty-sixth Ulster Division's terrible sacrifices at Thiepval on the first day of the Somme offensive in July 1916. Where other historians opt for the sweep of the grand narrative, Orr's microhistory examines the impact of the war on those who fought and on the towns and townlands across Ulster from whence they came.

Brief articles about the Irish experience in the First World War continue to appear sporadically in Irish history journals like *Irish Sword, History Ireland* and *An Cosantóir,* and *Irish*

Times columnist Kevin Myers (one of the few public curators of Irish war memory) writes frequently about the war in his regular newspaper columns. Despite these efforts, though, even by the late 1980s historians like David Fitzpatrick could still lament the general air of apathy toward the war in the Irish Republic. In his introduction to a collection of essays written chiefly by his own students in a Trinity College workshop, Fitzpatrick notes how the Great War's impact "on ordinary Irish people is largely ignored, so reducing a social catastrophe, which left few people untouched, to the status of a minor if unfortunate disturbance" (1988, viii). Since then, notable efforts have been made to redress this neglect with the appearance over the last ten years of a number of books recounting Ireland's wartime military history. Among the more notable of these military reevaluations is Tom Johnstone's *Orange, Green, and Khaki: The Story of the Irish Regiments in the Great War, 1914–1918* (1992), A. E. C. Bredin's *A History of the Irish Soldier* (1987), and Terence Denman's history of the Sixteenth (Irish) Division—*Ireland's Unknown Soldiers* (1992). Denman has also weighed in with a biography of parliamentary nationalist and Irish officer Willie Redmond, one of the war's many forgotten casualties, in his book *A Lonely Grave: The Life and Death of William Redmond* (1995). Thanks to the efforts of another Irish journalist, Myles Dungan, war memories from the other ranks have been preserved for posterity as well in his two books—*Irish Voices from the Great War* (1995) and *"They Shall Not Grow Old": Irish Soldiers Remember the Great War* (1997). Thomas Hennessey's *Dividing Ireland: World War 1 and Partition* is another book that takes a look at this extremely complex period in Irish history. While Hennessey focuses on the period's political changes, his book's central idea is that the Great War "transformed" the whole nature of the Irish Question and altered preexisting notions of "Irishness" and "Britishness," which underwent further "polarisation" (1998, xxi). As this book was going to press, another noteworthy history of Ireland's role in the Great War appeared. Keith Jeffrey's *Ireland and the Great War* (2000) reexamines Irish participation in the Somme and Gallipoli campaigns as well as the impact of the Easter Rising. Jeffrey's book also provides an excellent analysis of Irish war art, music, and monuments and how commemoration of the war was subsequently politicized in Irish memory.

Fortunately, the significance of Ireland's role in the First World War also continues to be explored by Irish writers. The earliest and most popular Irish war novels were Patrick MacGill's thinly fictionalized accounts of his own experiences on the Western Front, in such works as *The Amateur Army* (1915), *The Great Push* (1916), and *The Red Horizon* (1916). More recently, Jennifer Johnston's novel *How Many Miles to Babylon?* (1974) examines the political and cultural relationship between the Anglo-Irish and "Kiltartan poor" through the experiences of two young Irishmen who enlist together and are later killed on the Western Front, while playwright Sebastian Barry's novel *The Whereabouts of Eneas McNulty* (1998) follows the postwar fortunes of an Irish veteran of both world wars who, because he served Britain, finds himself a political pariah in his own country. On the stage, meanwhile, George Bernard Shaw's *O'Flaherty VC* (1917), Sean O'Casey's *The Silver Tassie* (1927), Frank McGuinness's *Observe the Sons of Ulster Marching Towards the Somme* (1985), and Sebastian Barry's *The Steward of Christendom* (1995) also explore the various paradoxes surrounding Irish involvement in the great conflict.[4]

The final scene in Barry's play in particular illustrates some of the overarching themes of this study. The play's protagonist, Thomas Dunne—a Catholic loyalist and former chief superintendent of the Dublin Metropolitan Police during those tumultuous years from 1913 to 1922—is a permanent resident of a "county home" (insane asylum) in Baltinglass. (The year is 1932.) During the course of the play, he experiences brief periods of clarity and largely escapes complete dementia by reclaiming scenes from his past. On several occasions Thomas's son Willie, who was killed in the war, appears on stage as a child (Thomas only remembers Willie as a thirteen-year-old boy) dressed in khaki and puttees. At the end of the play, while Thomas recalls the first time his own father actually expressed his love for him, Willie reappears, slides in beside Thomas as he lies in his cot and then they both sleep. The scene typifies the challenges that have moved Irish poets to write so frequently about the war. Thomas and Willie represent a strand of Irish political identity other than the ones codified by unionism and nationalism. Both men, both Catholics, served in the forces of the Crown, and their historical narrative has been subsequently sidelined in favor of a more homogeneous version of Ireland's past. Thomas's vision of his soldier child also demonstrates the difficulty of confronting the past and distinguishing between personal memory and historical fact. The role reversal at the end of Barry's play, where the dead son comforts his deranged father, reminds us that we can only begin to understand the complexities of Irish identity by acknowledging

Irish history's paradoxes and contradictions—where commonly perceived roles (like who is the father, who the son) either defy categorization or challenge popular perception.

Despite these standout works, though, little has been written about Irish war poetry. The few extant biographies of soldier poets like Francis Ledwidge, Lord Dunsany, and Tom Kettle do provide some interesting background information, but naturally their focus is on the life rather than the poetry. Despite this paucity of criticism, a number of contemporary critics have written about Ireland's Great War verse with considerable acuity.

To date, Fran Brearton's *The Great War in Irish Poetry: W. B. Yeats to Michael Longley* (2000, published while this book was in its final stages) is the only book-length study devoted to Irish war poetry. While Brearton's book is chiefly preoccupied by how the war has been imagined in Irish poetry, she restricts her focus to the work of six poets (W. B. Yeats, Robert Graves, Louis MacNeice, Derek Mahon, Seamus Heaney, and Michael Longley), largely with the goal of demonstrating the extent to which the war's images and memory contribute to their "aesthetic theory" (vii). In her treatment of Yeats and MacNeice in particular, Brearton cogently illustrates how their work impacts "recent Northern Irish poetry" (vii). With Mahon, Heaney, and Longley, she examines how the war engages them imaginatively as they struggle with the "pressures" of responding to "events in Northern Ireland over the last thirty years" (viii). As Brearton admits, her book follows a "particular Northern trajectory" (viii). Besides Yeats and Graves, she does not examine how Irish poets outside Ulster respond to the war. Certainly, as we shall see later, Brearton's comment that the war verse written by Irish soldier poets is not where we will find "Ireland's best war poetry" (41) is valid. However, her view that to "attribute too much importance to Irish soldiers' war literature may be to offer a misleading, or at least a very limited, picture" (41) is puzzling considering the fact that her book privileges the work of only six writers, all of whom enjoy membership, and deservedly so, in the Irish and British literary canon. Yet the value of Brearton's book lies in its authoritative analysis of how the war contributes to the historical and cultural resource of these canonical poets. Naturally in a book like this present study, which surveys the war verse of over thirty Irish poets from both sides of the Irish border, the aim is to explore the chief themes that preoccupy Irish war poetry in an attempt to further identify the wide range of Irish responses to the war.

In *Poetry in the Wars* (1987), Edna Longley also takes up the cause of war poetry in general when she argues that war verse has been unfairly discounted by "structuralists and other Modernists" who dismiss it as a "vulgar . . . version of history" (1987, 12). In *The Living Stream: Literature and Revisionism in Ireland,* she devotes a chapter ("The Rising, the Somme, and Irish Memory") to examine how the Easter Rebellion and Battle of the Somme have been "processed" by political and sectarian ideologies (1994, 69). Apart from a cursory glance at several Irish war poems, however, her discussion seems more preoccupied with defending her revisionist convictions and exposing the curative orthodoxies of nationalist and unionist culturespeak. Still, her point that Irish history continues to be ransacked to serve contemporary political agendas will be one of the chief preoccupations of this book.

Tjebbe Westendorp and D. G. Boyce have also written insightful essays about the Irish literary response to the war in which they chart the Great War's influence on the current situation in Northern Ireland. Westendorp's "The Great War in Irish Memory: The Case of Poetry" argues that an artistic and spiritual kinship exists between contemporary Ulster poets and the major English soldier poets of the Great War. He supports this argument by demonstrating how Ulster poets continue to draw on the war's memory and iconography in order to register their disaffection with contemporary existence (1991). Like Westendorp, Boyce (in his monograph *The Sure Confusing Drum: Ireland and the First World War*) explores how the war has been appropriated as a metaphor for current sectarian unrest in Northern Ireland, and he argues, like Edna Longley, that "in Ireland, politics and literature are inseparable" (Boyce 1993, 24). In the course of his discussion, Boyce takes a brief look at some of the most recent treatments of the war in Irish literature, namely in Johnston's *How Many Miles to Babylon?*, McGuinness's *Observe the Sons of Ulster Marching Towards the Somme*, and Seamus Heaney's elegy "In Memoriam Francis Ledwidge" (*Field Work*). Convinced that this "renewed interest in Ireland and the Great War" was sparked by the onset of the recent Troubles, Boyce contends that the war continues to play a critical role in "the forging of Irish identities" (1993, 24).

Another major Irish critic who has addressed Irish writers' response to the war is Declan Kiberd who allots a short chapter to the subject ("The Great War and Irish Memory") in his wide-ranging study *Inventing Ireland* (1995). After a cursory glance at Ledwidge and George Russell (AE), Kiberd concerns himself with Sean O' Casey's *The Silver Tassie*, a work which he feels was O'Casey's last major accomplishment. In his analysis of the play's themes, Kiberd argues that O'Casey's aim was not only to examine the effects of war on civilians and soldiers but to demonstrate that the war affected the lives of those in the trenches and on the home front equally.

Obviously this study is indebted to the work Brearton, Longley, Westendorp, Boyce, and Kiberd have done so far. As already noted, another key influence is historian Keith Jeffrey who takes a multidisciplinary approach as he examines how Irish memory of the war has been preserved in music, painting, and architecture (war monuments especially). Like Longley, Jeffery explores the politics of Irish war memory. However, his contention that Irish war literature's "main literary theme[s]" are "demoralisation," "distance," "disengagement," and "detachment" (1993, 140–41) is too narrowly prescribed. Despondency, ambivalence and "disengagement" form only a part of the dizzying array of Irish responses to the war, and while the quality of the poetry is often uneven, its cultural and historical subtexts reveal that literature can often be a fruitful guide to understanding how contemporary public assumptions have evolved.

Before identifying the chief themes of this study, a word or two about my own theoretical biases. Anyone looking for Lacanian perspectives, Derridaesque deconstructions, Bakhtinian architectonics, gender autopsies or any other highly theoretical analytical approach will be sorely disappointed. My chief concern is to ascertain what Irish war poems reveal about Irish attitudes toward the war, even if these attitudes are not indicative of any widespread consensus of opinion. While concurring with the idea that literature cannot be unequivocally equated "with the particular cultural situation in which it originates" (Bradley 1988, 36), I do believe, like Thomas Flanagan, that poems are "shaped" narratives that encapsulate a poet's "response to circumstance, to the present, and any present [that] carries within itself the sense of some past, if not of the past itself" (1988, 13). In this sense, Irish war poetry, with all its ideological imprints and anachronic revisions, reveals the extent to which the Irish conflict continues to be exacerbated by self-sustaining political myths that dominate contemporary politics on both sides of the Irish border. Whether we acknowledge it or not, memory of the war continues to inform some of the ongoing dialogues about Ireland's future, and somewhere between unionist appropriation and nationalist amnesia, the political ambiguities surrounding Ireland's role in the war need to be reexamined in order to challenge unionism and nationalism's constricted and politically expedient narratives. It is only appropriate then that any attempt to disturb these coaxial narratives of Ireland's role in the Great War should take a pluralistic approach by grafting together various modes of inquiry, hence blending the aesthetic with the cultural and political. Irish poet-critic Gerald Dawe has rightly cautioned against the danger of attributing too much cultural significance to everything Irish (1993, 43–44), so the aim here will be to strike a balance by examining the poetry's aesthetic and political significance and the conscious and unconscious interplay between both.

As for the selection of poets, I followed two guidelines. First of all, I chose those who were the most voluble in their response to the war and those who offered a perspective not found elsewhere (a key omission here is Louis MacNeice whose response to the war is thoroughly critiqued in Fran Brearton's *The Great War in Irish Poetry*). Second, to avoid pointless disputes over who is Irish, British, Ulster/British or Irish/British, I included the work of writers who call whatever part of the "island" of Ireland they lay claim to as home. Another rule I followed was to offer pertinent biographical sketches, if possible, on the lesser-known poets while skimming over such background materials on the better-known writers whose biographical details can easily be obtained elsewhere. While the general approach is chronological and thematic, a few further points need to be made with regards to what observations can be deduced from examining Irish war poetry. As personal and public fictions demonstrate, inaccurate memories of the war have created their own counter narratives, and by assuming their own reality, these conflicting versions of the past continue to inflame sectarian animosity. In Northern Ireland, appropriating the past has become a nationalist and unionist pastime where all games become binary games that paralyze constructive discourse. Sadly, ritual memory of the Great War in both nationalist and unionist communities has become almost irreparably politicized. Anachronistic readings of the war certainly produce personal fictions which are both historical (getting the details right) and ahistorical (coating the event with an ideological signature). The result is that the political and cultural tensions that lie submerged within the larger drama of the Great War continue to reveal how constrictive views of Irish history and identity lie at the heart of the Irish conflict. This idea that the Irish sense of the past "seems inextricably bound to a crisis of identity" (Eyler and Garratt 1988, 7) is one of the more common themes in contemporary Irish literature, but by conducting closer readings of Irish war poetry, we may be able to recognize the extent to which our "received impression of historical events is nothing more than the product of historians and poets . . . juggling 'possibly inaccurate memories'" (Weekes 1990, 186).

Among the other conclusions to be drawn will be the belief shared by most Irish commentators on the Great War that instead of establishing stronger relationships across the sectarian and political divide, the war actually aggravated hostilities between unionists and nationalists. There was to be no miraculous reconciliation between both sides in the trenches on the Western Front: apart from mutual respect for each side's bravery on the battlefield, the old grudges survived the war with a greater intensity. In this respect, the war only briefly averted possible violence in Ulster over Home Rule; in the long run, it played a key role in ensuring that the constitutional dispute in Northern Ireland would fester into this millennium. Yet some critics still look back to the first decades of this century as some kind of ambrosial golden age of national amity. One only has to look at the divisive manner in which the war has been preserved in modern Irish memory to realize how naïve and romantically retrospective are the views of nationalist critics like Desmond Fennell who talk about rediscovering the "satisfactory national self-definition that we lived and worked with during the first [decade] of the century" (1994, 252). Those determined to construct coherent national identities will find that the Great War resists any attempts to create what John Kerrigan calls "anachronistic forms of nationalism" (1997, 17). What Irish war poetry does demonstrate is that there were and still are various strains of Irish patriotism, and, as we shall see, some of the earliest poetry written in Ireland about the war sees no conflict between Irish and British affiliations as Irish nationality is preserved within and subordinate to a United Kingdom identity.

Setting aside the political implications of Irish war poetry, I will also explore how the war impacts Irish verse and its aesthetic development. Samuel Hynes argues that one of the major "discontinuities that the war would create would be the break with the literary past that would become a principle of postwar Modernism" (1990, 33). However, closer study of Irish war verse reveals that for many Irish poets, no such discontinuity seemed to exist as many writers continued to write in the popular styles associated with the Irish Literary Revival. There were other Irish writers (like Thomas MacGreevy) who (as a result of the war and the subsequent modernist ascendancy) quickly shed traditional notions about language, subject, and technique, but Irish modernism was more of a phenomenon led by Irish writers living abroad rather than any kind of widespread domestic movement.

The need to examine how Irish poets respond to the Great War is part of an ongoing effort to look beyond the sterile narratives of military offensives, and strategic gain and loss, and explore how the war affected ordinary and not so ordinary Irish men and women. Evidence that interest in the war is undergoing something of a revival throughout Northern Ireland and the Republic is borne out by the fact that quite a number of public debates and retrospective celebrations have been staged over the last few years. In 1996, one of the topics up for discussion at the West Belfast Festival (Féile an Phobail) was "on the lessons of 1916—both the Easter Rising and the Battle of the Somme" (Morrison 1996, 30–31) while in the same year, plans were announced to build a peace park (later named the Island of Ireland Peace Tower) in Belgium to honor the thousands of Irishmen from both sides of the political divide who died in the Great War. Amazingly, it took eighty years after the war ended to erect a memorial of this kind to commemorate all the Irish war dead. While the Northern Irish government dedicated the Ulster Tower at Thiepval in 1927 to the memory of those members of the Thirty-sixth Ulster Division who never returned home, this most recent monument (featuring a 109-foot round tower overlooking Messines Ridge with four gardens representing Ireland's four provinces) is the first major memorial on the Western Front to honor the south's war dead. The completion of this peace park at Messines Ridge (where men from the Thirty-sixth Ulster Division and the Sixteenth Irish Division combined for a successful attack on 7 June 1917) is especially poignant as its construction was coordinated by a group called A Journey of Reconciliation led by loyalist spokesman Glen Barr and former Irish T.D. Paddy Harte. The project was finally completed in early October 1998, and a month or so later, on 11 November, Irish President Mary McAleese stood shoulder to shoulder with Queen Elizabeth as they both officiated at the joint Irish and British dedication service.[5]

Other public manifestations of renewed interest in the Great War were punctuated by a week-long series of events held in July 1997 in Dublin and Meath to commemorate the life and poetry of Irish soldier poet Francis Ledwidge, while in the same year, RTE broadcast an award-winning documentary (*Behind the Closed Eye*) based on Ledwidge's life. Throughout the Irish Republic, what would have been unthinkable twenty years ago has also come to pass with the formation of such historical groups as the Royal Dublin Fusiliers Association. But all this attention given to Irish memory of the war has not been without its share of dissension. While no objections were raised in June 1998 when the Athy Heritage Centre in County Kildare unveiled a permanent exhibit to commemorate the memory of the two thousand or so Athy men who fought in the war, a few months earlier (March 1998), plans to build a war museum in Tipperary met with resistance when some locals condemned the project as nothing more than a memorial to the British Empire and those Irishmen who misguidedly supported it.[6]

So as a new millennium begins, this book-length study of how Irish poets write the Great War aims to contribute to the ongoing efforts to reassess the war's legacy in the contemporary Irish imagination. To aid this general objective, the book is divided into seven chapters that examine how Irish attitudes toward the war have evolved during the past eighty years or so. Chapter two surveys the prevailing misconceptions about Ireland's role in the First World War with particular emphasis given to how unionist and nationalist mythographies pervade Irish war poetry and appropriate the war for ideological reasons.

After identifying the various inherited untruths about the war, chapter three focuses on the poetry published by Irish soldier poets during the war. While the main thrust here will be to examine how these poets respond to the political ramifications of their enlistment in the British army, their attempts either to transcend or endorse the war will also be examined. It will become apparent that Irish soldier poets often oscillate between two extremes: they condemn the brutality and moral chaos of the war, but they also subscribe to a martial high-mindedness. Though adept at writing movingly about their slain comrades, they still see the war as the supreme test of valor. Despite the saber rattling and frequently crude craftsmanship, however, perhaps the true value of these poets' work lies in its contribution to our overall historical awareness about the kinds of literature

produced by the war's participants. Even if most of the war poetry written between 1914 and 1918 is imaginatively anemic, as
George Parfitt notes, bad war poems can be important for what
they reveal about "cultural materialism" (1990, 162).

Chapter four, then, takes a look at the home front response
to the war. A number of Irish women published volumes of war
poetry during the conflict with most of them registering the customary extremes of glorification or revulsion. But even luminar-
ies like Yeats and Joyce reacted to the violence, and their atypi-
cal attitudes toward the war demonstrate how complicated Irish
views about the war became as the casualties mounted and the
situation at home deteriorated.

In chapter five, I will examine how the mythologizing process
about the war was well underway in Irish poetry during the
decade or so after the war. While postwar poetry often glorifies
the deeds of the Irish war dead or tries to justify the war effort
at a time when the future of the Irish Free State still seemed uncertain, poets like Thomas MacGreevy embraced the high modernist mode in responding to their war experiences from an extremely fragmented point of view.

Chapter six will explore the most recent responses to the
Great War as contemporary Irish poets return to the "nightmare
ground" to write moving elegies about loved ones whose lives
were shattered by the war and, in the act of doing so, examine
how their own lives have been affected by the residue of the war's
psychical trauma. Another preoccupation will be to look at how
the Great War provides a rich iconography for Irish poets as they
explore new ways to respond to Ulster's violence and define their
own identities amid the ongoing conflict in Northern Ireland. As
already noted, the overarching connections between the past and
the present suggest that a special kinship exists between Irish
(and particularly Ulster) poets and the major war poets (Westendorp 1991, 131), for they share the burden of speaking out and
reaffirming the value of art during times of violence.

Finally, the last chapter—chapter seven—briefly traces how
the iconography of the Great War continues to provide a range
of figurative devices for Irish poets as they respond to contemporary issues and problems. Then, by way of conclusion, observations about the significance of Irish poetry about the Great
War will be discussed with particular emphasis given to the idea
that the presence of sectarianism in Irish cultural utterance often turns the private rite of poetry into a public act of cultural
essentialism. An understanding of how a major tragedy in Irish

history can produce such a range of viewpoints may also explain why even today the notion of Irish cultural and political hybridity continues to provoke stiff resistance from extremists who would wish us to believe that the labels "Irish," "Ulster," or "British" are necessarily and mutually exclusive.

2
Myth and Memory

MY INTEREST IN THE GREAT WAR AND ITS LITERATURE BEGAN AROUND ABOUT the first time I heard my parents and grandparents talk about someone even they could vaguely remember. This was at a time when, as already mentioned, Graves's *Good-bye to All That* was one of the texts my classmates and I were assigned as part of our preparation for "O" level English literature. The cover of our copy of the book featured *The Menin Road* (1919), one of celebrated war artist Paul Nash's bomb-blasted landscapes of the Western Front, and I often imagined my great-grandfather as one of the two soldiers in the foreground stepping anxiously between the shell holes, trying to stay alive in a nightmare world far beyond my schoolboy imagination. My great-grandfather, Rifleman David McGrann MM, was killed during Third Ypres. The only photograph of him in his army uniform (along with the Military Medal he had been awarded posthumously) disappeared years ago, lost, misplaced, or simply forgotten.

In later years I often wondered why our family's war hero had become a rarely spoken about ghost. One reason is obviously the fact that very little is known about his war service. As a veteran member of the Ninth Battalion of the Royal Irish Fusiliers, he probably saw action at the Somme, as the Royal Irish Fusiliers were among the "first of the local regiments to go 'over the top' . . . [on] that fateful morning" in July 1916.[1] Of course, he has not been totally forgotten. His name is inscribed on war memorials in his hometown of Lurgan, County Armagh and at Tyne Cot, just outside the Belgian town of Ieper (Ypres). His name also appears in the list of those who were decorated for their bravery in combat in Cyril Falls's *The History of the Thirty-sixth (Ulster) Division*. But I still wanted to know why so little was ever spoken about him, even if he had been dead for over sixty years at that time, and why the family did nothing to commemorate him every November.

The first clue about my family's acute case of historical amnesia emerged when I realized the significance of where the town's war memorial is situated. It lies in the center of Lurgan, in the shadow of the Church of Ireland's tall spire, and each July and November, the local Orange lodge lays a wreath at the foot of the monument in memory of the town's war dead.[2] On the memorial's scroll of honor, there is my great-grandfather's name inscribed alongside the names of all the other "loyal sons of Ulster" who died during the war. Here perhaps was the chief reason why he, like so many others, was subsequently forgotten, especially among his own community. As a Catholic nationalist who served in the British army, David McGrann is a historical aberration, trapped forever between two hostile traditions: an enigma to those who like the contours of their local politics rigidified and adversarial. Not surprisingly, to this day McGrann's surviving family and subsequent grandchildren and great grandchildren have never attended any of the town's biannual memorial services. No doubt apathy and sheer disinterest partly explain this neglect on their part, but the highly charged political and sectarian atmosphere that surrounds these occasions has played its role, too.[3]

This tribalizing of the memory of the Irish war dead became an industry on both sides of the Irish border shortly after partition.[4] As others have already noted, in Northern Ireland the Great War was appropriated as another sacred chapter in unionist mythography as Ulster Protestants commemorated *their* war dead as defenders of the empire. As a result, memorial services in the six counties soon took on an imperial and sectarian ethos: while the Somme was to assume its place beside the Boyne on the banners of the loyal Orange lodges, after the war, it replaced the Siege of Derry "as the great symbol of Ulster's willingness to pay the ultimate price for king and country" (McBride 1997, 71). That the war was to be consecrated in Ulster Protestant memory was inevitable, as many of the subsequent war monuments that were erected were (and still are) located close to or within the grounds of Protestant churches.

In Catholic churches throughout Northern Ireland, on the other hand, there is little acknowledgement that local parishioners fought (and died) in the war. In Lurgan, for instance, the Catholic church's only explicit gesture to commemorate its local war dead was to dedicate the altar railings to their memory. Sadly, these commemorative railings were later removed and never restored during subsequent refurbishments of the church interior (Clendinning 1999). Catholic churches in the Irish Republic share this reluctance to register any kind of remotely ostentatious act of war memory. While Protestant churches erected memorials to their congregations' war dead, most Catholic churches still do not "contain memorials" (Leonard 1988, 60). Further evidence of this historical amnesia can be found in some Catholic cemeteries, particularly in Northern Ireland, where many families with strong republican sympathies saw to it that the military headstones (especially designed and paid for by the Commonwealth War Graves Commission) commemorating their dead soldier ancestors were replaced by family gravestones (Clendinning 1999). In some cases, the bare facts of an old soldier's war service were retained ("A Soldier of the Great War"), but for many others, no record of their war service remains.[5] Apparently some people did and still do not feel comfortable with the fact that their grandfathers or great grandfathers served in the British army. The same sort of historical whitewashing can be found when one examines the war memorials in the Irish Republic. While Ulster unionists celebrate their war dead who died for king and country, as Keith Jeffery points out, in the Irish Republic, inscriptions on most remaining war memorials identify no specific reason for the terrible sacrifices, and when they do, they simply proclaim that the dead died for "Ireland" or the "freedom of small nations" (1993, 148).[6]

Equally problematic for Northern Irish Catholics were the subsequent Remembrance Day services whose ceremonies and symbols formed part of an elaborate imperial choreography. According to the local tribal customs, to participate in the memorial services' imperialistic ritual was to align oneself with the unionist majority, so naturally many Catholics shied away from making any public expression of remembrance lest it be construed as an act of solidarity with unionism. It has already been noted that most war memorials in Ulster are located adjacent to or within the grounds of Protestant churches, but even more intimidating for any Catholic who may be interested in participating in these commemorative services is the fact that they are generally conducted by the local Orange lodge (Jeffery 1993, 150). So, from very early on, commemorative services quickly adapted to the realities of local politics. In 1928, when the town of Lurgan dedicated its war memorial in the presence of the Duke of Abercorn, the then governor of Northern Ireland, the Catholic Ex-servicemen's Association (the Catholic counterpart to the loyalist British Legion) held their own separate church service prior to the main ceremony, which was presided over almost exclusively by unionist dignitaries (Clendinning 1999). In the subsequent wreath-laying ceremony, the Catholic church was the only local church that did not lay a wreath on the steps of the new war memorial (1999). Especially significant is the fact that Catholics formed their own veterans organization, thus indicating the extent to which memory of the war continued to reinforce existing sectarian divisions.

Even the war's most enduring icon, the poppy, continues to foment division. For most Northern Irish Catholics, the poppy is sadly synonymous with the Orange lily: a supremacist emblem commemorating their sacrifices but not ours. Even as recently as 1983, dispute broke out over commemoration services in Dublin as some felt the ceremony was imbued with too much of an imperial ethos; apparently selling poppies is still regarded as a flagrant act of imperial triumphalism. This perception of the poppy as imperial icon made the headlines again during the early 1990s when the governor at H.M. Prison, Belfast forbade the wearing of poppies by prisoners due to possible tensions between loyalists and republicans (McCartney and Bryson 1994, 179).

Clearly sectarianism and tribalism continue to distort Irish war memory as some link the war to what Keith Jeffery describes as a "Unionist blood sacrifice in the North" (1993, 153). This falsification of Ireland's role in the Great War certainly has been costly to community relations: as already noted, while Ulster unionists embrace a "predominantly Protestant type of commemoration," nationalists feel uncomfortable with what they perceive as a blatant "imperial symbolism" coloring most remembrance services (153). Sadly, though, the politicizing of Irish war memory has not been confined to war memorials, commemorative services, and the wearing of poppies.[7]

In a society where wall murals serve as public expressions of community allegiance and help demarcate the political and sectarian boundaries of a geopolitical landscape, it is not surprising that in this form of street art the Great War should be appropriated to reinforce tribal identity as well. In his richly illustrated studies of Northern Irish wall murals, *Politics and Painting: Murals and Conflict in Northern Ireland* (1991) and *Drawing Support: Murals in the North of Ireland* (1994), Bill Rolston explores how the war helped strengthen "unionist identity" (1991, 24). In both of his books, which include several photographs of murals commemorating the Ulster Division's heroics at the Somme, we see how the war was to become another defining moment for

Ulster unionism. One mural in Dunloy, County Antrim features the celebrated charge of the Ulster Division at Thiepval on 1 July 1916 (1994, 13). This image appears to be a crude copy of celebrated Ulster painter William Conor's portrait of the Somme attack, which, shortly after the battle, appeared on commemorative postcards that were sold to raise funds for the Ulster Volunteer Force (UVF) Hospital fund (J. Wilson 1981, 14–15). Evidence of more direct transhistorical expropriation can be seen on a wall mural in Dee Street in Belfast, where a Thirty-sixth Ulster Division soldier is depicted standing side by side with a contemporary member of the outlawed UVF, a pictorial which links the Great War and the "struggle of the current . . . as part of the one loyalist fight" (Rolston 1991, 45). Even in the heart of Belfast, on Donegall Pass, there is an elaborate mural commemorating the Somme, replete with soldiers standing at ease, resting on their rifles with heads bowed, while in the background, scenes of arm-to-arm combat are depicted in the usual battlefront landscapes of barbed wire and exploding shells.[8]

Wall murals have certainly played their part in ensuring that memory of the Great War assumes an exclusively unionist persona in Northern Ireland. Street names and the names of places with political significance were also given titles associated with Great War battles and British army generals.[9] Streets in towns and cities across Northern Ireland still carry the names of places forever linked with the war: there is a Messines Park in Derry City; a Cambrai Heights in Lisburn; and a Cambrai Park in Waringstown. In Belfast, several street names recall the city's links to the Great War: there is a Cambrai Street, a Picardie Avenue, and a Servia Street.[10] Sadly, some of these places, like the war memorial in Enniskillen (scene of the horrific bombing of an Armistice Day service by the IRA in 1987) and Cambrai Street (where the Shankill butcher gang committed one of their grisly murders in the mid-1970s) will also be forever linked with sectarian atrocities. In Northern Ireland, shrines of remembrance commemorating one generation's sacrifices have become the killing zones of another generation's sectarian extremists.

If memory of the war has been violated by further bloodletting and unionist wall murals have hijacked Irish memory of the war for the unionist cause, further evidence that the Great War has been completely appropriated by the unionist tradition is the way its battles and major figures have come to be associated with British power in Northern Ireland. Of the two major British army barracks in Northern Ireland, the one in Lisburn is named after the village of Thiepval, the Thirty-sixth Ulster Division's objective during the Somme offensive, while the name of the other one, in Armagh City, sports the surnames of General Hugh Gough, a veteran of Napoleonic and Indian campaigns, and General Hubert Gough, the avidly pro-union and generally incompetent commander of the British Fifth Army during the battles of Cambrai (June 1917) and Third Ypres (August 1917) where the Irish Divisions incurred such heavy losses. That most of these place names are situated in predominantly loyalist areas (or have links to the security forces) suggests the extent to which the war's memory has become the sole property of one side of the community in Northern Ireland. This association between the politics of place names and Ulster's sectarian demographics appears to confirm John Wilson Foster's point that in Ulster, "landscape is a cultural code" that "perpetuates . . . the instabilities and ruptures" of contemporary Irish politics (1991, 149).

In the Irish Republic, memory of the war and of the thousands of Irishmen who fought and died in it has fared even worse, for instead of wholesale appropriation, there has been, until very recently, almost a universal effort to forget the war.[11] Determined to create its own sense of nationhood during the immediate postwar years, the Free State had little use for the memory of Irishmen who served in the British army, and it did not take long until the war was reduced to a sideshow in republicanism's Easter doxology. In the words of Irish historian F. X. Martin, nationalist amnesia about the Great War became aptly known as the "Great Oblivion" (1967, 68). Yet such willful historical excisions were not always the case. Throughout the 1920s, Armistice Day services in Dublin still drew large crowds and the construction of a national war memorial was begun in 1931, but as relations between the Northern Ireland and Free State governments deteriorated, memory of the war soon became an ideological football kicked around for the sake of political expediency. Just as the Easter Rising evolved into a defining historical moment in the Republic's efforts to create a satisfactory nationalist self-image, any public acknowledgment of Ireland's role in the Great War was generally frowned upon. As already noted, over the years, while the political situation in Northern Ireland continued to petrify, the Armistice Day services in Dublin came to be regarded as an outmoded and thinly disguised celebration of Ireland's imperial past. Even the National War Memorial at Islandbridge (designed by Edward Lutyens) fell into a disgraceful state of dilapidation, a public eyesore that emblematized a nation's desire to selectively eradicate the less agreeable parts of its complicated past. Fortunately such attitudes appear to be changing as by the early 1990s, Ireland's monument to her Great War dead was restored to its former grandeur (J. Bowman 1993, 7).

Another fact that the Irish government can hardly be proud of is that it was not until 1996 that an Irish president (Mary Robinson) participated in wreath-laying ceremonies at Westminster Cathedral to commemorate the thousands of Irish soldiers who died during the war.[12] Further signs that nationalist attitudes about the war are under reconstruction can be gauged by the fact that another Irish president, Mary McAleese, a Northern Catholic herself, proudly wore a poppy while laying a wreath at London's Cenotaph Memorial during the November 1998 commemoration ceremonies. Prior to the subsequent dedication of the new memorial at Messines, President McAleese noted that Ireland's war dead came "from every part of this island, [and that] nobody owns their memory."[13] Sadly, the chief victims of all this tribalizing of Irish war memory are the soldiers themselves. For many years after the war, there were towns like Lurgan where sepia prints of grandfathers and great-grandfathers who fought with the British army on those lunar hellhole landscapes of the Somme and Ypres still adorned the walls and gathered dust on side tables in many Catholic homes.[14] But time and history have rendered the war dead's memory obsolete: like historical orphans, these men peer out from their ornate frames, forever captured in a political No Man's Land not of their making.

Despite the divisive nature of Irish memory of the Great War, its enduring images of troops leaving for the front are no different from English memory: there are the requisite bands, the flag-waving, the cheers, and the overwhelming sense of imminent adventure. In her memoir, *Liquorice All Sorts*, Muriel Breen recalls her childhood memories of the Ulster Division's departure for France over eighty years ago. Her reminiscence of that distant event captures the pageantry and pomp that in retrospect would soon become all the more ironic. As the troops march to the boat, she remembers "[a] happy, happy band of brothers, thousands and thousands of them. I can hear the bands and see the flags. I remember the windows along the route packed with people and flags and more flags" (1993, 116). It is appropriate that Breen's description of such precombat euphoria should evoke an imaginary bygone world of chivalry with its echoes of Shakespeare's *Henry V* and the soldier king's stirring speech to his troops in the field before Agincourt ("we happy few, we band of brothers").

But, with sad hindsight, she knows this "ceremony of innocence" will not last. Her brief recollection ends with the sober acknowledgment that "Three quarters [of these men] never came back" (116). Likewise in James Kelly's memoir, *Bonfires on the Hillside*, the author's memory of the war ranges from stereotypical images of "khaki-clad soldiers singing 'Tipperary'" to numbing recollections of men at the Belfast War Hospital on the corner of the Grosvenor Road "struggling along on crutches in 'hospital blue' uniforms, pale, emaciated, some shell-shocked, some minus limbs, no longer smiling, the wreckage of war" (1995, 3).

It does not take the distance of retrospect to recognize the extent to which the war was to alter life in Ireland forever. In a letter to the *Irish Times* in December 1917, the poet AE (George Russell) spoke for many when he noted how the world of pre-1914 seemed "now to the imagination as far sunken behind time as Babylon or Samarcand." Perhaps Virginia Woolf's description of the war as a "chasm in a smooth road" (1960, 167) is the only view of the war that would gain widespread acceptance on both sides of the Irish border today. Instead, half-truths and myths about the Irish war experience still persist thanks to years of political appropriation, historical selectivity, and literary propaganda. These inherited versions of the part Ireland played in the First World War continue to influence how Irish poets write the Great War, too, but as we shall see, Irish poets have also played an integral role in shaping how memory of the war has been preserved in the Irish imagination. With so much early Irish war verse being purposefully polemical, it is not surprising that Irish war memory quickly became processed by rival unionist and republican mythographies.

Perhaps the most enduring unionist myth about the Great War surrounds the Ulster Division's attack on Thiepval during the early hours of the Somme offensive when several thousand loyal "Sons of Ulster" gave their lives in a supreme act of imperial devotion to king and empire. Of course there is nothing mythical about what happened to the men of the Ulster Division on that July morning. The facts speak for themselves: several thousand dead and several thousand wounded in what must rank as one of the most heroic frontal assaults of the war. As memories of past victories or defeats enter the realm of myth, moments of error and human frailty inevitably get elided from the heroic narrative, and in this regard, Ulster memory of the Somme is not any different. The Ulster Division's penetration of the Schwaben Re-

Loyalist heroes or nationalist pariahs? Two members of the 1st Battalion of the Royal Irish Fusiliers. Western Front. This page: a private serving as a personal attendant (batman) to an officer. Facing page: a lance-corporal sitting on a trench ladder. © Royal Irish Fusiliers Museum.

doubt overextended the range of their supporting artillery, with the result that "many men of the 36th" were killed by 'friendly fire'" (T. Bowman 1996, 50). Given the unimaginable terror and chaos of the scene, understandably not all of the troops charged the German lines fearlessly, as some "officers had to threaten to shoot some men who were trying to retreat" (50). But folk memory has little use for such details. Like nationalist memory of the Easter Rebellion, noble sacrifice and defiance against all odds lie at the heart of Ulster unionism. To this day, tribal glorifications of the Rising and the Somme betray a lack of understanding of both tragedies; as popular memory resists reinterpretation, remembrance of 1916 has yet to reach a level of public maturity. What is also interesting is how the Somme has been incorporated into the greater Ulster loyalist folk narrative where death on the battlefield is commemorated as some sort of ritualistic act reaffirming Ulster Protestants' covenant with the Union and faith in their preordained political destiny. To this day, the idea that Ulster Protestants share a manifest destiny has become irreparably linked with the sacrifice at the Somme. One recent wall mural located in "the Sandy Row area of Belfast" pays tribute to the UVF and the Thirty-sixth Ulster Division, replete with a scriptural quotation from Deuteronomy 7:2: "And when the Lord thy God shall deliver them before thee[,] thou shalt smite them and utterly destroy them[,] thou shalt make no covenant with them nor show mercy unto them" (Southern 1998, 14). The mural "affirms that the chosen people of God can in no way be defeated nor deflected from the course of their objective" (14). Consequently for loyalists, the Somme is not the name of a disastrous British offensive during the Great War but another glorious chapter in the ongoing struggle to maintain the union and deliver Ulster from its political and religious enemies. Ironically, like their nationalist counterparts, loyalists share this flair for aggrandizing a setback (the Somme); for loyalists, and even more so for nationalists, "defeat" often becomes a paradoxical synonym for victory.

This idea of a chosen people fulfilling their biblical destiny is further dramatized in Frank McGuinness's acclaimed play *Observe the Sons of Ulster Marching Towards the Somme*, which one critic describes as "a sensitive insight into the centrality of sacrifice for the Union" (Richards 1991, 142). But this belief that thousands of Ulstermen died at the Somme out of an almost fanatic love for empire is not a recent one. Certainly unionist support for the war was, for the most part, "unqualified," demonstrating, as it did, an "automatic acceptance of the righteousness of

British actions" (Hennessey 1998, 123). But during and shortly after the war, pro-imperialist poets like F. S. Boas and Samuel McCurry eagerly appropriated Ulster's losses for political gain. For them, the Somme not only confirmed Ulster's unconditional allegiance to the empire, but it was further proof that while Ulster Protestants remained "steadfast and true," their Catholic neighbors sat at home and collaborated with Sinn Fein conspiracies. During the war, several Ulster newspapers contributed to this brand of expedient sectarianism by spreading the lie that many nationalists refused to enlist. In Pamela Clayton's study, *Enemies and Passing Friends*, she notes how the editor of the *Londonderry Sentinel* "painted the picture of Ulster Unionists volunteering while nationalists stayed at home and took their jobs" (1996, 126). Of course, this kind of sectarian essentialism conveniently ignores the fact that there were Catholics in the Thirty-sixth Ulster Division and glosses over the casualties incurred by the largely nationalist Sixteenth Irish Division at the Somme in September 1916 (Leonard 1996, 259). Unfortunately the notion of Protestant duty to empire and Catholic treachery still dominates unionist memory of the war, but such views do not hold up under further scrutiny.

In fact, by the midsummer of 1914, there was a very real danger that Ulster unionists would take up arms against their own government. In order to maintain a union no longer recognized by the constitution to which they pledged allegiance, the UVF made elaborate plans to resist the implementation of Home Rule. This regional loyalty reveals a major distinction between Ulster loyalism and British patriotism. In his book, *The Strange Death of Liberal England*, George Dangerfield's lively reconstruction of the events leading up to the Home Rule impasse clearly implies that Ulster "loyalty was loyalty to Ulster" and that all the "talk of British citizenship, and crown, and Empire, and constitution was simply a way of finding synonyms for the Protestant Ascendancy" (1935, 78). It seems then that the sacrifices on the Somme were motivated primarily by autarkic allegiances rather than by devotion to the larger abstractions of Britain or empire.

In McGuinness's *Observe the Sons of Ulster Marching Towards the Somme*, the appropriately named central character, Kenneth Pyper (at once a Pied Piper leading his men and a piper of loyalism's "true blue" martial tune) rallies his comrades in the Ulster Division (the vast majority of whom were former UVF members) just before the Somme offensive by reminding them of their "homeland": "We're not in France. We're home. We're on our own territory. We're fighting for home. This river is ours. This land's ours. We've come home" (1986, 73). History and myth commingle in Pyper's quixotic address as the Somme is linked to the Boyne, *the* river of mythic significance in Protestant folk memory. The real war here is the battle to save Ulster, a battle that transcends all borders of time and space. This racial spirit of a chosen people is later mythicized, as the battle and the war become part of the prevailing unionist mythography. Memory of the war is not quarantined in some historical enclosure as an event that ended with the subsequent Armistice. Instead, it occupies the present as part of an ongoing struggle to protect a political and religious identity. Past and present form a continuum where, like the rest of Ireland, Ulster is "a land without history because the troubles of the past are relived as contemporary events" (McAuley 1991, 46).

Of course republican mythography has played an equally culpable role in distorting Irish memory of the First World War. Up until very recently, the idea that nationalist sympathies lay solidly with the Easter rebels and that few nationalists actually enlisted in the British army was the popular perception, but revisionist historians have eagerly demonstrated that this picture of popular solidarity with the rebels has little credibility. For a start, the number of rebels who took to the Dublin streets during the Easter Rebellion pales in comparison to the thousands of Irishmen who served in the British army during the Great War. F. X. Martin has pointed out that by "mid-April 1916 there were over 265,000 Irishmen serving, or in alliance, with the British forces, while the Irish Volunteers could only count around 16,000 men in its ranks" (1967, 68). Martin goes on to estimate that "over eighty percent of the [Irish] people were in sympathy with England's war effort" (68), a figure that hardly confirms the myth of a populist republican struggle against British rule. Men like parliamentary nationalist Tom Kettle served with the British army on the Western Front while even nationalists of a more extreme persuasion like Erskine Childers and Tom Barry also enlisted (Dungan 1997, 22). Even during the Easter Rebellion, there were many more nationalists killed "on the Western Front that week in the Hulluch gas attack than in Dublin" (Dungan 1993, 68).

In *Seventy Years: Being the Autobiography of Lady Gregory*, we find further corroboration of this general anti-German sentiment among ordinary Irish people. In her chapter entitled "The Folklore of the War," Lady Gregory records the views of local Galway people who spoke out against rumored German atrocities (1974, 511). She also notes that such was the extent of prowar fervor that even an ardent nationalist like John Dillon was moved to sing "God Save the King" (515). It appears, then, that many Irish men and women were supportive of the war effort, but this does not mean that all Irish Catholics saw the war as a test of imperial loyalty the way their Protestant neighbors did. Again in Lady Gregory's autobiography, she shares a more telling anecdote about how popular sentiment could be both supportive of the war effort yet still pro-nationalist. One scene early in the war that she recalls was the occasion one Boxing Day morning (December 26) when a group of Wren Boys appeared on her doorstep. Instead of bringing a dead wren, one Wren Boy was dressed up as a German soldier who the others chased off "in triumph firing imaginary shots at him with a holly bough" (519). Later, though, they "sang a song about the [Irish] Volunteers and how . . . [they would] fight Carson's men and turn them upside down" (519). This anecdote demonstrates how nationalists supported the war against Germany. However, contemporary attitudes toward the war were divided to some extent, too, as in the very same pages of Lady Gregory's autobiography, we find her make mention of Edward Martyn's report that there was "a strong feeling for the Germans among the people" (513).

Naturally there were those among the Irish intelligentsia who saw through the fervent anti-German propaganda spewed out by the British press. In a poem entitled "Pat and Fritz" (1974, 520–21), written in early 1915, Lady Gregory questions the war aims of both sides and the tragic allure of "desperate glory" for Irishmen and Germans alike:

> Oh shining angel, in the fight
> It was for Germany he died
> And I for England, wrong or right,
> On God or on the Devil's side,
> How would we know?[15]

Later in the poem, the speaker, with considerable irony, notes the price of Europe's blind allegiance to contending imperialist ideologies:

> Give over Fritz and Pat your fear
> We got report the way you died;
> We want good soldiers here as there
> From this day out you'll know your side;

> Solomon's wisdom could say
> "These all are wrong, all these are right"
> Down where your body's making clay;
> But we upon this airy height,
> The King of Friday giving laws,
> Are well contented with our cause.

In the final stanza, a bitter note of resignation undercuts the recruitment hysteria that swept through Britain in the early months of the war:

> Here the recruiting sergeants come,
> Here are the ribbons and the drum
> So right about and through the door,
> It's now you'll have your fill of war!

As an antiwar statement, Lady Gregory's little squib must have stood out against the prowar jeremiads and sentimental elegies that were so popular at the time. Later in her autobiography, she describes the "inexplicable" conflict as "a sacrifice of the best for the worst" (521), and her sentiments suggest that not everyone viewed the war as an opportunity to demonstrate the sincerity of his politics.

On the whole, the majority of the Irish populace backed the war effort, and even the immediate crisis brought on by the Easter Rising initially had little impact on prevailing sentiment, especially among the thousands of Irish troops on active service. Throughout 1916, concerns were raised by the British High Command that Irish troops' loyalty may be suspect. However, Patrick Pearse's claim that Irish regiments had been defecting to the rebel cause "was clearly nonsense," and Roger Casement's attempts to recruit Irish POWs in German prison camps for his Irish brigade were to prove to be a miserable failure (Denman 1992, 142). Casement was to later defend his recruiting activities in Germany, arguing that his work there was to keep Irishmen out of the war and "from volunteering for a world war that had no claim upon their patriotism or their honour" (1958, 148). Despite his protestations, Irish troops regarded him and his German associates as the villains responsible for the Rising (Leonard 1996, 262). But fears still lingered that the "loyalty of the Irish battalions stationed in Ireland was now suspect" (Denman 1992, 142). These concerns proved groundless, though; in fact "reserve battalions from several Irish regiments were used in the first few days of fighting in Dublin [during Easter Week]" (142), and the "overwhelming majority of nationalists serving in the army at the time thought of Pearse, James Connolly, the socialist leader of the Citizen army, and their comrades as traitors, German dupes, or hooligans" (McCaffrey 1989, 16).

Among Irish officers, unionist and nationalist alike, the reaction to the Rising was generally the same: they regarded it as a "stab in the back" and were angry at this "disruption to the war effort" (Leonard 1996, 259). Unionist officers naturally saw the Rebellion as an act of betrayal (259), while nationalist officers were deeply resentful that the Rising had eclipsed the "cause of Irish constitutional nationalism" (264). Attitudes toward the Rebellion among the rank and file nationalists of the Tenth and Sixteenth Divisions, however, were more mixed. Any distress caused by the carnage in Dublin was largely confined to the troops' concern that Irish people were being shot by the very army in which they served, and while many showed "no great sympathy with the rebels . . . , they got fed up when they heard of the execution of the leaders" (Denman 1992, 143).

It has also been demonstrated that the Rising did subsequently dampen recruiting in Ireland (Dungan 1997, 28), but despite these rumblings of discontent, the predominantly nationalist Tenth and Sixteenth Divisions never presented a security risk. While the Easter insurgents occupied the General Post Office in the center of Dublin, on the Western Front "the Germans tried hard, but with little success, to subvert Southern Irish troops," even going so far as to use "loud-hailers" to broadcast anti-British slogans and encourage defection to the German side (Middlebrook 1972, 57). During the subsequent Somme offensive in July, the Sixteenth's performance removed any doubts about its commitment to the war effort. And though throughout the rest of the war, men in the division certainly "talked a lot of politics" and on occasion displayed green flags with yellow harps with no crowns, their loyalty was never really at issue (Denman 1992, 140). The violent repression of the Rebellion, while it did not directly affect "front-line morale in Irish units[,]" did have "a long-term alienating effect on the nationalist 'psyche'" (Leonard 1996, 263).

If Irish soldiers' immediate reaction toward the Rising was generally unfavorable, overseas, the response among the Irish diaspora was equally hostile. As Thomas Rowland points out, because the full details of the Rising took several weeks to circulate abroad, in America, there was at first little attention paid to the events of Easter Week in Dublin. When reaction did come, it was not favorable as most Irish-American Catholics were appalled when they learned of the Rebellion, regarding it as nothing more than a "foolhardy fiasco" (1996).

Consequently, it would appear that the Easter rebels did not enjoy any broad-based platform of support from the Irish people both at home or abroad. Of course, all this was to change in the aftermath of the Rising and the subsequent executions. As for the many thousands of Irish nationalists who were killed during the Great War, as we have seen, in the years following partition their memory was largely consigned to the dustbin of history. Paranoia about eradicating the memory of Ireland's colonial past was officially sanctioned by the Irish State's 1937 Constitution, which promoted constricted views of Irishness, thus helping Northern Irish unionists further foster "the notion that Ulster was [exclusively] British" (T. Brown 1992, 75). Inevitably, Free State irredentism and the imperialist fervor of Northern Ireland's war commemorations reinforced the idea that the Great War was essentially a British cause.

The result is that history has not been kind to the memory of the thousands of Irish nationalists who fought in the Great War. They are an uncomfortable reminder that Irish republicans did not represent the political views of the majority of Irish people during the war years. The nationalist view of the war as an exercise in British imperial aggression is equally as erroneous as unionism's imperial sacrifice. Even more complicating is that many of those nationalists who went off to fight in the war were also self-divided in their reasons for enlistment. In his elegy for Irish soldier poet Francis Ledwidge ("In Memoriam Francis Ledwidge"), Seamus Heaney explores the reasons why nationalists like Ledwidge supported the war effort, and the "whole question of belonging permeates the poem" (T. Foster 1989, 90). Ledwidge, Heaney implies, represents an historical enigma: that of an Irish Catholic nationalist who goes to an "ambivalent death" (90). Heaney's portrait of Ledwidge as the Celtic bard who followed a "sure, confusing drum" overlooks the fact that there were many Irish Catholic nationalists, like Tom Kettle, who were committed to the war and who saw no contradiction between serving Ireland and the empire. Heaney's implication that allegiance to Ireland and loyalty to empire were mutually exclusive illustrates the extent to which Ireland's past continues to be laundered for selective narratives by nationalist as well as unionist apologists. Furthermore, these acts of historical distortion have rendered another bitter irony, for, as Keith Jeffery notes, "the nationalist and unionist casualties of the Great War [have be-

come] . . . more divided in death than they had ever been in life"
(1993, 153).

Unionist appropriation and nationalist amnesia have produced other misconceptions about the Irish soldier of the Great War.
Chief among these are the oversimplified reasons given for enlistment: unionists fought for king and country while nationalists fought for the rights of small nations, including their own
small nation's quest for Home Rule. One reason why thousands
of Irishmen, who had been previously prepared to fight for Home
Rule, joined the British army was because, as Roy Foster notes,
Irish Parliamentary Party leader John Redmond recognized that
here was the opportunity to "prove that Home Rule was fully
compatible with loyalty to Crown and Empire" (1988, 472). In
response to Redmond, many Irish National Volunteers enlisted
with the belief that they were actually fighting to preserve the
implementation of Home Rule after the war.

Apart from these political motives, there were other more
immediate incentives to enlist. First of all, there was already
a storied connection between the British army and Irish Catholics. When men like Francis Ledwidge and Tom Kettle enlisted
in their respective Irish regiments, they were actually taking
part in a tradition that had existed for generations. For reasons
of national security, it had been illegal to recruit Irish Catholics
throughout the eighteenth century, but this practice was usually ignored when a regiment was "destined for foreign parts"
(Bartlett 1993, 69). Subsequent Catholic Relief Acts and eventual emancipation (1829) enabled Irish Catholics to obtain com-
missions in the army as soldiering offered economic opportunity.
In fact, "by 1830, over 40 percent of NCOs and below of the
British army was composed of Irishmen" (81). This tradition of
soldiering as a career was still popular among Irish youth during
the decade before the Great War as many small Irish provincial
towns were known as "soldiers' towns." James Deeny, a retired
Irish doctor, recalled why service in the British army continued
to appeal to generation after generation of his fellow townsmen:

> Whether it was the Crimean, Afghan, Boer, or other smaller war of
> the Empire, the Lurgan men were always there. In my time it used
> to happen in this way. A boy leaving primary school at fourteen had
> only one hope, to be taken on somewhere as a message boy. Before the
> advent of telephones, small boys had one vocation only and that was
> to "run messages." When he became sixteen years of age and it was
> necessary to stamp his card for insurance he was let go and someone

else was taken on. If he was a Catholic (as people in this position generally were) he had then only one alternative, to go lie about his age and enlist. In a few months he would return, completely changed after good food for the first time in his life, drill, company and sport. (1989, 28)

For many men, the promise of a steady wage ("taking the king's shilling") made the British army an attractive career choice. Many linen workers across Ulster, for example, saw the opportunity to enlist as an escape route from what was already a fairly arduous existence. Loom workers in particular regarded army life as a brighter alternative. In the linen factories, the average workday ran from 6 A.M. to 6 P.M., and salaries could reach eleven shillings a week, paid fortnightly (Clendinning 1999). Potential recruits would have been easily impressed by a recruiting sergeant dressed in black padded boots and khaki. In some instances, ceremonial regalia would have been trotted out to further impress the less eager. Inevitably, many men were quickly won over by the promise of a fortnight's advance pay, a fortnight's holiday, and a new pair of boots (1999).[16]

While the financial incentive may have proved hard to resist, others felt the pressure of family expectation. Many families had a tradition of service in the British army. Fathers, grandfathers, and uncles may have seen service in such exotic locales as Egypt, South Africa, and India, and maintaining the family tradition would have provided considerable leverage for enlistment. While many men would have signed up for the "duration of the war," like their forefathers before them, other men who were already in the colors had enlisted for seven, eleven, or twenty-one years. Twenty-one year veterans could expect to spend fifteen of those years in the colors with the remaining six years in reserve (Clendinning 1999).

The prospect of joining a distinctly Irish brigade helped motivate many Irishmen to enlist for active service, too, and there were a number of options. A man could join any one of the three newly formed divisions (the Tenth, Sixteenth and Thirty-sixth) or other regular Irish regiments in the British army like the Connaught Rangers or the Irish Guards. But others, like Irish scholar and Member of Parliament, Tom Kettle, were inspired by a more lofty idealism.

Ironically, Kettle was in Belgium negotiating for firearms for the Irish Volunteers when the war broke out. His eyewitness account of German atrocities in Belgium convinced him and many others that the war was a moral issue. For Kettle, the German occupation of Catholic Belgium was another assault on a small nation's liberty; Belgium was like Ireland—"a nation in chains" (Harris 1968, 14). Convinced that neutrality was inconceivable, Kettle regarded German aggression as a "challenge to civilization" (14). Not surprisingly, most of his war poems seek to whip up support for the war by portraying the conflict as a battle between freedom and tyranny.

Whether unionists or nationalists enlisted for political reasons or not, ultimately it appears certain that many "other Irishmen joined for the more traditional reasons of a steady wage, adventure . . . foreign travel, [and] family tradition" (Denman, 1992, 180). Sometimes, however, the chief motive was nothing more than a momentary whim. Summing up his own reasons for enlisting, Monk Gibbon spoke for many in the crowd who were not inspired by any grand ideal: instead, "The war was just something that one went to" (1968, 14). Looking back years later, another Irish veteran soberly remarked that, " 'You hear some old soldiers talk about love of King and country but if you want me to let you know, most men did it because of the monotony of life and because it was a chance to be in the crowd'" (Orr 1987, 225).

Such a lack of conviction about and understanding of the conflict was probably more common than we realize. In George Bernard Shaw's prorecruitment drama *O'Flaherty VC*, the eponymous hero, when asked to explain "what the war is about" (1962, 134), can only respond, "Arra, sir, how the divil do I know what the war is about?" (134). Then at the end of the play, when O'Flaherty becomes embroiled in an argument with his mother and a young parlor maid, the war hero comically longs for the relative serenity of the front: "Some likes war's alarums; and some likes home life. I've tried both, sir; and I'm all for war's alarums now" (151). Whether, according to Shaw, some men ran away to the war "to escape from tyrants and taskmasters, termagants, and shrews" (126), others, especially in Ulster, were literally press-ganged into service. In quite a few towns, local linen magnates would form volunteer battalions by "conscripting" their own workers, who, if they valued holding on to their jobs, acquiesced with their employer's "suggestions" (Clendinning 1999). In Lurgan, for example, the Sixteenth Battalion Royal Irish Rifles' Pioneer Corps was formed with the assistance of Sir William Allen, who was co-owner of the town's largest linen factory (1999).

Of course there were others who were either largely unaffected by economic hardship and personal pressure or were oblivious to political principle. While many of Redmond's Irish National Volunteers answered their leader's call to enlist, there were some, though sympathetic with the allied cause, who "evinced little desire to come forward and join the army" (Denman 1992, 35). The farming classes were especially reluctant to join up as wartime demand for grain made farming quite a profitable enterprise. Not surprisingly, many of the young men whose deaths moved Katharine Tynan to write hundreds of consolatory elegies typically came from the urban poor.

If there were many motives to enlist, when it came time for unionists and nationalists to do their share of the fighting, some leaders regarded the war as an opportunity to find a common ground between the two political camps. When John Redmond made his offer of "full Irish support for the war effort," it was based on the hope that a cooperative effort with the Ulster Volunteers in a "joint action against Germany would weld Irishmen together" (R. Foster 1988, 472). Ironically, when the UVF was formed in 1913, even nationalist extremists like Patrick Pearse applauded the Ulster Volunteers in the naive belief that Ulster unionists and southern nationalists could unite and "get rid of the English" (467). Of course such thinking completely ignored the reason why Ulster unionists armed themselves in the first place. Yet throughout the month of August 1914 there was the strange spectacle of Ulster and National Volunteers joining together to "give a rousing send-off to departing troops" (Orr 1987, 39). In some cases, members of the local Orange lodge and the Ancient Order of Hibernians would parade together "for the first and last time in over three hundred years, and went off to the railway station and to the war" (Deeny 1989, 28). Local poetasters also did their best to encourage this cross-community war effort:

> Now here's to Edward Carson, and
> Likewise John Redmond, too,
> Sure they have joined hand in hand to
> Make the German rue. (Clendinning 1994)

At the front, troops from both sides of the political divide did generally respect each other. One veteran from the Thirty-sixth Division acknowledged this mutual regard years later:

The 16th Division played a vital role alongside of us. We'd always the greatest respect for them—except for the odd hardliner that's always there—we'd great regard for the 16th. The 16th were with us at Messines . . . [and] some of the 16th had their wee dug-out, and we went across, a couple at a time, to have a yarn with them and they came across too, a couple at a time, always leaving a couple at the first aid post—and we became great friends. (Hall 1993, 22)

And in individual cases, hard-line attitudes were altered somewhat, particularly when Irish troops from both persuasions were given the chance to fight side by side. In Major Bryan Cooper's account of the Gallipoli campaign, he notes how the Irish Tenth Division consisted of men from different creeds and political factions (1993, 137). Furthermore, Cooper claims that "old quarrels" and "inherited animosities" were often "forgotten" (138). Belfast shipyard poet Thomas Carnduff also recalls how one of his brothers who served with the Thirty-sixth Ulster Division bore "an extraordinary antipathy towards all his southern countrymen," but after the Battle of Messines Ridge, where the two largely loyalist and nationalist Irish divisions bore the brunt of the frontal assault together, Carnduff's brother held a "fierce admiration for the courage and comradeship of the Connacht men that remained with him through all the troubles that followed" (1994, 158).

This notion that a newly discovered bond between unionists and nationalists could somehow be exported home after the war was championed by John Redmond's brother Willie whose death at Messines in June 1917 it was hoped "would reconcile north and south in Ireland" (Denman 1995, 115). AE also sought to link the war dead with those who died in the Easter Rebellion as heroes whose sacrifice provided the opportunity for a new Ireland to emerge from centuries of sectarian hostility. But despite this desire to locate a point of common ground on which to build a new future, the reality is that the war actually exacerbated unionist and nationalist relations.

For a start, the whole issue of recruitment was used by both sides in a curious game of one-upmanship as Sir Edward Carson and John Redmond vied with each other to curry favor with the British government. The intent of course was to ensure that when the war ended the respective political goals of unionists and Home Rulers would be suitably rewarded. As Irish recruiting figures (except those in "loyal" Ulster) fell from 50,107 during the first six months of the war to 19,801 over the next twelve-month period, the issue of recruitment in Ireland became a serious political controversy throughout 1915 (Callan 1987, 42). By January 1916, "a bitter dispute over Irish recruitment broke out between the Ulster Unionists and the Irish party" (Denman 1992, 132). After several unsuccessful attempts to force the government to release Irish recruitment figures, the unionists felt that their suspicions were vindicated when the official numbers were given out in the Commons in January of 1916. Up until 15 December 1915, Ulster had provided 49,760 recruits while the combined total of the other three provinces numbered approximately 45,000 (133). Carson argued that these figures indicated Catholic Ireland's failure to match Ulster Protestant contributions to the war effort (even though no sectarian distinctions were made in the released totals). Such claims only increased tensions and helped circulate the erroneous belief that Irish, and especially Ulster, Catholics stirred up trouble at home while their Protestant neighbors did their patriotic duty.

Recruiting procedures were equally instrumental in preserving the sectarian/political divisions on the home front. During the war, a total of "140,460 men enlisted in Ireland in the British armed services" (Callan 1987, 42). However, the British government made several blunders with regard to Irish recruitment during these years. As secretary of war, Lord Kitchener was particularly insensitive to "the complex subtleties and loyalties of Irish politics and Irish sensitivities" (Denman 1992, 178). Nowhere was this indifference to local politics more evident than with the use of recruitment posters.

Early posters "circulating in Ireland had had no Irish content and mainly appealed to Empire loyalty":

> Lord Kitchener says "The time has come, and I now call for 300,000 recruits to form new armies. God Save the King." (Tierney, Bowen and Fitzpatrick 1988, 48)

This situation was quickly rectified by the end of 1914, when "the content of recruiting posters" began to appeal to Irish patriotism:

> You are strong and active,
> You who are fit for the fray,
> What have you done for Ireland?
> Ask of your heart today. (48)

Posters that had been used elsewhere in the United Kingdom were also adapted to the Irish situation: the appeal "To the Women of London" became "To the Women of Ireland" and the call to "Join the Army Today" read "Join an Irish Regiment To-day" (48). Other familiar icons were exploited to drum up support for the war as Irishmen were called on to defend their wives and sweethearts. Typical of the "Sporting imagery of British social discourse" (Eksteins 1989, 120), the war was even likened to an international soccer match:

> Grand international match
> Great Britain, Ireland and Allies
> v Germany, Austria, and Allies
> Are you playing the game? (Tierney, Bowen, and Fitzpatrick
> 1988, 48)

Recognizing that patriotic appeals were proving less effective as the war dragged on, government propagandists then used a variety of other ploys to boost enlistment. Stories of German atrocities and local testimonials (usually in the form of picto-rial appeals) from "military men, politicians and (contrary to common belief) Catholic clergymen" were circulated (Tierney, Bowen, and Fitzpatrick 1988, 55). In the south of Ireland, army recruiters, eager not to offend nationalist sentiment, employed the "emotive colour green" and avoided orange in their poster design; in fact, the color green "dominated more than half of the 1918 posters but only one-fifth of those printed in 1915" (54). Likewise, clearly identifiable Irish insignia (shamrocks, wolf-hounds, harps etc.) gradually replaced "Royal Arms" or the "Crown" (54).

While these strategies were designed to boost enlistment fig-ures, another effect was that they foregrounded the political iconography that marked the boundaries between the two tra-ditions. By favoring one set of cultural and political markers for another, Irish public opinion was reminded that unionism and nationalism could not be reconciled by any common denomina-tor. Another irony is that despite the fact that both unionists and nationalists were fighting ostensibly for the same cause, their motives for doing so were, as we have already seen, quite dif-ferent. Despite Redmond's romantic notion that unionists and nationalists would serve side by side as fellow Irishmen, the three new Irish divisions formed during the war were initially almost exclusively Protestant or Catholic in composition until heavy casualty rates dictated that reinforcements be "made up with whatever men" could be found (Middlebrook 1972, 271). The losses incurred by the Thirth-sixth Ulster Division and the two other Irish divisions (Tenth and Sixteenth) were subsequently replaced by English recruits.

The aftermath of the Easter Rising also raised serious questions about Britain's intent to keep faith with the future implementation of Home Rule, and Sinn Fein was quick to exploit the public's outrage after the execution of the Easter Rising's leaders, claiming, among other things, that but for the Rising, conscription would have been enforced in Ireland, thus ensuring that many more Irishmen would be "'manuring the fields of France'" (Denman 1992, 137). When compulsory registration of all males did come into effect in Great Britain in early 1916, registration in Ireland remained optional (133). But as recruiting figures continued to plummet, enforcing conscription in Ireland seemed necessary to some in government circles. Redmond's response was unequivocal: he "warned the government in October 1916 that conscription would be resisted in every village in Ireland" (137). Others were fearful that coercing a large number of disaffected Irishmen to join the army would not only affect the morale of those already in service, but would also represent a threat to national security given their questionable loyalties.

In retrospect, the likelihood that some political compromise in the Irish Question could have been achieved as a result of frontline collaboration between the largely unionist Thirty-sixth Division and the nationalist Tenth and Sixteenth Divisions was remote. The deteriorating situation at home, the issue over conscription, and the general segregation of unionists and nationalists in separate divisions muted any prospect of significant rapprochement. In fact, Southern Irish recruitment figures continued to decline throughout the duration of the war, and by August 1918, the six-month period of enlistment returns numbered only 5,812 (Callan 1987, 42). Obviously the Easter Rising had an impact on recruitment. In the south of Ireland, enlisting in an Irish regiment prior to the Rebellion was generally regarded as a nationalist gesture; after 1916, however, it was gradually construed as a sign of one's alleged pro-British loyalties. Subsequent attempts to enforce conscription in Ireland, especially in the aftermath of the executions of the Easter Rising leaders, only encouraged further anti-British sentiment, undermined the Irish Parliamentary Party's position, and bolstered support for Sinn Fein. Despite the fact that Ireland still possessed a fairly large body of eligible men for service, the government "decided against Irish conscription" for two reasons: "first, the enlarged garrison necessary to enforce conscription would have offset the number of men enlisted; [and] secondly, conscription would have jeopardized the Irish Convention which had been searching for a solution to the Irish [Home Rule] problem since July" 1917 (Ward 1974, 109). Nevertheless, when the German offensive of March 1918 inflicted heavy allied casualties, the need for reinforcements became even more acute, and British Prime Minister Lloyd George became further convinced that Irish conscription was "necessary to the war effort" despite its cost: Home Rule (111).

When the New Military Service Bill was introduced in the House of Commons on 9 April 1917, its "provision of Irish conscription" led to a walkout of Irish Party M.P.s who clearly felt that Home Rule must precede any attempts to enforce conscription in Ireland (Ward 1974, 114). The feasibility of Irish conscription became more and more questionable as Sinn Fein's antirecruiting campaign led to its proscription in July 1918 and the internment of many of its leaders (120). Despite increasing hostilities, the government pressed ahead with its "dual policy" of conscription and Home Rule, and by October, the firm date of December 1 was set for Irish conscription (124–25). Clearly the risk of destroying the Irish Parliamentary Party's chances in the November general election was considered worth taking (Sinn Fein won a landslide victory), but all this was preempted by the November Armistice.

In hindsight, the government's handling of the Irish conscription crisis was particularly inept. Lloyd George defended his policy because he felt "conscription was necessary to get the Tories to accept Home Rule, but in fact he well knew that when the crisis broke in France Home Rule was introduced to help the passage of conscription, not the reverse" (Ward 1974, 128). On the whole, the government's bungled recruitment policy in Ireland demonstrated an overall insensitivity toward Irish affairs. Given the country's political turmoil and the delicate nature of Irish support for the British war effort, it should have been obvious that Ireland could not be treated like any other region of the United Kingdom. The only practical policy to pursue given the volatility of the Irish situation and the incendiary nature of Home Rule would have been to exempt Ireland from conscription and leave "Irish affairs . . . in abeyance for the duration of the war" (128). As a result of the mismanaged Irish policy, Redmond's Parliamentary Party went the way of the stegosaurus, and Sinn Fein's political ascendancy led Ireland down the road to the Irish Treaty in December 1921 (129).

Despite the individual acts of comradeship and mutual respect shared by unionist and nationalist troops during the war, the war did not briefly reconcile political differences between unionists and nationalists. Far from offering an opportunity to resolve local disputes during a global conflict, the war further exacerbated the existing feelings of mistrust and sectarian enmity between both sides. As British army veterans, many Irish nationalists found postwar Ireland a hostile environment. Only a small number of officers "became prominent in Sinn Fein or the IRA after the Armistice," but some continued to serve with the British army or "found civilian careers outside Ireland after the war," while some later returned to serve in the new Free State Army at the outbreak of the "Civil War" (Leonard 1996, 264). For enlisted men, prospects were much bleaker: unemployment and silence about one's war service.

As the recruitment and conscription crises further alienated unionists and nationalists, it is understandable that Irish war poetry should reflect these divisions and fault lines that run through Irish war memory. But another attractive war myth that surfaces in Irish war poetry, especially in the individual elegies, is one that Robert Wohl's book *The Generation of 1914* attempts to dispel. Wohl argues that the notion that Britain's best and brightest perished in the war has "provided an important self-image for the survivors from within the educated elite and a satisfying and perhaps even necessary explanation of what happened after they returned from the war" (1979, 115). Wohl goes on to note that the myth's adherents see Britain's subsequent postwar sociocultural decline as a contributing factor to the Second World War (113). The temptation to look back at the war and see it as the destroyer of British pedigree and culture obviously is, as Wohl maintains, an attempt to explain current miseries by escaping into retrospect. Furthermore, Wohl believes that this "lost generation" myth can be dismissed as "elitist nonsense" for, if anything, death in the trenches was "meted out at random to brave and cowardly alike" (113).

In the Irish context, Yeats's elegies for Robert Gregory support this idea that the war robbed Britain and Ireland of its best and brightest. Yeats suggests that the loss of men like Gregory had profound repercussions on Ireland's political and cultural identity. As arguably the best poems written by any Irish poet about the war, these tributes to Gregory ("our perfect man") subscribe to a certain political and cultural hierarchy, and his death symbolizes the Anglo-Irish elite's political and cultural decline. Yeats's war poetry implicates the war's role in the demise of Anglo-Irish culture and the negation of any prospect for the survival of a healthy political, ethnic and cultural diversity in Ireland. Such a portrayal tends to gloss over the fact that after the founding of the Irish Free State in 1922, the Anglo-Irish did participate in the administration of the new regime (including Yeats himself). Some of them even took posts in the newly formed Irish army while the "central, local government and public services also received an intake of returning ex-soldiers who were invaluable in the many details of administration" (Harris 1968, 207–8). Also, like Yeats, other prominent Anglo-Irish figures entered political life: for example, General Bryan Mahon who led the "first ever Irish division to war became a Senator" (208).

Tribal readings of the Irish role in the war have also infiltrated Irish pop culture. Not surprisingly, Irish folk music has led the way in politicizing war memory. In the Easter Rising ballad "The Foggy Dew" (the words of which were written by Canon Charles O'Neil), we are told that it was "better to die 'neath an Irish sky than at Suvla or Sud el Bar" (Loesberg 1979, 60, 15).[17] Michael MacDonagh, the aforementioned author of *The Irish at the Front*, was convinced that the memory of Irish troops would be revered in the years to come. After recounting the Dardenelles fiasco, MacDonagh wrote: "Because of those [Irish] dead Gallipoli will ever be to the Irish race a place of glorious pride and sorrow" (1916, 102). On this note he was not alone. Major Bryan Cooper who served with the Tenth Irish Division at Gallipoli, was also optimistic that Ireland would "not easily forget" Irish sacrifices in the Dardenelles (1993, 139). Subsequent events were to prove both men sadly wrong as no official memorial service for the Irish dead at Gallipoli is held in the Irish Republic today. On the contrary, popular memory of Irishmen who died during the Turkish campaign is usually defamatory. In "Gallipoli," a song recorded by popular Irish folk band The Fureys (1984), the elegist's lament at the death of a young Irish soldier who was "blown to Kingdom Come on the shores of Gallipoli" is transformed into a nationalist propaganda exercise:

> You fought for the wrong country, you died for the wrong cause
> And your ma always said it was Ireland's great loss.
> All those fine young men who marched to foreign shores
> To fight the wars when the greatest war of all was at home.[18]

As these lines imply, the Gallipoli dead have become the scape-goats of republican mythography.

We also see this historical distortion of Ireland's war dead in Irish drama and film. In his acclaimed play *Dancing at Lughnasa*, Brian Friel accurately alludes to the stigma of collaboration that was to haunt Irish war veterans. Father Jack, a repatriated priest from Africa who served during the war as a "chaplain to the British forces in East Africa," lives with the fact that his "brief career in the British Army was never referred to in that house" (1990, 8). And this is some sixteen years after the war has ended. Of course, as we have already seen, Ulster Protestant war memory provides a stark contrast to nationalist Ireland's lingering shame. The Somme takes its place alongside the Boyne and Aughrim on Orange Order banners. But the war is also celebrated in loyalist ballads where Great War icons are processed by sectarian and racial idioms.[19] In one scene from Irish director Thaddeus O'Sullivan's film *Nothing Personal* (1995), a paramilitary moll sings a tribute to Billy McFadzean (one of four members of the Thirty-sixth Ulster Division to be awarded a VC for gallantry during the Somme offensive) in a bar somewhere in loyalist Belfast. According to Bill Rolston, this song (simply titled "Billy McFadzean") borrows its melody from the republican tune, "James Connolly," and it commemorates "the sacrifice made by loyalists [at the Somme] in order to stay British" (1999, 49). Surrounded by loyalist gunmen, the singer's performance links the heroism of an Ulster war hero of yesteryear with the present-day defenders of the faith. Yet as David Fitzpatrick has pointed out, the Easter Rising and the Somme share more than just a common melody. In his book *The Two Irelands 1912–1939*, Fitzpatrick notes that both events share a sense of fighting against "overwhelming odds," an acceptance of defeat with "dignity," the suffering of "appalling losses," and the sense of martyrdom for a just cause (1998, 61). Another legacy of the Somme and the Easter Rising is how both events continue to be exploited and distorted by both sides' paramilitaries. The many wall murals in and around Belfast featuring images of the old UVF alongside their modern-day namesakes and the rhetoric of Pearse accompanied by the ubiquitous balaclava-clad republican volunteer indicate the extent to which these past defeats are viewed as part of the same ongoing struggle.

Obviously such examples of how Irish history is constantly appropriated to serve loyalist and republican ideology reaffirm the validity of Edna Longley's argument that the past continues to divide the Irish imagination. Memory of the war has been submerged by the subsequent mythmaking industry of unionism and nationalism. In his book, *Pleasant the Scholar's Life*, Maurice Goldring argues that the more a nation is defined racially (race, culture, religion, and language), the more it is likely to exclude "others and thus militarises [its] political life" with the chief goal being the "protection of the community's cultural borders" (1995, 138). Surely these divergent memories of the Great War have played their part, too, in maintaining current political divisions in Ireland. And like the ongoing debates over what constitutes Irishness, Irish memory of the war continues to be distorted by those who search for what Edward Said describes as "a more congenial national origin than that provided by colonial history" (1994, 220). Said goes on to argue that those who wish to create "a new pantheon of heroes and (occasionally) heroines, [and] myths" do so in order to accommodate the "reappropriation of a land by its people" (220). Maybe this is why our image of the Western Front, where we visualize thousands of tiny sepia figures crawling through the mud in a never-ending, deadly game of territorial gain and loss, is such a fitting analogy for the endless jockeying for position in Ireland's ongoing political and cultural wars. In the ensuing discussion we will see how many of these aforementioned appropriations, misinterpretations, myths, and misperceptions continue to pervade the diverse range of responses articulated by Irish poets about such a controversial period in Irish history.

3

The Soldier Poets

THE GENERAL PUBLIC'S MEMORY OF THE SOLDIER POETS OF THE GREAT WAR usually consists of sepia prints of khaki-clad English officers of public school pedigree, but the truth is that many of the soldiers who wrote and published poetry during the First World War came from various backgrounds. The thousands of poems published in local and national newspapers throughout the United Kingdom during the war were mostly written by men who never considered themselves poets and who responded to their immediate war experience with the occasional hastily written verse that covered "a wide range of outlook" (Powell 1993, xiv). In contrast to the poetry writing fever that gripped many English troops during the war, Irish troops were less inclined to write poetry. As in the rest of the United Kingdom, many small town newspapers did publish poems sent home from the front by local men on active duty, but the number of Irish soldiers who actually wrote about their war experiences during the conflict is small in comparison to England's thriving war poem industry. Lower literacy rates, fewer numbers of Irishmen in uniform in comparison to the total number of English enlistees, and, for some, a greater sense of ambivalence toward the war may explain why Irish soldiers were not as prolific poetasters as their English counterparts, but such explanations remain purely speculative.

The fact is that the majority of Irish soldiers seldom wrote poems about their war experiences.[1] For instance, none of the personal war diaries or the Regimental Gazette in the Royal Irish Fusiliers Regimental Museum contains any poems about the war. But those who did send home the odd poem from the front were virtually guaranteed publication in their hometown newspaper. Of course reciting poetry had always been an extremely popular form of local entertainment throughout Ireland; while many semi-illiterates could recite most of Oliver Goldsmith's "The Deserted Village" (a particular favorite), the more creative could publicly declaim their own compositions (Clendinning 1999). These local bards took their poetry recitation so seriously that when called upon to perform their work at a social gathering, great care was taken not to recite the entire poem for fear of imitation or, worse yet, not being asked to perform publicly again because their work was now completely known (1999). As for the tradition of publishing poetry in the local newspaper, this practice flourished throughout Ireland well into the 1940s and 1950s. Publishing his poems in the local paper was where Francis Ledwidge first gained some notoriety.

Another particularly strong tradition was that of the street poem. Prior to and during the Great War, many streets in small Irish towns would have had their own poem, a sort of street ballad that listed the names (and quite often the nicknames) of the street's residents along with their trades and any other noteworthy exploits worth mentioning (Clendinning 1999). In some cases, neighborhood rivalries introduced an element of satire into these street poems as the names of characters from other streets would be cited in very unflattering terms (1999). This practice of incorporating the names of local characters in a poem was soon adopted by Irish soldier poets themselves, many of whom probably had prior experience as street bards. An example of this kind of adaptation of street verse to the experience of the war is a poem by Lurgan man Bob McDowell, who served with the Royal Irish Fusiliers. In McDowell's poem "The Hill Street Tommies," the street bard compiles a heroic catalogue of friends and neighbors who left the local linen mill "to fight the foe":

> There's big Bob Lunn and Donaldson,
> Who could make boots with any other,
> And the Blizzard Boy, his mother's joy,
> Who could never keep out of bother.
> There's Bobbie Gordon, solid man, old
> Tom Black and Campbell.
> When these lads brave cross o'er the waves
> The Germans in their boots will tremble. (Clendinning 1994)

Irrespective of their quality, these kinds of automatic war ballads are noteworthy because of the attitudes they reveal about the war itself. The cheery campfire coziness typifies the stock response to the war by many Irish soldier poets from the lower ranks, even after many of their comrades were buried in "some foreign field."

What the home front saw. This photograph of the "The Roman Road," a main communication trench used by Irish soldiers near Auchonvillers, was taken during the summer months. In winter, the trench became a morass. © Royal Irish Fusiliers Museum.

What the soldiers saw. Irish officer (Captain Le Mare, 1st Battalion Royal
Irish Fusiliers) in a waterlogged trench. Beaumont Hamel. February 1916.
© Royal Irish Fusiliers Museum.

As we have just seen, the recurring themes of most soldier poetry seldom rise above the sentimental or the propagandistic.
One poem, "A Wee British Tommy," written by a "soldier lad in
the trenches" and published in the *Armagh Guardian* in February 1915 typifies the kind of poetry that appeared in many Irish
newspapers during the war:

> A wee British Tommy
> Writes home from the front;
> A few lines to the mother he loves;
> "Keep up heart mother dear
> For the God we all fear
> Is watching us from above."
> As I lie in my 'dug out
> Just off the main trench,
> My boots full of water
> And clothes simply drenched,
> I pray to my God that he will not wrench
> The boy from the mother he loves.[2]

In what was a fairly formulaic response to the war, the common
themes of homesickness and trench fatigue were usually complemented by bouts of saber rattling, performed as much for the
soldier poet himself as for the folks back home:

> Is it not death? From the Germans I fear
> For I'm equal to them one to three,
> And I've faced them in scores
> Like my dad did the Boers
> And I'll make them respect, even me.
> I have fought both at Mons,
> The Marne and the Aisne,
> I have fought for the coast
> And I'll fight yet again,
> But if when the roll's called
> I am found with the slain
> Pray, remember "the mother I love."

This kind of jingoistic bravado was extremely common in the
poems sent home from the front. In another poem "written by
an Irish Fusilier" and also published in the *Armagh Guardian*
(January 1915), the war effort is portrayed as a truly *United*
Kingdom effort:

Now here's to good old Ireland and bonnie Scotland too,
The boys of merry England and the Welsh taffies so true.
The Yankees are all watching us and the Irish people too,
To see how we fight for the cause of our right
And the fame of the red, white, and blue.

Like this example, many war poems written by poorly educated soldiers had weak endings which usually opted for "ideological propriety" (Featherstone 1995, 41) over originality. But local communities cared little about the quality of the poetry sent from the front. What was important were the reassurances, the testimony to duty, honor and respect. The *Armagh Guardian*'s prefatory comment to "A Wee British Tommy" noted that the poem was published "as it is written and though the metre is faulty the sentiment is of merit."

However, there was a small group of Irish soldier poets who did publish volumes of verse between 1914 and 1918, and it is their work in particular that will be the chief focus of this chapter. Not surprisingly, most of these soldier poets relied heavily on the inherited idioms and figurative devices of nineteenth-century English verse while the more sophisticated ones tended to imitate what was currently in vogue. This meant that their work was generally Georgian in theme and technique, a term that quickly became a pejorative to the early modernists who regarded Georgian poetry as nothing more than a second-hand offering of romantic escapism, simplicity, and ruralism.

Generally speaking most of the themes and stylistic features of those Irish soldiers who saw themselves as poets rather than occasional versifiers are largely indistinguishable from the kind of popular verse written by their English counterparts. While some of these poets explored "the sufferings of soldiers at the front, . . . one of the main, though much neglected, themes of war literature in English" (Rutherford 1989, 72), all of them participated in the traditional discourses about the war (escapism and propaganda). One preoccupation was the desire to transcend the war, to view it as a bad dream, but this fixation with romantic escape was shared by all ranks. Irish writer Alexander Irvine, who served as a YMCA padre during the war, recalled gazing toward Amiens from his position on the Somme every morning "to see if the cathedral was still standing" (Smyth 1980, 11). Depressed by the devastation that he saw there, Irvine recalled closing his eyes on one occasion and imagining a new cathedral where the ruins of the old one were. With a typical soldier's sense of irony, though, Irvine remembered that his fleeting vision of a reborn Amiens was soon shattered by a heavy gun barrage (1980, 11). If some soldiers daydreamed to momentarily forget the death and destruction all around them, others clung to the hope that as the situation was so bad it had to end soon. In a letter written from his hospital bed in Marseilles, a Lurgan soldier, Sergeant Lowery, tried to describe what he had witnessed during the heavy fighting that took place around Ypres from October to November of 1915:

> I can't describe the sensation of putting a bayonet through another man, but it certainly means that if you don't the other fellow will, and I can't say it has troubled me very much. . . . I could tell some nasty stories but I think this is enough for the present. Just a word about Ypres, I saw it in its beauty, and in its death throes. Such was the scene of desolation. The cathedral was twice the size of the Catholic one in Armagh and more magnificent also, but it is gone now. I wish it was all over[;] it's too terrible to last long. (Clendinning 1994)

There are many letters like this written by Irish soldiers that make no attempt to misrepresent what was going on at the front. But while some Irish troops were less likely to rhapsodize about how the war resembled some grand Homeric scouting expedition, there were others, especially early in the war, whose letters were the prose equivalent of a John Hinde postcard. In a letter home to his wife, another Lurgan soldier, Private Henry Lunn, who was "a well-known local footballer associated with [Lurgan team] Glenavon," wrote:

> We are having a good time out here, considering everything. Our regiment has got a band and every time we come out of the trenches we enjoy its music very much, while we have a gay old time playing football behind the firing line, and travelling on motors to other districts to play other regiments. There is no mistake we fairly enjoy ourselves, and sometimes we do not realise there is a war on at all. (Clendinning 1994)

Of course it is the narrative gaps in Private Lunn's letter that betray his efforts to spare his wife further anxiety. But when Irish soldiers turn to verse, there is little room for blunt honesty or well-intentioned disingenuousness. It is as though the beauty of poetry cannot accommodate the carnage of war.

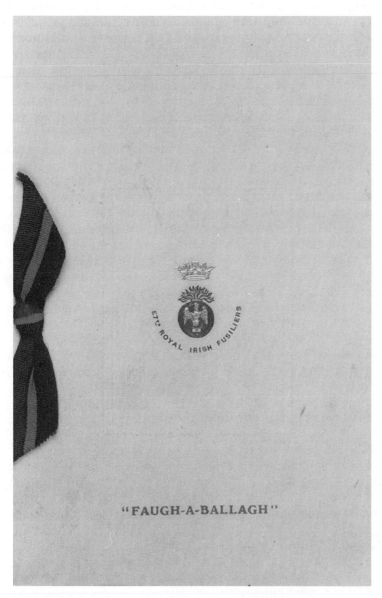

"FAUGH-A-BALLAGH"

Another example of how the army created a cosmetically appealing image of the war's alleged benignity. Christmas cards like this one were distributed by the 1st Battalion Royal Irish Fusiliers in 1915. © Royal Irish Fusiliers Museum.

As we shall see, escapist fantasy and patriotic tub-thumping dominate Irish soldiers' poetry, but what often sets their work apart from English soldier poets is their attempt to explain why they, as Irishmen, volunteered to fight. For some, enlistment was an uncomplicated affair requiring little political debate, while others struggled to reconcile their divided loyalties to Ireland and to the war against Germany. Above all else, most of these poets' response to the war is colored to some degree by local politics, and we find evidence in their war poems of submerged unionist and nationalist mythographies.

Apart from exploring the major themes of Irish soldier poetry, we will also survey its chief stylistic features. A few generalizations can be made about the fixed forms, figurative devices, and techniques favored by Irish soldier poets. For a start, they were enamored with the aesthetic appeal of an English pastoral poetry, and this brand of poetry, which propagated the "myth of an England essentially rural and essentially unchanging[,] appealed across political lines to both Conservatives and Imperialists, and to anti-Imperialists, Liberals, and Radicals" (Featherstone 1995, 29). Irish soldier poets also preferred the lyric and the swinging rhythms of the ballad, and they drew extensively on the iconography of popular Victorian verse with its edification of such imperialist pieties as honor, chivalry, and sacrifice. (Irish soldier poets also affected the campy italic typeface and extremely odd patterns of indentation fashionable in popular Georgian verse.)

By borrowing heavily from the English tradition, Irish soldiers' war poetry is predictably dominated by pastoral landscapes, and a fascination with the local flora and fauna either of the front or of home. In the marching songs of Tom Kettle and Patrick MacGill, for instance, we encounter parody and mimicry of the jaunty rhythms of Kiplingesque imperialist propaganda, but what is particularly ironic is how soldier poets like Kettle, who was an ardent supporter of Home Rule, adopt what George Parfitt describes as the "nationalistic public style" usually associated with arch-imperialists like Henry Newbolt and William Watson (1990, 10). Perhaps it is not surprising then that Irish soldier poets' literary referents should be so decidedly "English" considering the likelihood that any instruction they received in the art and craft of poetry was no doubt largely confined to the traditions of the English lyric and English romanticism. As a result, their poetry rarely strays beyond the derivative, with its obsession with English pastoralism and a predilection for Greek mythology.

With the possible exception of Francis Ledwidge, most Irish soldier poets wrote in a style that made the characteristics of Georgian poetry look decidedly innovative by comparison. One soldier poet who typifies this betrothal to an archaic English aesthetic was Willoughby Weaving, an Oxford graduate who served as a lieutenant in the Royal Irish Rifles (one source lists him serving with the Royal Irish Fusiliers) before being invalided home in 1915. During the war, he published two volumes of verse containing poems about the war. *The Star Fields and Other Poems* (1916), Weaving's first collection, received high praise from the poet laureate Robert Bridges who, in a commissioned introduction, noted of Weaving that "there can scarcely have been a more genuine and prolific poet in the trenches" (1916, viii). As Bridges' "protégé," Weaving's nature poetry "achieved wide popularity" (Gardner 1964, 184), and Bridges was especially fond of Weaving's fidelity to the elegiac, the chivalric, and the pastoral. In *The Bubble and Other Poems* (1917), Weaving's second wartime volume of poems, there is no discernible shift in his treatment of the war as he remains faithful to his ultraromantic ideal. Weaving's obsession with medieval vernacular was hardly unique. Even the better-known war poets sometimes fell into archaism. For example, before finding his voice as an ironist, some of Siegfried Sassoon's early war poems reveal an antiquated predilection for "jarring medieval English words" (Quinn 1994, 161). What distinguishes Weaving from many of his Georgian contemporaries, however, is his rejection of the colloquial voice. Every line seldom wavers from the regal or the romantic, and his poetry's literariness reveals a hybrid style, commingling romantic and Victorian nostalgia with neoclassical decorum. A contemporary reviewer for *The Dublin Express* haughtily noted that Weaving's poetry differed significantly from "the verses of other soldier poets" whose popular verse was "the production of only partially educated men" (Weaving 1917, 147). By comparison, Weaving's poetry, was judged to be "the work of a ripe classical scholar" (147), and the elegies he wrote for fellow soldiers killed in action literally seethe with the elements of traditional pastoral poetry.

We see evidence of Weaving's classical education in "In Battle," one of a sequence of sonnets from *The Star Fields and Other Poems* (1916, 158). Ostensibly a war poem, Weaving's short narrative communicates nothing about his experiences at the front or the realities of mechanized mass slaughter. Instead, in his evocation of the martial pieties of honor and sacrifice, he describes a

scene from the *Aeneid* where the hero Aeneas confronts the evil
Rutalian King Turnus in a battle to decide the future of Rome:

> As dives a black wind down upon the sea
> Came all the dark Rutalian chivalry,
> Athwart Aeneas' brazen ranks, relying
> Upon their chieftain's eagle heart and eye,
> Who in their foremost rank, with red plume flying
> And haughty sanguine face and voice defying,
> Rode—Turnus!—in his golden panoply.

Opting for analogy in order to draw connections between historical events that shaped the future of empires (Roman and
British), Weaving depicts a classical dichotomy between the
forces of good and evil with Aeneas's allied army of Trojans and
Etruscans representing Britain and her allies and the Rutalians,
with their demonic leader Turnus, as the classical counterparts
of the Kaiser and his German hordes. Weaving's language is also
retrospective in its resemblance to the studied archaisms of Lord
Macauley's *Lays of Ancient Rome* (1842). Ultimately, though, the
poem buries the Great War under an avalanche of myth and romantic rhetoric and by doing so illustrates Paul Fussell's conclusions about the sources and overall inadequacy of this kind
of war poetry. According to Fussell, in his magisterial work *The
Great War and Modern Memory*, the popular literature of the
time favored the "feudal language" of Tennyson's *Morte* and the
"pseudo-medieval romances of William Morris" (1975, 21). We
see Weaving's predilection for this sort of "raised" language with
his "black wind" cavalry and "brazen ranks" of warriors.

Fussell maintains that such language was inappropriate to the
subject of the war, but Weaving evades this charge by almost
avoiding the Great War altogether. All of his war poems celebrate the glory of sacrifice and the importance of honor without ever describing the front line. Instead, his landscapes are
remote and timeless. The closest he comes to actually situating
his war poetry at the front is in the poems, "The Hill by Hooge"
(1917, 84) and "Between the Trenches" (13), but despite their titles, neither poem directly engages the trauma or the conditions
of the firing line. Apart from the odd reference to a "shell" or a
"soiled stretcher," both poems mourn the death of comrades in
a language thickly larded with the epithets of romantic sentiment: the dead are inevitably always described as "phantoms,"
"shades," or "spirits." Certainly there is a fixation with "death"

in the abstract in Weaving's war poetry as he romanticizes the tragedy of shattered lives. His war poetry abounds with chivalric euphemisms for "death." His soldiers never actually die: they hear "the sweeter music," travel "beyond life's veil" (Tennysonian echoes here), enjoy a "splendid fate," depart for a "greater destiny," or become "A glory for ever." Overall, the constant reference to myth and the orchestration of artificial diction support Fussell's contention about the ineffectiveness of such language, for no amount of myth could ever expiate the horror of the daily massacres on the Western Front. Then again, what poetry could? Weaving's war poems ultimately reveal an attachment to the poetic sureties of a Victorian world that rapidly receded into the haze of retrospect as the war raged on.

Weaving's work illustrates the extent to which some Irish soldier poets resorted to a language that could not "accommodate" an experience that was "too vast," "too various," and "too powerful" (J. Johnston 1964, 13). Anachronistic ideas about chivalry, sacrifice, and honor were so deep-rooted in the popular conscience that they still gripped the contemporary imagination long after the obscenities of the front rendered them absurdly obsolete. One would look hard to find the kind of antiwar bitterness of a Sassoon or Owen in Irish soldier poetry; on the contrary, most Irish soldier poets seldom stray beyond the notions of the war as a purifying force or as another opportunity for adventure. But, as we shall see, while many of these poems record cheery, Boy Scout accounts of life at the front, they reveal other submerged tensions ranging from subtle protest to an almost complete loss of faith in the war effort altogether. Political controversies surrounding Ireland's war role also feature prominently in Irish soldier poetry. One example is how poets like Francis Ledwidge and Tom Kettle struggle to reconcile what they perceived to be the apparent incongruities between their nationalist sympathies and their enlistment in the British army.

Perhaps the best known of all the Irish soldier poets is Francis Ledwidge who personifies the internal divisions of Ireland's Great War experience. Up until very recently, he was regarded as a minor Irish offshoot of Georgian poetry, but lately, his reputation as a poet of significance has been resurrected. During the summer of 1997, the eightieth anniversary of his death near Ypres in late July 1917 was marked by a special service held just outside his hometown of Slane in County Meath. This effort to commemorate Ledwidge has also been matched by a rekindled interest in his poetry. While his *Selected Poems* appeared along with an appreciative introduction by Seamus Heaney back in 1992, some of his poems were also included in Heaney and Ted Hughes' collaborative anthology, *The School Bag,* where Ledwidge keeps company with exalted elegists like Tennyson, Milton, and Gray (1997, 508–9). Apart from frequent appearances in various anthologies, an updated edition of Ledwidge's *Complete Poems* appeared in 1997 with an additional sixty-six poems not included in the 1974 edition.[3] All this attention would not have surprised Ledwidge's contemporaries, though, for during his own lifetime he enjoyed a popular readership. When his first collection *Songs of the Fields* appeared in 1916, it "rapidly sold out" (Dole 1983, 205). Of his remaining three volumes, one was published while he was still on active duty (*Songs of Peace* in 1917), and *Last Songs,* his third volume, appeared the year after his death in 1918. A fourth volume, the *Complete Poems,* was published as early as 1919 and has thrice been revised and reissued.

Few poets can claim both commercial and critical success, but when it first appeared, *Songs of the Fields* received glowing front page reviews in *The New York Times Book Review* and the *Times Literary Supplement,* and noted Georgian poet-critics like John Drinkwater and T. Sturge Moore wrote generally favorable critical essays about Ledwidge's poetry. After his death, eulogistic reviews appeared in several prominent publications. In an obituary wistfully entitled "Lost Music," the reviewer in the August 1917 issue of the *Times Literary Supplement* mourned the loss of another talented voice, while in a essay in *The English Review* (1918, 127–37) fellow Irish writer and war poet Katharine Tynan recounted her meeting and correspondence with Ledwidge prior to his death. Other noteworthy admirers were Edward Marsh who included several of Ledwidge's poems in his anthologies of *Georgian Poetry* and fellow soldier poet Ivor Gurney who, despite being confined in a mental hospital in Kent after the war, later wrote musical scores for a number of Ledwidge's poems (Stephen 1996, 140). Another famous devotee was Irish patriot Roger Casement who read a volume of Ledwidge's poems while locked up in the Tower of London in the days before his execution for treason in August 1916 (Inglis 1973, 369).

Unfortunately, over eighty years after Ledwidge's death, the advent of modernism has effectively relegated Georgian poets like him to the margins of literary history. So why all this effort and enthusiasm to retrieve him from the literary scrap heap? Perhaps the answer to that question reveals more about current trends in literary criticism than it does about the perceived literary value of Ledwidge's work. Despite Seamus Heaney's disclaimers of mere ethnic affection for Ledwidge in his prefatory comments to the *Selected Poems*, it appears that Ledwidge's poetry, especially his war poetry, has regained an audience chiefly due to its cultural and ideological significance. Certainly Heaney's remarks appear to bear this out, for he readily admits that while "Ledwidge is neither a very strong or a very original talent" (1992, 20), he still "represents conflicting elements in the Irish inheritance which continue to be unresolved" (19). Heaney's point here, that these "conflicting elements" need to be resolved, operates under the assumption that Ledwidge's Irishness and Britishness cannot coexist. This kind of thinking betrays the tendency to plaster anachronistic nationalist notions of Irishness on the past. While Ledwidge was eager to establish his Irishness, his experiences hardly typify the attitudes of many of his fellow Irish soldiers as their sense of "Britishness in . . . the Empire was flexible enough to accommodate other identities within it" (Hennessey 1998, xxi). The fact remains, though, that Ledwidge felt sufficiently insecure about his involvement in the war that in his war poetry he tried to reconcile the political ironies of his role as an Irish nationalist in the British army. His attraction to Irish myth and local landscapes reveals a man desperately trying to locate an Irish political and cultural identity in opposition to the suffocating presence of a British culture that he can never truly shake off.

There was certainly little in his background to suggest that Ledwidge would become a best-selling poet. The son of a Boyne Valley farm worker, he was born into a family of eight children and left school when he was only thirteen ("Francis Ledwidge" 1987, 105). While drifting through a number of manual-labor jobs over the next few years, he enjoyed some early success when local newspapers began publishing his poems. His subsequent "discovery" by unionist peer Lord Dunsany gave birth to this cozy image of him as a peasant poet, but Dunsany also helped further his education and introduced him to other writers like AE and Katharine Tynan (105). While this unlikely duo (a unionist peer and a road laborer) shared a love of poetry, Ledwidge was no unionist. On the contrary, even though he never joined Sinn Fein, he did help organize the local corps of the Irish Volunteers, and when the Volunteers split over whether or not to support the war effort, Ledwidge followed Irish Parliamentary Party leader John Redmond's call to sign up for active duty by enlisting in the Royal Inniskilling Fusiliers in October 1914.

There has been considerable speculation over what motivated
Ledwidge to enlist, especially since he was already a member of a
militia (albeit a poorly armed one) that was preparing to fight, if
need be, for Home Rule. Alice Curtayne, Ledwidge's biographer,
argues that the poet's friendship with Lord Dunsany played no
role in his decision to enlist. In fact, in one of the first letters
he wrote home while on active service, Ledwidge expressed no
qualms about his decision to join up. For him, the war was simply
a struggle to save the world from the threat of evil:

> Some of the people who know me least imagine that I joined the
> army because I knew men were struggling for higher ideals and
> great emprises, and I could not sit idle to watch them make for me a
> more beautiful world. They are mistaken. I joined the British Army
> because she stood between Ireland and an enemy common to our
> civilization and I would not have her say that she defended us while
> we did nothing at home but pass resolutions. (Curtayne 1972, 83)

Of course Ledwidge's idealism only partially explains why he enlisted. A more personal and certainly more plausible reason was
the breakup of his relationship with a local girl, Ellie Vaughey,
whose family did not warm to the prospect of their daughter mar-
rying a road laborer. Her subsequent marriage to John O'Neil, a
local farmer, and sudden death less than a year later in Manchester deeply hurt the romantic Ledwidge, and the war provided
him with the opportunity to escape if not to forget (Jeffares
1982, 184).[4]

In the three years he had left to live, Ledwidge saw action on
three fronts. He served on the Gallipoli peninsula from July to
October 1915, then was reassigned to Serbia and Salonika from
October 1915 to April 1916 before being evacuated home, suffering from exhaustion. After an extended convalescence in Ireland,
he was sent to the Western Front in January of 1917 where he
was killed by shellfire in late July while working behind the lines
on a road-building detail ("Francis Ledwidge" 1987, 106).

No doubt Ledwidge's reputation as a poet benefited from the
literary establishment and general public's interest in anything
written by those in uniform: indeed, "By mid-1916 booksellers
were reporting that the public was eagerly buying slender volumes of works by the less well-known poets, especially if the authors had been killed in action" (Ross 1965, 143). Of Ledwidge's
first three volumes, only the second and third were written while
he was in the army. As a result, *Songs of the Fields* contains no

poems directly about the war, while in *Songs of Peace* and *Last Songs*, the war is rarely treated overtly. While most of these poems consist of landscape descriptions registering the customary escapist sentiments of most Georgian war poetry, other tensions also surface. A number of poems support the war effort by championing those martial absolutes of chivalry and sacrifice while a few offer a particularly politicized Irish perspective as Ledwidge tries to justify Ireland's role in the war and link this sacrifice to the martyrdom of the executed leaders of the Easter Rebellion.

Still, some critics question whether Ledwidge is a war poet at all because the war's presence is frequently quite oblique in his work. Other commentators even make the claim that his war poems never approach the lyrical (Dungan 1997, 118). A more accurate view is that Ledwidge's attempts to escape the horror of the front actually confirm the war's inseparable contiguity to his experience, and his war poetry frequently reveals a variety of sentiments, attitudes, and techniques. On other occasions, he tries to reconcile his part in the conflict with his nationalist sympathies, and, as already noted, some of his war poems tackle the self-perceived ironies of his roles as an Irish Catholic nationalist fighting for a British cause and as an Irish poet wholly dependent on English forms and idioms.

In *The Great War and Modern Memory*, Paul Fussell spends an entire chapter examining how "literature" so dominated the language of the war in letters, trench vernacular, poetry and prose that it seemed "impossible to write an account of anything without some 'literature' leaking in" (1975, 173). In the majority of the poems that Ledwidge wrote while on active duty, we find that so concerted is his attempt to preserve his memory of a rural world untainted by the destruction of war that it is the war itself that only occasionally leaks in. The same has been said of Edward Thomas. In the few war poems that Thomas wrote, the war is usually placed firmly in the background as a threat to unceasing rural rituals or is the cause, only half hinted at, of human absences. But like Thomas, Ledwidge's war poems periodically feature metaphorical landscapes that communicate indirectly the pain and suffering of the war.

As Ledwidge wrote a considerable number of his war poems while on active duty, it is not surprising that their preoccupation with scenes of rural tranquillity indicates how desperate he was to locate oases of order and coherency amid the prevailing chaos and bloodshed of the front. In a sense, most of Ledwidge's war poems celebrate the edifying and restorative powers of pas-

toralism, but they are never irresponsibly escapist or consciously
dishonest in their depiction of the reality of war. Rather, Ledwidge's war poetry attempts to preserve the aesthetic sensibility
that the war threatens to obliterate. His poetry is an act of faith
in the poet's gift to detect rare moments of beauty amid the front
line waste land.

We see this responsiveness to brief glimpses of beauty at the
front in "The Home-Coming of the Sheep" (1974, 185), a poem
he wrote while on active duty in Salonika in 1915. It features
a fairly traditional description of a pastoral scene replete with
shepherds and sheep. But in the poet's brief observation of Greek
boys bringing their flocks home from the hillsides, we detect how
the war intensifies his desire for the natural rhythms of rural life
and landscape:

> Before the early stars are bright
> Cormorants and sea-gulls call,
> And the moon comes large and white
> Filling with a lovely light
> The ferny curtained waterfall.
> Then sleep wraps every bell up tight
> And the climbing moon grows small.

The preciosity of these lines implies that quite often Ledwidge's
desire to write moving verse was not matched by a refreshing
verbal facility for description, but any image of evening tranquillity must have been particularly preferable to the terror of
nighttime artillery bombardments. Irony also prevails as Ledwidge's language encloses the action in an extended sequence of
pastoral congruities, but the proximity of the war forces us to
read the poem as an ironic tableau. Like a battalion of soldiers,
the sheep wander

> . . . wide a little piece
> Thro' the evening red and still,
> Stopping where the pathways cease,
> Cropping with a hurried will.

And later, when the sheep are on parade, they are guarded by
shepherd boys who (with "shouldered crooks" like rifles) "Close
them in a single row, / [and] Shout among them as they go."
Herded together, the docile sheep resemble troops suffering from
combat fatigue just before the imminent, ritual slaughter. This
pastoral impulse also preoccupies Edmund Blunden's war po-

etry in a celebration of what Fussell calls an "English Arcadia," but Fussell defends Blunden's escapism because it is not driven by self-indulgent sentimentality or a subscription to any agenda other than the recognition of the beautiful (1975, 254–69). Ledwidge's testimony to the beautiful not only reminds us of what war deprives us of but also demonstrates how the war made it virtually impossible in the future to read without irony such phrases as the "evening red" or the description of sheep in the parlance of military drill. As Fussell points out, the war altered the formerly innocent connotations of literary language (23), and this was a change that was symptomatic of a much larger shift in attitude as the war destroyed the illusion of a world perceived to be literal and constant.

Another poem "Autumn Evening in Serbia" (1974, 51), also written at the Balkan front in October 1915, illustrates Ledwidge's practice of using descriptive landscape to register emotion. A quick glance at the poem's two stanzas, however, reveals little evidence that there is a war going on. Even the bucolic scene described seems contrived given Ledwidge's own accounts of the bitterly cold Balkan campaign. In his letters home, he confided that he wrote many of these poems in stressful conditions, "some of them indeed under shrapnel" (Curtayne 1972, 142). Despite this disparity between image and experience, the poem does resonate with an inescapable sense of foreboding signified by Ledwidge's description of the dying day and the imminence of the new season. The first stanza begins with a description of evening and concludes with a fairly trite personification:

> All the thin shadows
> Have closed on the grass,
> With the drone on their dark wings
> The night beetles pass.
> Folded her eyelids,
> A maiden asleep,
> Day sees in her chamber
> The pallid moon peep.

Once again, it appears we have another good example of Georgian escapism, but despite the fact that the war is banished to the background, the accumulation of ominous images (the "thin shadows"; "dark wings"; and "night beetles") undercuts the desired tranquillity. Even the moon is sickly "pallid." Several of these meditative-pastoral poems that Ledwidge wrote at the front reveal tensions where connotative disturbances in the language disrupt the dreamy, dissociative quality of the verse. Despite Ledwidge's attempt to recognize beauty and transcend the horror of the war, though, such connotative patterns threaten the serenity of the idyll. Ledwidge cannot totally filter out the war. He seems drawn to describe the temporality of things: in this case, the close of day, a time reference that also drives the narrative in "The Home-Coming of the Sheep."

In the second stanza of "Autumn in Serbia," the narrative shifts from the notation of time passing to a description of landscape:

> From the bend of the briar
> The roses are torn,
> And the folds of the wood tops
> Are faded and worn.
> A strange bird is singing
> Sweet notes of the sun,
> Tho' song time is over
> And Autumn begun.

These lines typify Ledwidge's propensity for terse expression. There is no evidence that he was familiar with the work of the Imagists, but, as he said himself, he preferred to use not only "short words, but short lines, too, and short poems" (Curtayne 1972, 193). Images of decay clearly predominate. We encounter a ravaged landscape with "torn" roses and a "faded and worn" tree line, and Ledwidge's description of nature's fragility seems inextricably linked to his own sense of vulnerability. Even his use of that familiar romantic trope, the singing bird, strikes a somber note. In this context, it is a "strange bird," one the poet is unfamiliar with, and his eagerness to locate reminders of home in the surrounding landscape is ultimately disrupted by this unknown bird whose alien melody reminds him of his own mortality as "song time is over."

In her book *Remembering, We Forget: A Background Study to the Poetry of the First World War*, Hilda Spear accurately describes this kind of poetry as "ultra-romantic" (1979, 52). She goes on to criticize Ledwidge for his "complete dissociation" and "air of conscious 'separateness' which make his verse seem empty and lacking in vitality" (52). Spear then concludes that Ledwidge sacrifices "truth" for "expression" (53). From our distant perspective (an eighty year marination in the modernist mode),

Ledwidge's war poems frequently sound derivative, but Spear's claim that they are dissociated from their context (the war) insinuates that there actually is an appropriate idiom for war poetry and Ledwidge does not speak the language. Of course one can argue that no language could ever adequately describe such carnage, and Spear's point might be that some idioms are more appropriate than others. However, Ledwidge's war poems are never completely dissociated from their context. Instead, he reaffirms the importance of beauty during times of terror and destruction. His escapism cannot be equated with "'separateness'" or isolation from the war. The recurring images of decay and the temporality of all living things in his poetry suggest that complete transcendence is impossible. Even the poet's cache of images and distilled memories bear the war's smudge and smell.

Rather than dull Ledwidge's poetic sensitivities, the war actually intensifies them. We learn again from Fussell how the war shattered previous notions about sunrises and sunsets with their "tokens of hope and peace and rural charm" (1975, 52). In Ledwidge's war poems, there are only twilights. Days always approach their end. Darkness is constantly imminent. Resignation reigns. Beneath the surface appeals of Ledwidge's foreign landscapes, we detect the strain of a voice looking for psychological relief: the poems, for all their tired language and stylistic infelicities, reveal subtle incongruities between what is being described and how it is being described.

Above all, though, Ledwidge's war poetry reveals his attempt to piece together the shards of a fragmented self. While the war left an indelible mark on the lives of its survivors, for some poets it also destroyed confidence in language. The tensions between Ledwidge's apparently idyllic landscapes and their shadows and darknesses indicate how his devotion to inherited idioms began to unravel. We see the strain of maintaining the standards of a prewar aesthetic ideal in his poetry which can no longer inoculate itself against the obscenity of the war. The misery leaks in.

In a short pastoral lyric entitled "A Fear" (1974, 148), presumably written during the summer of 1914 but not published until the winter of 1915 "when Ledwidge was dug into a bitterly cold mountain ridge in Serbia on starvation rations" (Bolger 1992, 9), the poet evokes images of misery that anticipate the real horrors that were soon to follow. The poem's two short stanzas recount the speaker's walk in "the woods" and the disturbing afterthoughts of his experience. Unlike the two previous poems we examined, the locale of this poem appears ambiguous as though we hover somewhere between dream and reality.

The first four lines describe a surreal forest where the trees appear to undergo a stage of ghoulish transubstantiation. Limb and bark become flesh and blood:

> I roamed the woods to-day and seemed to hear,
> As Dante heard, the voice of suffering trees.
> The twisted roots seemed bare contorted knees,
> The bark was full of faces strange with fear.

According to Alice Curtayne, Ledwidge was "in the current fashion . . . in his continuous favor of classical references" (1972, 192), but his allusion to Dante's *Divine Comedy* with its blood-shedding trees goes beyond the decorative to cross-connect pictures of suffering that communicate to us the subsequent violence, mass murder, and trauma of war. We cannot help but translate these images as prescient glimpses of horror from the front, ranging from the shattered landscape ("twisted roots") to the trauma of combat ("faces strange with fear").

The second stanza intensifies the nightmare and introduces the poem's disturbing conceit:

> I hurried home still wrapt in that dark spell,
> And all the night upon the world's great lie
> I pondered, and a voice seemed whisp'ring high,
> "You died long since, and all this thing is hell!"

Throughout the poem, the speaker is unsure whether what he sees is real or a dream. He "seemed to hear" the crying voices; he hurries "home" transfixed by a "dark spell"; and this ominous voice "seemed" to whisper "high." Trapped between waking consciousness and the nightmare of illusion, the speaker discovers all in the end when the conceit is revealed: "You died long since and all this thing is hell!" The speaker's personal tour of hell and the poem's general narrative structure faintly resemble Wilfred Owen's later poem "Strange Meeting." Like Ledwidge, Owen's speaker uses conditional verbs like "seemed" to show his temporary sense of disorientation, and ironically he, too, discovers that he stands in "hell" as both poems' speaker-victims become shades.

In "A Fear," Ledwidge foresees not only the horror of war but the jingoistic spirit that was to drive many young men to enlist. When the speaker takes refuge at "home" after escaping the nightmare world of the forest, he realizes that there can be no escape, for all night long he ponders the "world's great lie." Like Owen's rejection of the "Old Lie" in "Dulce et Decorum Est," Ledwidge questions Horatian sacrifice and its vain promise of glory.

At the confluence of two aesthetic ideals, the poem's language and technique reveal an interesting blend of styles. On the one hand, Ledwidge's use of allusion seems right out of T. S. Eliot's modernist handbook. The reference to Dante draws cross-cultural parallels between two very real and horrifying impressions of hell and enables Ledwidge to achieve a rare concentrated focus as he compares Dante's macabre forest to the horrors of a battlefield. At the same time, though, Ledwidge cannot cast off his reliance on dated poeticisms. Archaisms like "wrapt," the affected syncope of "whisp'ring" or the gothic flavor of a "dark spell" creep in. This allegiance to a poetic decorum seems oddly out of place given the poem's very immediate condemnation of violence.

As we can see, the idea that Ledwidge's war poems were removed from the entire theater of conflict does not hold up under closer analysis. On the contrary, he wrote a number of poems that directly address the war, but they are generally not as successful as those poems where he takes a more circumspect approach. Most of his more overt war poems celebrate the type of chivalric piety we associate with cenotaph inscriptions and the Christian necrology, and like Rupert Brooke and Julian Grenfell, Ledwidge sometimes views the war as a purifying agent that offers an opportunity for valor.

Both of these sentiments are present in Ledwidge's most anthologized war poem, "Soliloquy" (1974, 188). As its title suggests, the poet indulges in the romantic retrospection of lost innocence and youthful possibility:

> When I was young I had a care
> Lest I should cheat me of my share
> Of that which makes it sweet to strive
> For life, and dying still survive,
> A name in sunshine written higher
> Than lark or poet dare aspire.

Here is another poem preoccupied with the promise of glory and honor as Ledwidge envisions his name on a roll of honor, a fate that will ensure a legacy greater than any poet's. But when these youthful aspirations fail to transpire and dissipation sets in, it is the war that ironically offers an opportunity for redemption.

At this stage, the poem resembles a recruiting poster: "Tomorrow will be loud with war, / How will I be accounted for?" Then the concluding propagandistic flourish:

> It is too late now to retrieve
> A fallen dream, too late to grieve
> A name unmade, but not too late
> To thank the gods for what is great;
> A keen-edged sword, a soldier's heart,
> Is greater than a poet's art.
> And greater than a poet's fame
> A little grave that has no name,
> Whence honour turns away in shame.

The war is viewed as an opportunity to make up for wasted youth and lost ambition, and here lies the central irony. The poet prefers the glorious anonymity of the war dead to a "poet's fame," but what is particularly odd is how Ledwidge sets aside his acknowledged nationalist sympathies in order to endorse the war effort: an act that contradicts the antiwar sentiments expressed earlier in "A Fear." As we shall see later, Ledwidge gradually grew disillusioned with his decision to enlist, so it would seem natural to expect that his self-doubts about serving in the British army would provoke a range of dissentient voices within his war poetry. In this case, perhaps his prowar ardor is an attempt to reconcile his conflicted loyalties while writing a public poem celebrating heroic sacrifice.

Whatever the case, this devotion to a prowar creed is sustained in another short poem that ignores the human cost of the conflict in its praise of a lofty abstraction. In "A Soldier's Grave" (1974, 189), written in France in early February 1917, Ledwidge euphemizes a dead soldier's interment to the extent that death itself is denied. The first stanza portrays the casualty who dies in the "lull of midnight" and is lowered from the heights, where he was killed, by "gentle arms," which lift him "slowly" "Lest he should hear again the mad alarms / Of battle, dying moans, and painful breath." At the grave, the "soft" earth is decorated with "flowers" so that the dead soldier may have "better rest," and when "Spring" comes a lark will "turn her dewy nest" in the dead soldier's "sweetly arrayed" grave.

Ultimately, death is reduced to a romantic abstraction. The unconscious irony of the euphemism "better rest" is typical of the poem's attempt to divert attention from the human loss. This is not death. Instead, the poet transforms the corpse into a deity of nature as life springs forth from the soldier's grave. And yet there is something conspiratorial here. The delicate phrases and fragrant ceremony contrast with the butchery of the soldier's killing. Soldiers don't die; they simply rest better. In all its verbal simplicity, the poem transcends pain with the promise of eternal rest, a consolation lost on the thousands of unknowns who were buried where they died.

In another group of Ledwidge's war poems, the poet explores his role in fighting for what he came to regard as a dubious cause. As a member of the Irish Volunteers and friend of Thomas Mac-Donagh and Joseph Plunkett, two of the signatories of the Easter Proclamation, Ledwidge feared that his service in the British army would later be judged as a betrayal of his nationalist allegiances. In particular, he was eager to reconcile his decision to enlist with his sense of guilt over the events of Easter Week and the death of his friends.

Nationalist mythography traditionally links Irish identity with landscape. In *Northern Voices: Poets from Ulster*, one of the earliest studies of recent Northern Irish poetry, Terence Brown argues that confusions over identity are quite often "partially" resolved through an "identification with Irish landscape" (1975, 210). As Ledwidge's war poems illustrate, this association between land and identity is hardly new. In his monumental study *Landscape and Memory*, Simon Schama notes that "National identity . . . would lose much of its ferocious enchantment without the mystique of a particular landscape tradition: its topography mapped, elaborated and enriched as a homeland" (1995, 15). Of course, love of landscape is a recurring feature of Georgian poetry in general, but while Ledwidge shares this pastoral affection with his English contemporaries, it is not the singing birds of Gloucestershire that capture his attention. As the war drags on, it is the landscapes of his native Meath that are "freshly remembered."

Evidence of Ledwidge's faith in a "landscape tradition" can be found in his letters from the front as the poet became increasingly nostalgic. In a letter to Katharine Tynan dated 19 June 1917, he writes, "If you go to Tara, go to Rath-na-Rí and look all around you from the hills of Drumcondrath in the north to the plains of Enfield in the south, where Allen Bog begins, and remember me to every little hill and wood and ruin, for my heart is there" (Curtayne 1972, 183). Despite growing up in an area littered with historical sites like the megalithic ruins at New Grange and Tara, Alice Curtayne notes that Ledwidge initially "made no study of [them]" (31). Instead, he showed more interest in the "pastoral scenes" *around* New Grange and the Boyne (31), inspired as he was by the local landscape and fauna. In a short poem entitled "Home" (1974, 30) written not long before his death, Ledwidge refuses to be overwhelmed by the carnage around him by recreating a sense of home:

> A burst of sudden wings at dawn,
> Faint voices in a dreamy noon,
> Evenings of mist and murmurings,
> And nights with rainbows of the moon.
>
> And through these things a wood-way dim,
> And waters dim, and slow sheep seen
> On uphill paths that wind away
> Through summer sounds and harvest green.
>
> This is a song a robin sang
> This morning on a broken tree,
> It was about the little fields
> That call across the world to me.

While it can be argued that these lines could just as well be describing a scene in the Chilterns as a landscape in the heart of County Meath, it is his native home that preoccupies Ledwidge and not some unspecified, antiseptic pastoral idyll. The focus here on a miniaturized Irish rural world not only establishes a sense of identity through a parochial intimacy with hedgerows and fields but also serves what Simon Featherstone describes as a "counterpoint to . . . imperialist nationalism . . . by providing a defined set of home-grown values to replace those of an imperilled empire" (1995, 29). In another poem, "In France," written while Ledwidge was stationed at Ebrington Barracks in Derry in 1916, the poet again transcends memories of the front by invoking visions of his homeland in the first and last stanzas: "The silence of maternal hills / Is round me in my evening dreams;" and "The hills of home are in my mind, / And there I wander as I will" (1974, 31). Ledwidge may have borrowed an English aesthetic replete with its garden Arcadia vocabulary, but it is his recollection of an Ireland of the mind that counters the immediacy of the war, a war that Ledwidge increasingly began to associate with an intrusive British presence that he felt undermined his Irishness.

This desire to reaffirm his Irish identity was complemented by the use of Irish materials in his verse. While the result is an uneasy commingling of English pastoral and Celtic sources in the last work, Ledwidge's attempts to move beyond the Anglo influences that dominate his historical and cultural resource indicate that he was clearly on the verge of committing himself to his own brand of cultural essentialism. In the essay "The Poetry of Ledwidge," John Drinkwater contends that Ledwidge's first collection of poems was marred by the poet's mimicry of English pastoral poetry (1918, 180–89). But in "The Dead Kings" (Ledwidge 1992, 70), written in January 1917 shortly after Ledwidge was posted to the Western Front, the borrowed English pastoral is replaced with a subject and technique typical of the "Gaelic-romantic strand" in Irish poetry "which assumes, generally speaking, a cultural identity based on the past and the Irish language" (Bradley 1989, 2).

The poem's setting at Rosnaree, the supernatural visitations of the dead Irish martyrs Pearse and MacDonagh, and the memory of a "lost Arcadia" echo the folkloric qualities of Yeats's early work (Curtayne 1972, 193):

> I listened to the sorrows three
> Of that Eire passed into song.
> A cock crowed near a hazel croft,
> And up aloft dim larks winged strong.

The use of internal rhyme, a feature of gaelic poetry, illustrates another one of the first tentative steps Ledwidge took to shed his borrowed English poeticisms. However, his poetry was still steeped in English Romanticism, a fact that illustrates Declan Kiberd's observation that the culturally colonized are often "more susceptible to the literature of the parent country than the inhabitants of that country itself" (1995, 115). The poem also evokes that mainstay of nationalist mythography where present difficulties can be partially mitigated by retreating into a nostalgia for Ireland's gaelic past: the "Eire passed into song."

Certainly Ledwidge's motives for turning toward the Irish landscape and other features of traditional Irish verse were political. In these poems, the war is either relegated to the distant background or ignored altogether. In many ways, his reaction against his cultural co-dependence led him to view the war as another reminder of Irish political and cultural subjugation. A number of poems grapple directly with the ambiguity of his role as an Irish nationalist serving in the British army, especially during a time of great tumult in Ireland. It is possible to trace how Ledwidge's attitude toward the war evolves as things heat up on the political scene back home. While it is hardly surprising that he did not write any poems during his tour of duty on the Gallipoli peninsula from July to October 1915, the few poems that he did complete during his assignments to the Balkans and the Western Front attempt to justify his reasons for fighting in the war.

In two poems, "At Currabwee" (1974, 158) written in Derry in December 1916, and "The Irish in Gallipoli" (174), written in late February 1917 in France, we see Ledwidge try to come to terms with why he played no part in the events of Easter Week. In the Gallipoli poem, he justifies the sacrifices Irish soldiers made not only on this rocky peninsula but during the entire war. As a propaganda piece, the poem does not support the war effort from a British standpoint but instead explains why so many Irishmen volunteered to go and fight at all. In an attempt to glorify Irish sacrifices during this ill-fated campaign, Ledwidge begins by alluding to the rich history of the Western Turkish seaboard: the "Aegean cliffs" are "Lighted by Troy's last shadow, where the first / Hero kept watch." These references back to distant antiquity imply that Ireland's sons share the noble stature and valor of those ancient Greek and Trojan heroes.

In the second stanza, the reasons for the Irish sacrifice at Gallipoli are laid bare: these men fought "Neither for lust of glory nor new throne." Instead, Irishmen "war when war / Serves Liberty and Justice, Love and Peace." Irish nationalism and British patriotism are abridged by the larger and more abstract ideal of fighting for global freedom. Also interesting is how these lines appear to contradict Ledwidge's previous statements in his first letter home when he claimed he was not fighting for "higher ideals" (Curtayne 1972, 83). This shift in attitude may be explained by the poet's political dilemma in writing a war poem: while eager to commemorate the Irish war dead, he may have been reluctant to sound a pro-British note. So he opts instead for politically circumspect language and, like other war versifiers, goes no further than portraying the war as a popular Christian crusade. In the last stanza, in responding to the charge that Irish soldiers died for nothing, Ledwidge anoints the Irish dead by linking their sacrifice to the greatest sacrifice, Christ's death on the cross:

> Who said that such an emprise could be vain?
> Were they not one with Christ Who strove and died?
> Let Ireland weep but not for sorrow. Weep
> That by her sons a land is sanctified
> For Christ Arisen, and angels once again
> Come back like exile birds to guard their sleep.

Ledwidge's orchestration of Christian simulacra is typical of the kind of Christian iconography often seen in Great War poetry. In Adrian Caesar's study of the major war poets, *Taking it Like a Man,* he argues that conflating Christ the martyr with the war dead helped justify the mass slaughter while promoting the idea that in its role as a missionary force fighting to save souls, the British army annexed "power to the Christian State" (1993, 225). Of course these "ideological responses to suffering," Caesar notes, were "in place well before the outbreak of hostilities" (229). It wasn't long before the notion of Christian sacrifice soon became a synonym for imperial sacrifice as well. In Ledwidge's poem, however, there is no implication that imperialist loyalties lay behind the Irish sacrifice at Gallipoli. These men died for universal liberty. Like Christ, they died for mankind rather than for any flag or political agenda. Determined to avoid the customary imperialist pieties of most English war verse, Ledwidge also seems reluctant to depict Ireland's role in the war as subordinate to mother empire, and this final stanza celebrates the Irish war dead in much the same way nationalist mythography eulogizes its dead heroes by commemorating the blood sacrifice as an act that purifies and sanctifies the homeland.

In the poem "At Currabwee," he again tackles the ambiguity of his role as an Irish nationalist in British uniform. Like several of his war poems, this one reveals a Chinese box effect where within a framework conflict (the Easter Rebellion), we find another conflict (the Great War) and within that conflict yet another: Ledwidge's self-recriminations about his nonparticipation in the cause that really mattered most to him—the struggle for Irish independence.

The poem is actually an elegy for the leaders of the Easter Rebellion like MacDonagh, Plunkett, and Pearse, whom Ledwidge knew personally. In the poem's fourth and final stanza, the poet links his own actions in the war to the sacrifices of the Easter insurgents by describing how Plunkett and Pearse were spurred

on by the ancient voices of the "faery" to pursue their dream of
Irish nationhood:

> And I, myself, have often heard
> Their singing as the stars went by,
> For am I not of those who reared
> The banner of old Ireland high,
> From Dublin town to Turkey's shores,
> And where the Vardar loudly roars?

In "The Irish in Gallipoli," the reason given for Ireland's involvement in the war was the fight for such ideals as "Liberty,"
"Peace," and Christian charity. But now the motive to fight is
for Ireland as it was Ireland's "banner" that was raised at Gallipoli and in Northern Greece (location of the Vardar River).
Ledwidge wants to believe that he fought for the same cause
as those who took over the center of Dublin during the Easter
Rising. What he chooses to ignore is the fact that Irish soldiers
helped suppress the rebellion in Dublin. Ledwidge did believe,
like many other former members of the Irish Volunteers, that
he was doing his part to advance the cause of Home Rule. But
the republican rhetoric of the Easter Proclamation exceeded the
semiautonomous dictates of any Home Rule settlement. Above
all, though, we see a shift in Ledwidge's attempt to validate his
decision to enlist. His enthusiasm for the war gradually gives
way to a more strident nationalism.

According to Alice Curtayne, in the months prior to his death,
Ledwidge continued to wrestle with how his role in the war may
be misinterpreted. Home on leave shortly after the Rising in May
1916, he was deeply affected by the news of the executions and
the devastation he saw in the Dublin streets. Reluctant to return
to active duty, he went to Dublin's Richmond Barracks to pick
up his equipment and a travel pass in order to report for duty in
Derry, but his hopes for a leave extension were dashed when he
got into an altercation with an officer who made some derogatory
remark about the Rising. The result of the ensuing dispute was
that Ledwidge was court-martialed in Derry and lost his lance
corporal's stripe (1980, 121). In a short poem simply entitled
"After Court Martial" (1974, 141), he wrote:

> The Present is a dream I see
> Of horror and loud sufferings,
> At dawn a bird will waken me
> Unto my place among the kings.

These lines reflect his growing disillusionment with the war and emerging sympathies with Irish republicanism. By early 1917, Ledwidge believed "that he would have to get out of the British army as soon as possible" (1980, 120).

His most direct statement of disengagement from the war can be found in "The Dead Kings," the first two stanzas of which recall a dream where Ledwidge sees his friends, these "dead kings," return to tell him stories of "ancient glory." Again, the poem's setting at Rosnaree is significant as Ledwidge describes the Celtic burial ground there as a sacred, semimythical place:

> All the dead kings came to me
> At Rosnaree, where I was dreaming,
> A few stars glimmered through the morn,
> And down the thorn the dews were streaming.

This shift from a bardic localism to nationalist mystique was nothing new in Ledwidge's work. In 1913 he wrote several articles for the *Drogheda Independent* about places of interest in the Boyne Valley, and in these short pieces, Ledwidge often "use[d] landscape as a peg on which to hang his social and political thinking" (Curtayne 1972, 59).

Of course the poem's real intent is to celebrate an ancient Irish heroic narrative of resistance and to mourn the loss of Irish freedom:

> And I, too, told the kings a story
> Of later glory, her fourth sorrow:
> There was a sound like moving shields
> In high green fields and the lowland furrow.

As the poem gains speed, we see further evidence of Ledwidge's subscription to nationalist myth where the past is viewed as an idyllic preconquest world and the Irish as a bardic race:

> And one said: "Since the poets perished
> And all they cherished in the way,
> Their thoughts unsung, like petal flowers
> Inflame the hours of blue and grey."

Certainly one of the basic constructs of nationalist mythography is this faith in a predawn gaelic world where Irish boundaries and ethnic essences were mapped, cohesive, and secure. Of course, in Ireland, popular history and myth are frequently synonymous, but nationalism's romantic recreation of Ireland as a place bonded by a gaelic-speaking rural ethos ignores the reality. Like many other revisionist critics, Vincent Cheng points out that Ireland has never been a nation in the sense that it was a place inhabited by a so-called indigenous people who saw themselves as one people linked together by language, religion, ethnicity, and a common economic interest. Cheng asks: "When was Ireland ever not either a colony of some foreign power or other, or else a loose collection of rival and warring tribes or kingdoms?" (1995, 216). Ledwidge's vision of Ireland is certainly of the gaelic-romantic variety. His imagined Ireland is an island inhabited by "a historically-continuous community with a homogeneous national character" (216).

But where does the Great War figure in all this? Only in the poem's last two lines is the war mentioned:

> And one said: "A loud tramp of men
> We'll hear again at Rosnaree."
> A bomb burst near me where I lay.
> I woke, 'twas day in Picardy.

Gone are the attempts to vindicate the Irish involvement in the war. Ledwidge simply pays tribute to those who have become part of a nascent republican mythology. The last line with its sudden shattering of the poet's vision of a dreamy Celtic Arcadia is especially ironic for it reminds us not only of Ledwidge's sense of exclusion from this Celtic warrior brotherhood but also his sense of cultural and political dislocation on a foreign battlefield wearing a foreign uniform. (The poem's last two lines also ironically foreshadow Ledwidge's own death from an exploding shell while he worked on road detail behind the front lines.) As the political situation at home became more volatile, Ledwidge became more ambivalent about the war. By linking these dead martyrs to an ancient Ireland, an Ireland before the Norman and Anglo-Saxon invasions, he enshrines the nationalist myth of a nation bonded by an agreeable self image, an image complicated by the Great War, which nationalist extremists subsequently reduced to just another episode in Ireland's ongoing struggle against colonial subjugation. The exploding shell in Picardy represents a presence that is both destructive and alien. What is also important about this poem is how it reveals Ledwidge's growing discomfort as an Irish nationalist serving in the British army. There is no attempt to justify the Irish role in the war; instead, Ledwidge recalls the dead Easter insurgents and can only dream of their "glory."

Certainly, as Eavan Boland also points out, "the war never featured overtly in his poems" (1990, 38), but evidence of his growing disengagement from the war can be seen throughout Ledwidge's last war poems as a dialogue is waged between the warring parts of his political and artistic identity. The shift from English pastoralism to Celtic sources suggests that he, more than any other Irish soldier poet, tried to embrace the styles and techniques of the Irish Literary Revival. In a letter he wrote in early June 1917 to Lewis Nathaniel Chase, a University of Wisconsin English professor, Ledwidge mentions his discontent at being "called a British soldier while [his] own country has no place amongst the nations but the place of Cinderella" (Curtayne 1972, 180). But if "The Dead Kings" reveals Ledwidge's emerging disaffection with the war, it is not an antiwar poem; it does not condemn the lie of false glory. Rather, it shifts allegiances to the cause of Irish freedom, an issue that, as we have seen, Ledwidge felt increasingly more earnest about.

And yet his letters continue to reveal his confusing loyalties. In late June 1917 in a letter to Katharine Tynan, he appears to support the war effort again, describing "every honour won by Irishmen on the battlefields of the world" as "Ireland's honour" (Curtayne 1972, 182–83). The context of the letter is important, too, for Tynan was worried about her son who was on active service in Macedonia, and, to spare her further worry, Ledwidge may have been tactfully noncommittal about his true feelings towards the war. Ultimately, however, in poems like "The Dead Kings," the war functions either as a dramatic backdrop to the greater cause of Irish independence or as a threat to the poet's sense of place and ethnicity.

Besides the evidence of Ledwidge's growing republican sympathies, we see subtle changes in his literary technique. As already noted, most of his war poems favor the English lyric and the English concept of a garden Arcadia. This explains why many of his war poems possess this residue of decorative pastoralism where nostalgia replaces thought, and the use of an artificial mode suppresses any intuitive inclination to portray things as they are. Ledwidge's technique, for the most part, dictates the nature of his expression, and his poetry reveals the extent to which English ideas about refinement and culture dominated Irish cultural utterance.

Overall, Ledwidge's war poems reveal conflicting ideologies. As

for technique, his absorption of the English pastoral tradition is
so complete that he seems unable to liberate himself from writing
the kind of emotionally agreeable landscape poetry that his contemporary critics praised him for. If anything, he trades one set
of poetic "orthodoxies" for another, thus implying that the landscape affectations of the Irish Literary Revival were really only
imitations of a cold English Pastoral with an Irish locale.[5] Inevitable comparisons to John Clare drew attention to Ledwidge's
gift for describing the minutaie of the field and stream, and Lord
Dunsany baptized him "the poet of the blackbird" in his introduction to *Songs of the Fields* (1916, 11). But the later war poems
show the strain of accommodating outmoded techniques when
confronted with new and terrifying experiences.

The war poems also reveal cross-cultural conflicts in Ledwidge's politics, and they illustrate the kinds of self-dividing
conflicts other constitutional nationalists faced during the war
years. Inevitably, Ledwidge's war poetry offers glimpses of the
many paradoxes of the Irish situation where the lines between
ethnic and cultural identities blur. If we look closely enough,
we can also see how the tensions in Ledwidge's poetry function as a kind of synecdoche for the entire Irish problem: his
internal debate over Ireland's role in the war reminds us of the
conflicting influences that frustrate any attempt to construct a
narrow definition of Irish ethnic and cultural identity. In this
regard, Seamus Heaney accords Ledwidge the highest tribute:
"it is because of this scruple, this incapacity for grand and over-
bearing certainties, and not because of the uniform he wore,
it is for this reason that Ledwidge can be counted as a 'war
poet' in the company of Wilfred Owen and Siegfried Sassoon"
(1992, 11).

In his book *War Poetry: An Introductory Reader*, Simon Featherstone observes that Scottish war poetry "generally contained a
mixture of patriotism with an accent of Tartanry . . . and a sentimental affection for an idealized Celtic homeland" (1995, 83).
At first glance, Ledwidge's poetry appears to project little more
than some misty appreciation for the landscapes of home as well.
But, as we have seen, this is not entirely accurate as his war
poems contain submerged political and cultural tensions that reveal the importance of examining minor war poetry for dialogues
other than the binary narratives of patriotic or pacifistic verse.
And while the war is rarely treated overtly in Ledwidge's poetry,
when it does seep in, it renders his nostalgia for a prewar rural
landscape all the more plaintive and ironic. In a letter written

to Edward Marsh less than a month before his death, Ledwidge sounds an apocalyptic note:

> If you visit the Front don't forget to come up the line at night to watch the German rockets. They have white crests which throw a pale flame across no-man's land and white bursting into green and green changing into blue and blue bursting and dropping down in purple torrents. It is like the end of a beautiful world. (Curtayne 1972, 184)

Over eighty years after the end of that "beautiful world," Francis Ledwidge is still remembered. On 31 July 1998 (the same date on which he was killed in 1917), in conjunction with the town of Boezinge (Boesinghe) near Ieper (Ypres), the In Flanders Fields Museum erected a small memorial at the place where he was killed. This is the spot where Ledwidge's first grave was, at the junction of the Roulers railway and the track leading to Artillery Wood in Boezinge.[6] Today, his grave lies three miles or so north of Ieper (Dungan 1997, 119).

At home, meanwhile, he remains an enigma: nationalists warm to his "political 'reconversion,'" particularly after his court-martial, while "his earlier ambivalence" about the war casts "him in the role of a revisionist icon" (Dungan 1997, 115). In a war whose repercussions are still with us, Ledwidge's political and cultural disorientation reveal the futility of subscribing to identity politics within the Irish context. Perhaps part of Ledwidge's appeal is how he transcends Ireland's political fault lines and demonstrates the extent to which British and Irish identities overlap. How appropriate then that the plaque erected in his honor on the Boyne Bridge in Slane should straddle that contentious river, for Ledwidge's greatest legacy as a war poet is to remind us of the political and cultural crosscurrents that make up that "living stream."

Another poet who struggled to reconcile his nationalist sympathies with the war effort was Tom Kettle (1880–1916) whose educational and social backgrounds contrast starkly with the country-bred Ledwidge. Son of a wealthy landowner and land reformer, Kettle graduated from University College Dublin in 1902, studied law, and edited *The Nationist*—a weekly Irish review—before being elected to parliament for the East Tyrone constituency in 1906 (Powell 1993, 130). In 1910, he was appointed professor of national economics at Dublin University and in 1911 "resigned his seat at Westminister" in order to devote more time to his academic duties (131). But this did not end Kettle's involvement in political affairs. He supported the 1912 Home Rule Bill and later joined the Irish Volunteers at their formation in November 1913 (132). By the summer of 1914, he was in Belgium buying guns for the Volunteers, and when war was declared, he remained there as a reporter for *The Daily News* (132). He later returned to Ireland in November 1914, received a commission in the Royal Dublin Fusiliers, and traveled all over the country as a "recruiting spokesman" (133). In a number of speeches he made during this tour, Kettle clarified why he firmly believed that Irishmen should do their part for the war effort. At Navan in January 1915, he expressed the belief that a joint war effort with the Ulster unionists would make it possible to "find an easier way of settling their differences at home" (J. Lyons 1983, 275).

A few months later, he told an audience in Dundalk that the Irish were "on the side of England because England was on the side of God. They were fighting the people's war for the people's peace" (J. Lyons 1983, 275). By the end of his recruiting drive, he reiterated his belief that "he was not fighting for England or the colonies" but for Ireland (278). Despite Kettle's apparently solid convictions that he was fighting for the ideal of liberty and not for the cause of British imperialism, the constant personal attacks against him by Sinn Fein sympathizers took their toll. By the early summer of 1916, as he prepared for embarkation to France, his thoughts turned repeatedly to the events of Easter Week. During the Rising, Kettle was stationed at Newbridge Barracks, and the subsequent tragedy that played out on the Dublin streets left him bitterly disillusioned and "spoiled his dream . . . of a free Ireland in a United Europe" (McHugh 1960, 137). Like Ledwidge, Kettle was also intimate with some of the Rising's leaders, but when one of his friends, Francis Sheehy-Skeffington, (who had worked diligently to stop the insurrection) was murdered while in British army custody just two days after the rebels seized the General Post Office, Kettle began for the first time to doubt the choice he had made to support the war effort. During his last leave, he spoke about the Rebellion with some old family friends and observed bitterly: "These men will go down to history as heroes and martyrs, and I will go down—if I go down at all— as a bloody British officer" (J. Lyons 1983, 293).

Later, in July 1916, Kettle left for France, and by August, he was posted to the Somme where he was killed on the ninth of September during the successful attack on Ginchy by the Tenth

Irish Division. According to his biographer J. B. Lyons, speculation arose that "when Kettle went to the front he hardly cared what happened to him, welcoming in France the blood sacrifice Pearse sought in Dublin" (1983, 298). But Kettle had no such death wish. In a letter he sent to his brother just days before his death, he wrote "I am happy and calm and anxious to live," and his intent to return to Ireland to work tirelessly for peace was reinforced by what he saw at the front: "I have seen war, and faced modern artillery, and know what an outrage it is against simple men" (Kettle 1917, 35).

As his public role as a politician suggests, Kettle was not primarily a poet but rather an academic who wrote on a broad range of subjects. During his recruiting tour, he and Stephen Gwynn, M.P., published *Battle Songs for the Irish Brigades* (1915), a "collection of ballads by Davis, Mangan, and others," which also "included a few of their own poems" (J. Lyons 1983, 276). The only volume of poetry that Kettle published during the war that consisted entirely of his own work was *Poems and Parodies,* published posthumously, in December 1916. As a collection, it is a mixed bag of patriotic ballads and political satires, all chiefly concerned with Ireland's ongoing domestic crisis. As for style, "the imagery often resembles the Celtic Twilight school of AE" (Kime Scott 1979, 353). In one section, entitled "War Poems," Kettle does directly address the war as his subject. Contemporary reviewers "included AE and Katherine [sic] Tynan, neither of whom allowed false sentiment to influence their assessments" (J. Lyons 1983, 304). Tynan dismissed most of the poems as "verses à servir" while AE generously noted that Kettle's poems will continue to be "read more because they remind us of a lovable and many-sided man than for their own sake" (304). To be fair to Kettle, most of these poems were written prior to his departure for the front, and his attitude toward the war was certainly sobered by what he saw there. After a spell in the front lines, he soon voiced a much more resigned attitude toward the war: "In the trenches it is the day-by-dayness that tells and tries. It is always the same tone of duty. . . . And of course the nerve-strain is not slight. . . . In the trenches death is random, illogical, devoid of principle" (Ellis 1976, 190).

The few poems Kettle wrote for the collaborative work with Gwynn are also included in *Poems and Parodies*, and while they have little stylistic merit, they reveal several viewpoints about the Irish role in the war. In essence, "Kettle saw the Irish, north and south, taking part in a crusade and linked this romantically with the 'Wild Geese'" (Johnstone 1992, 191). One poem, "A Song for the Irish Armies" (1916, 84–86), which was originally titled "The Last Crusade," is nothing more than a recruiting instrument. Kettle portrays the war not as a conflict between warring nations and empires but as an epic struggle between Christianity and paganism, civilization and anarchy. The war is simply another chapter in an ancient conflict between good and evil:

> Not for this did our fathers fall;
> That truth, and pity, and love, and all
> Should break in dust at a trumpet call,
> Yea! all things clean and old.
> Not to this had we sacrificed:
> To sit at the last where the slayers diced,
> With blood-hot hands for the robes of
>   Christ . . .
> And snatch at the Devil's gold.

Despite the artificial high-mindedness of these lines and the proclivity for rhetorical bombast, we see Kettle appeal to Irish sentiment by implying that the war is a holy war. Like a good propagandist, he glorifies the allied cause as God's cause (they "lift the flag of the Last Crusade") while German aggression is described as "the tramp of / Cain." Kettle's portrayal of Germany as a godless race that worshipped "Iron" and "Odin" can be traced to his experiences in Belgium during the late summer and early autumn of 1914. Irish historian Brendan Clifford observes that Kettle's newspaper reports from the front during that autumn were among the first to create the impression "that Britain was at war with the philosophy of evil Nietzscheanism, which had become incarnate in the German state" (1992, 24). Kettle is reputed to have said that he cared more "for liberty than . . . for Ireland" (J. Lyons 1983, 278), yet, as his flagrantly anti-German sentiments expressed in this poem suggest, he was ironically very adept at producing British imperial propaganda.

During his stint as a newspaper correspondent in Belgium in the late summer of 1914, Kettle's anti-German sentiments were hardened by his eyewitness accounts of German atrocities. The wholesale destruction of Liège and Louvain—the "Athens of Belgium" (J. Lyons 1983, 253)—raised his prejudices against Germany almost to the level of hysteria. Reading through the reports he wrote for *The Daily News* at this time, we see how his passionate ideals overwhelmed any attempt at journalistic objectivity. He responded to German aggression with an assault

on German culture: "the big blonde brute [had] stepped from the
pages of Nietsche out on the plains about Liège"; the destruction
of the Belgian countryside was the result of Bismarck's "directive" to leave the vanquished only with "their eyes to weep with";
and German expansionism was the carrying out of "Treitsche's
doctrine of a chosen people" (253).[7] Ironically, Kettle responds
to Treitsche's racist doctrines trumpeting the Germans as the
"chosen people" with a xenophobic ferocity of his own. In his
recruiting songs, the Germans are portrayed as the barbarians
who trample over the rights of other nations and despoil European culture. No doubt, such sentiments were due to his im-
passioned sympathies for Catholic Belgium, another small country whose sovereign rights had been violated by a larger and
stronger neighbor.

Many of Kettle's war ballads feature such spirited denunciations of German aggression. They also try to resolve Ireland's
ambiguous role in the war by casting the conflict as a fight for
universal liberty. Furthermore, Kettle shared the sentiment expressed by many that Irish loyalty to the British Empire had
been too long taken for granted and that this present conflict,
which Irishmen were being called to fight in, may have a price.
He was particularly aggrieved by the scant recognition Irish soldiers received for their sacrifices in Britain's armies. In a parody of Kipling's "Tommy Atkins," Kettle's poem "Paddy" (1916,
75–78) echoes Kipling's condemnation of the British public's apathy toward her soldiers. But Kettle substitutes a bitter Irish
speaker for Kipling's "Tommy" and through the course of the
poem, "Paddy" lists Ireland's grievances and upbraids the British
government for regarding Irish soldiers as shock troops expend-
able for the protection of homeland and colonial frontier.

The Great War serves as a departure point for Kettle to air
his political concerns. While attacking British intransigence over
the Home Rule Bill and the anti-Irish prejudice of the British
press, this ballad commemorates the contributions Irishmen
made to past British military successes. Despite the poem's aim
to broadcast Irish grievances and attack the British for treating
the Irish unfairly, Kettle's politicization of the Irish war effort to
support the cause of Irish constitutional nationalism is undercut
by linguistic ironies in the poem. In short, Kettle's appropriation
of Kipling's dialect style indicates the extent to which the Irish
imagination was subjugated by a British imperial idiom. Also
ironic is Kettle's adaptation of the imperial voice to further his
Irish nationalist agenda. By assigning a contiguous role to the

Irish as the strong arm of the empire and never a role in its governance, Kettle unconsciously implies that Ireland's sovereignty should be granted only because of its willingness to play an auxiliary role in the whole colonial enterprise. As a result, his parody of British prejudices reveals his own subscription to prevailing Irish stereotypes (the Irish reputation for being good fighters, for example) and implicitly accepts that the likelihood of Home Rule depends entirely on the expedient outcome of British charity rather than as a result of Ireland's right to self determination.

"Paddy" begins with Kettle's reminder that Irish Home Rule has been frustrated by British parliamentary vacillation:

> I went into the talkin' shop to see about
>   the Bill;
> The Premier 'e ups and says: "We're
>   waitin' . . . waitin' still!"
> The Tories grinned, and Balfour strung
>   Our gamble Haman-high,
> I outs into the street again, and to meself
>   sez I:
> "O, it's Paddy this, and Paddy that, an'
>   A cattle-driven crew!
> But 'twas Murphy o' the Munsters!
>   when the trump of battle blew."

Kettle's next target is British prejudice against all things Irish:

> I looked into the newspaper to see about
>   the land . . .
> They'd room for cricket scores, and tips,
>   and trash of every kind,
> But when I asked of Ireland's cause, it
>   seemed to be behind . . .
> Yes! Sneerin' round at Irishmen, and
>   Irish speech and ways
> Is cheaper—much—than snatchin' guns
>   from battle's red amaze. . . .

Later, the British press is excoriated for ignoring Irish sacrifices on the battlefield as "The *Times* won't spare a Smith to tell / how Dan O'Connell died." Kettle successfully reminds his audience how Irish soldiers have been exploited by the British government for the war effort while at home Irish political rights continued to be denied, but as a parody the poem remains unconvincing because its very format deflects attention away from its target (British insensitivity to Irish affairs). As a dialect poem, it is also a nonstarter. If dialect is usually employed to reveal the speaker's persona, Kettle's Irishman is linguistically disoriented. We encounter inconsistencies in language ranging from the use of the decorative/formal ("Haman-high" and "red amaze"), to the informal ("talkin' shop"—the House of Commons), to the colloquial ("ain't"). There are also incongruities in the chosen dialect, for Kettle's "Paddy" speaks fluent cockney (the lingua franca of the British army) rather than the expected Hiberno-English, and this faithful mimicry of Kipling's "Tommy Atkins" indicates a passive submission to the English acculturation of Great War poetry. Kettle's unconscious immersion in the defining English culture signifies how difficult it was for him, like Ledwidge, to locate an authentic voice. In this case, the Irish persona is submerged by English vernacular.

If Irish writers found it difficult to articulate a peculiarly Irish response to the war, it is not surprising that the growing dissension in Ireland was due to the Great War being perceived as a British cause. Irish resistance to the war flourished as prowar apologists failed to draw up political and cultural distinctions between British and Irish soldiers. The cultural submissiveness of Kettle's narrative voice ultimately defuses the satirical edge of his parody. But perhaps the best poem that clarifies his distinctly Irish perspective about the war, and one that is relatively free of archaisms and an intrusive colonial voice, is a sonnet he wrote at the front several days before his death. In "To My Daughter Betty, the Gift of God" (1916, 15–16), he imagines a time in the distant future when his young daughter (1913–97) will ask why her father left his family to fight in a foreign war. The octet and sestet clearly delineate a dialectical structure whereby the first eight lines frame the rhetorical question—why Kettle fought in the war—and the last six lines provide the answer.

If the poem's chief objective is to explain Kettle's reasons for fighting, it also reveals his hopes for Ireland's future. In the opening lines, in contrast to the past, the future is described as "wiser days" and as a "desired, delayed, incredible time." Yet Kettle's optimism for Ireland's future is sobered by his anticipation of the human cost of such a prospect, and the following lines reveal a self-accusatory tone:

> You'll ask why I abandoned you, my own,
> And the dear heart that was your baby
>   throne,
> To dice with death.

Kettle then addresses those who will deride his decision to serve
in the British army:

> . . . And oh! they'll
>   give you rhyme
> And reason: some will call the thing
>   sublime,
> And some decry it in a knowing tone.

The poet dismisses any notion that he was seduced by sacrificial superlatives or blind patriotism ("the thing sublime") and
takes issue with his critics who, in their constricted view, "de-
cry" the legacy of those Irishmen who served with the British
army. Thoughts of posterity give way in the last six lines to the
immediate present—the trenches at Guillemont:

> So here, while the mad guns curse
>   overhead,
> And tired men sigh with mud for couch
>   and floor,
> Know that we fools, now with the foolish
>   dead,
> Died not for flag, nor King, nor Emperor,
> But for a dream, born in a herdsman's
>   shed,
> And for the secret Scripture of the poor.

These last four lines clarify Kettle's motives for fighting. For
him, the war transcends the local politics of the Irish situation;
he also sadly and accurately anticipates how the war was to be
preserved in Irish memory. Taking the moral high ground, Kettle memorializes the Irish dead by emphasizing the nobility of
their deaths. These men did not die for nationalist or imperialist imperatives; they died for an ideal. By conflating their cause
(the "dream") with the Christian ideal (the "herdsman's shed"),
Kettle, like Ledwidge, anoints the Irish war dead as heroes of a
much greater cause, as defenders of "the secret Scripture of the
poor." Anxious to protect the memory of the Irish dead, Kettle
anticipates how Irish soldiers of the Great War will be forgotten
and their war service distorted as a misguided sacrifice for the
British Empire. In a memoir written by his wife, Mary, which
appeared in a posthumous collection of Kettle's political writings
(*The Ways of War*) published the year after his death, she takes
poet Padraic Colum to task for his comment that Kettle died for

the wrong cause. On the contrary, she argues, "Tom Kettle died most nobly for the cause of Irish Nationality, in dying for the cause of European honour" (1917, 6). But subsequent republican and unionist mythographies have sadly confirmed Kettle's fears and Colum's prejudices.

As casualties of the Great War, Kettle and his fellow war dead have become casualties of Irish history, their cause forgotten, misunderstood, or distorted by nationalist and unionist triumph-alism. Consigned to historical oblivion as nationalists who fought for the wrong army, men like Kettle and Willie Redmond frus-trate the construction of nationalist and unionist hegemonies. The poem's political agenda, with its obvious intent to serve as Kettle's last political will and testament, also makes no attempt to condemn the war's necessity. The violence and hardships are acknowledged, but by invoking familiar images from the Chris-tian Nativity, Kettle suggests that the war is a crusade against evil and a portent of imminent redemption.

The poem's thematic conflicts are accompanied by a confusing blend of styles: the sentimental ("darling rosebud") gives way to the harshly realistic ("tired men sigh with mud"), and the per-sonal (the octet) yields to the didactic (sestet). But in its unflinch-ing attempt to speak the truth about the war and verify, even in a consolatory way, the reasons why men like Kettle fought and died, the poem illustrates how some Irish nationalists were pre-occupied with justifying the war effort from an Irish perspective rather than simply speaking out against the slaughter like some of their English literary counterparts. Unfortunately, essential-ist readings of Irish history gloss over the fact that many Irish nationalists like Kettle fought for the rights of small nations and ignore how this "uneasiness . . . [over] Irish/British identity" was a symptom of their "opposition to English dominance" (Feather-stone 1995, 82). Ultimately, Kettle saw the war as a conflict that subsumed all other parochial struggles.

Obviously Kettle's war poems carry on a dialogue about the one issue that dominated Irish politics between 1912 and 1916 and that is Home Rule. As a Redmondite, he believed that the war offered an opportunity to demonstrate that Home Rule did not involve disloyalty to empire. Most of his war poems are pred-icated on this good faith argument that Ireland's support for the British war effort would secure Home Rule. This spirit of reci-procity was shattered by the Rising, though. The firing squads of May 1916 shifted public sympathy to the rebels, and the consti-tutional nationalism of Redmond and Kettle became a washed-up ideology abandoned by the withdrawing tide of republican-ism. After Easter 1916, the Great War for many nationalists was a foreign conflict: the real war was at home.

Just as Ledwidge and Kettle were preoccupied by their strug-gle to locate a rationale for their belief in the war, an Irish sol-dier poet who seems to have shared none of their self-doubts was Donegal-born Patrick MacGill. From what we know about MacGill, he, too, shares little in common with the canonical sol-dier poets of the Great War. Born in 1890, he left school at the age of twelve and worked as a farm laborer (S. Brown 1970, 188). At fourteen, he began writing poetry for the *Derry Journal* before immigrating to Scotland to work in the potato fields (187). Over the next several years, he got by doing various menial jobs be-fore devoting himself to writing. His early works (a collection of poems and two novels) were largely autobiographical in nature and drew heavily on his experiences as a migrant worker. The popularity of these works led *The Daily Express* to hire MacGill as a reporter, but in 1913 he quit and took up editing work with the Chapter Library at Windsor Castle (May 1986, 295).

With the onset of the war, he enlisted in the London Irish Rifles but continued to write prolifically. During the war, he was pro-moted to sergeant and was wounded at Loos (Parfitt 1990, 68), yet he still found time to publish several war novels (*The Am-ateur Army*, *The Great Push*, *The Red Horizon* and *The Brown Brethren*—all of which enjoyed considerable sales) and a series of war sketches from 1915 to 1917 (S. Brown 1970, 187). The one volume of war poems he did publish during the war, *Soldier Songs*, is generally regarded as inferior to his war novels, which were praised at the time for their "scathing account of his ex-periences" in the London Irish Rifles (May 1986, 295).[8] Another highlight of his active service was his participation in one of the war's most famous attacks when his regiment purportedly drib-bled a soccer ball toward the German lines (Falls 1930, 215), a popular story that MacGill later revealed to be more myth than fact (Dungan 1997, 132). After the war, he continued to write, and in 1930, he left for the United States where he was unable to rediscover the kind of acclaim his early work enjoyed. He finally published nineteen novels and several volumes of poetry before his death in 1963 (May 1986, 295).[9] It is as a novelist, though, that MacGill is chiefly remembered. His first book is reputed to have sold over 120,000 copies in its first two weeks after publica-tion, and his harshly realistic descriptions of the lives of migrant farm workers have been compared in style and theme to the novels of Émile Zola. After years of being out of print, several of his early novels were republished in the 1980s, and there is even a MacGill Summer School held each year in Donegal devoted to the study of his work, with additional programs for creative writing that attract some of Ireland's best-known contemporary authors.[10]

However, as a purported voice of the other ranks, MacGill's poems reveal a confusing range of responses to the war. While he appeared to remain "sceptical about the goal of the war" and remained critical toward those "who had provoked [the] conflict" (Dungan 1997, 129), in comparison to Ledwidge and Kettle, he did not agonize over his own decision to enlist. Like many Irish men and women at the time, he was fairly comfortable with his Irish/British identity. Perhaps this is why his poems never engage the divisive issue of Ireland's role in the war: "Nor was he interested in Irish nationalism; for him the one burning social issue was the plight of the underprivileged who scrambled for existence" (Hogan 1979, 402).

Except for a few poems that reveal his homesickness for Ireland, MacGill's war poetry simply explores what George Parfitt describes as the thematic clichés of trench poetry: the compassion for the "poor bloody infantry," the admiration for Tommy's "cheerful endurance," and the reportage of " 'cockney' grumbling about mud and rations" (1990, 61). Unlike Ledwidge, practically every one of MacGill's poems treats the war directly but then only the conflict on the Western Front. For someone whose war novels were praised for their realistic depictions of life at the front, MacGill's war poetry is thematically indistinguishable from the type of popular verse written by most English soldier poets. While acknowledging that minor war poetry leaves "out vast tracts of experience the heights and depths of which were mapped by the likes of Owen and Sassoon," Martin Stephen's point that many of these minor war poets deliver as "vivid, honest, and truthful" portrait of life at the front "as the findings of the great authors" is certainly not borne out in MacGill's case (1996, 136). In *Soldier Songs,* MacGill does at times briefly discard his sanitized version of front-line experience in order to acknowledge the realities of survival, but read with the grain, his poems rarely stray from their Boy Scout brio. Many of these so-called songs, with their breezy rhythms and spirit-lifting cadences, are almost unnerving in their excessively jocund delivery as though MacGill had spent too many nights listening to the disposable platitudes and superficial sentimentalities of the music hall. We encounter little detail in his war poetry that shares the horror of his "harrowing experiences as a stretcher-bearer at Loos"; instead, what we get is a carefully rigged performance that showcases his skills as a sentimental versifier who gave "public recitals of his writing, heralded by pipes of the London Irish regiment, to tug the heartstrings of his audiences" (Cecil 1996, 231). Like many other soldiers, MacGill "remained firmly rooted in music hall culture" whose songs embraced the inoculating assurances of good faith and cheerfulness (Fuller 1990, 119 and 126). On another level, his complete adaptation of an English cockney voice and the subjugation of his own Irish identity reveal an attitude toward the war that is both politically and philosophically at odds with the stance taken by Ledwidge and Kettle.

Apart from the constraints of censorship, there may be several reasons to explain the gap between MacGill's hard-hitting war prose and his sentimental war verse (Jeffery 2000, 100). In his brief analysis of MacGill's casual orchestration of the clichés of the British Tommy's front-line experience, George Parfitt speculates that MacGill's lack of realistic details may indicate that he was either less appalled by the squalor of the front due to his laboring background or that he purposefully screened out the horrors for home front consumption (1990, 72). The first explanation seems very unlikely: conditions in the potato fields of Scotland could never have prepared MacGill for the evisceration and excreta of the front. The second possibility seems more plausible, yet as already noted, MacGill's war novels were praised for their "powerful" (brutal) accounts of the conditions in the trenches. Another possibility is that MacGill simply assumed that prose could better accommodate the shocking truths of the war than verse. He himself had no illusions about the disposable quality of his war songs. In a prefatory essay to Soldier Songs, he admitted that most of these poems were of "no import" precisely because "the crowd has no sense of poetic values; it is the singing alone which gives expression to the soldier's soul" (1917, 10). Whatever the case, Parfitt argues that the generalized effects of most of MacGill's poems remind us of how the war suppressed individuality (1990, 72). Popular war verse was tailored for the demotic and to "accentuate the positive."

MacGill's war poetry generally gives a simplified impression of infantry life at the front; his vaguely contoured descriptions, banal generalizations, and defused emotions wring all the trauma out of these glimpses of life in the trenches. Perhaps this is

why John Wilson Foster describes MacGill's poetry as termi-
nally "bad" (Greacen 1981, 14). Not surprisingly, the "persis-
tently cheery" rhythms "look like efforts at what Home expects"
(Parfitt 1990, 68). In "After Loos" (1917, 23–24) we see this dis-
sonance between the urgency of the experience and the language
of recollection:

> Was it only yesterday
> Lusty comrades marched away?
> Now they're covered up with clay.

This unfortunate use of buoyant end rhymes in an elegy is not
only a mistake in technique but a failure to register the de-
plorable authenticity and complexity of the violence. We also see
this failure to find a rhythm and vocabulary adequate to the situation in "La Bassée Road" (1917, 29–30) where MacGill depicts
a before-and-after glimpse of the troops who came "swinging
up . . . from bil- / lets in Bethune" but after the attack "Have now
got little homes of clay beside the / firing line." Any attempt at
irony is defused by the breezy rhymes and the folksy metonymy
("little homes" for graves) that whitewash the soldiers' deaths. If
MacGill practices self-censorship to spare the delicate sensibilities of the home front, his emotional disengagement falsely implies that the soldiers' sufferings were expiated by their burial.
There is no outrage here for order and decency. To borrow from
the warspeak of another conflict, MacGill implies that there is
"an acceptable level of violence."

The pervasiveness of these false simplicities and pseudo-
solemnities is also demonstrated in his playful treatment of the
terrible living conditions the troops had to endure in the
trenches. In "The Fly" (1917, 96) the speaker provides a jocu-
lar description of the hordes of corpse flies that made the troops'
lives miserable:

> They revel in your butter-dish and riot on
>   your ham,
> Drill upon the army cheese and loot the
>   army jam.

There is even the suggestion that killing flies is a welcome dis-
traction, for "There's never zest like Tommy's zest when / these
have got to die." But the widespread misery these pests caused on
the various fronts would not have been so cavalierly dismissed
by surviving veterans. Dysentery was so common at Gallipoli,
for instance, that, as one survivor later recalled, many men cried

openly because they were so dirty and could not "stop shitting" (Moorhouse 1993, 2). As someone who had firsthand experience of the war, MacGill's whimsical treatment of the front line's sickening pestilence and barbarity seems odd unless we accept the theory that he was eager to spare home front sensibilities. Or perhaps such poems illustrate the type of dark humor that was prevalent among the troops, a sort of grisly indifference that helped them cope with their terrible living conditions.

MacGill also dutifully honors that third major cliché of frontline reportage: Tommy's constant grumbling about the food and the mud. In "The Tommy's Lament" (1917, 45–46), he adopts the voice of the habitual complainer who whines about his pack ("Parading like a snail through France, / My house upon my bloomin' back") and his rations ("mongrel's feed"). Again, MacGill constructs a caricature picture of the British soldier, but the troops in the front lines often had little patience with "chronic grousers": for instance, one particularly "favorite reprimand" to a soldier's constant whining was "What do you want?—Jam on it?" (Brophy and Partridge 1965, 225). Yet MacGill's stereotypical portrait of the British Tommy cloaks any further understanding of what the war was like.

For someone whose novels offer a more realistic view of the war, the superficial nature of MacGill's war poetry remains puzzling. Like Ledwidge, he does occasionally indulge in escapist fantasies via recollection of remembered Irish landscapes, but unlike Ledwidge, MacGill wallows in nostalgia and sentiment. As previously noted, for many Irish poets, personal identity largely involves intimate connections to Irish landscape, and we see this same sentiment in some of MacGill's "songs." In "Death and the Fairies" (1917, 89), for instance, he contrasts the mystery of Irish folklore and landscape with the savage reality of the front: "every night the Fairies / Would hold their carnival," but now in "Flanders, / Where men like wheat-ears fall, . . . it's Death and not the Fairies / Who is holding carnival." MacGill obliquely explores how the war separates him from his cultural memory, and he sustains this dichotomizing between home and the front in "It's a Far, Far Cry" (1917, 37–38) where the flat topography of Flanders reminds him only of what he has lost:

> My heart is sick of the level lands,
>   Where the wingless windmills be,
>   Where the long-nosed from dusk to
>   dawn

> Are speaking angrily;
> But the little home by Glenties Hill,
> Ah! that's the place for me.

It is only in a handful of poems like these that MacGill's sense of cultural dislocation intrudes, but even here his disillusionment with the war never assumes the stridency of antiwar bitterness or political hostility.

On the contrary, at times, he directly endorses the "Old Lie." In "A.D. 1916" (1917, 73–74), for example, war is celebrated as an opportunity to sound "the shout of glory!" Not only does the poem acknowledge the war as a necessary agent for change— "The old life fails, but the new life comes"—but the very title suggests that all war is a part of an honorable tradition. This interpretation of the war as a necessary cleansing agent loses sight of what is actually being eradicated here: not so much a way of life (although that goes, too) but life itself.

If MacGill's poems are inconsistent in their perspective, probably the most significant distinguishing feature between his "songs" and the war poetry of Ledwidge and Kettle is how his enlistment in the British army never seems to be an issue for him. If anything, MacGill's Irishness is simply a variety of Britishness, and there is ample evidence to illustrate his subscription to the dominant theology where "England" is the defining icon for the entire British Isles. There has been a tradition of writing the British Isles "as a coherent whole, subsumed to the concept 'England'" (Parfitt 1990, 9). Writers ranging in caliber from Shakespeare (in *Henry V*) to W. E. Henley eagerly sponsored the idea of a hegemonic British patriotism (9). In MacGill's case, he appears to have "been swept into patriotic fervor by the prevailing climate of British opinion and the atmosphere of Windsor Castle" where he worked briefly in 1913 (Greacen 1981, 10). However, MacGill's affiliation with the British cause is not unusual, for quite often "pride in Empire and service in the army were synonymous in the minds of many Irishmen" (Dooley 1995, 37). Writer Seán O'Faoláin later recalled how he had "no consciousness of [his] . . . country as a separate cultural entity inside the Empire" (36). To assume that, prior to partition, most Irish Catholics were unambiguously nationalist is to accept the nationalist myth of an uninterrupted history of heroic resistance to British rule. The political reality is much more complex: as someone who was to later acquire nationalist sympathies himself, O'Faoláin admitted that, prior to 1916, he "was tremendously proud of belonging to the Empire, as were at that time most Irishmen" (36).

With the exception of those poems where MacGill indulges in bouts of homesickness for Ireland, he effectively annuls his own identity and adopts a decidedly English persona throughout the entire collection. His poems portray "stereotypical images of the nation to reinforce the 'need' for the war" and they also favor "extreme selection and the power of myth" (Parfitt 1990, 103). When home is mentioned, it is England as in "Letters" (1917, 53–58) where the speaker dreams that "We see the lights of London, of London and / of home." Even when Tommy thinks of love letters sent to the front, he imagines "An English maiden's letter to her sweetheart / at the War."

And when thoughts turn to what life will be like when the war is over, MacGill's soldiers think again of England as in "After the War" (1917, 111–12):

> When I come back to England,
>   And times of Peace come round,
> I'll surely have a shilling
>   And maybe have a pound.

The cumulative effect of all these references to England is to submerge other strands of Britishness. MacGill's exclusive use of a cockney dialect also marginalizes the "vast majority of the population" and implies that what was being fought for was "the protection of the privileges of the few" (Parfitt 1990, 107).

By writing many of his poems in the cockney dialect, MacGill conforms to the "Home convention that 'cockney' is what rankers speak when not using standard English" (Parfitt 1990, 69). Rather than trying to create an authentic trench voice, MacGill's soldiers simply mimic the popular concept of ranker speech made famous by Kipling. As an Irishman serving in the British army, though, MacGill's adoption of cockney as the vernacular of the front involves certain cultural ironies. For a start, he has written his "own brogue . . . out of *Soldier Songs*" (69). Furthermore, his handling of the ballad form with the cockney dialect contains some interesting political implications. Historically, ballads function as cultural icons that map out the boundaries and characteristics of regional or national pride and identity. In MacGill's case, though, this sense of identity takes on a fairly constricted English perspective. The very qualities we come to admire in the troops—their stoicism, selflessness, and humanity—are inseparably linked to their English cockney voice as in "Matey" (1917, 119–20):

> I'd sooner the bullet was mine, matey—
> Goin' out on my own,
> Leavin' you 'ere in the line, matey,
> All by yourself, alone.

The whole concept of front-line mateship is presented as an exclusively English experience. In "Ole Sweats" (1917, 25–28) these virtues of endurance and fortitude are also celebrated through a cockney voice:

> We've 'eld the trenches eighteen months and
>   copped some packets, too . . .
> But if our butty's still were out in Flanders
>   raisin' Cain,
> We'd weather through with those we knew
>   on bully beef again.

No wonder one of the sales advertisements at the end of *Soldier Songs* favorably compares MacGill's work "with that of Rudyard Kipling" (121). If ballads purport to be the "authentic echo of the voice of the people" (Fitzpatrick 1982–85, 60), MacGill's songs clearly indicate that the voice of the British soldier is an English one.

Perceptions of the war from an exclusively English perspective have also affected the way literary historians label British poetry of the Great War, for "English poetry of the war" usually means "poetry in English by residents of the British Isles" (Parfitt 1990, 17). Most of the popular verse written during the war and the work that has subsequently entered the anthologies is decidedly English in idiom and is mostly written by Englishmen, but MacGill appears to have been quite fluent in the official language of the war. But perhaps his predilection for the cockney voice can simply be explained by his immediate circumstances during the war—after all, he was a member of the *London* Irish Rifles.

Taken as a whole, MacGill's poems are not convincing as representations of the ranker voice (Parfitt 1990, 69). The frequent inconsistencies in dialect, where MacGill's cockney voice and standard English compete side by side as the true vernacular of the trenches, undermine any attempt at authentic orality. There is a certain degree of disingenuousness here also, for this verse has been carefully processed for the home front. However, MacGill's *Soldier Songs* are "significant both as gauges of morale and as contributions to the literature or sub-literature of war" (Rutherford 1989, 73).

Another impression these songs leave behind is their implicit endorsement of imperialism. War is frequently interpreted as adventurous and exciting; if the front is the arena where one proves one's worth, the corollary is that a period of peace stifles these noble instincts. In *Rule of Darkness: British Literature and Imperialism*, Patrick Brantlinger argues that a common theme of late Victorian literature is its lament that the colonial frontiers have been settled and that there are fewer opportunities for heroism (1988, 230). Despite MacGill's adoption of this late Victorian imperialist lament, his songs still remind us that the war is appalling, but they do not unequivocally denounce it. If anything, many of his war poems uphold the unionist myth that supporting the war is perceived as duty to the empire and flag, and MacGill honors the imperialist pieties Kipling identifies in his poem "McAndrew's Hymn" where "Law, Orrder, Duty an' Restraint, Obedience, Discipline" are worshipped as abstractions. MacGill's glorification of these absolutes and his failure to look beyond the received ideas about the war effectively bury his own voice amid the noise of the crowd. Ironically, he guarantees his own prediction that these songs "will not outlast the turmoil in which they originated" (MacGill 1917, 14).

If MacGill's songs are more representative of the kinds of verse that were popular during the war, recent reevaluations of the poetry of the Great War generalize that the more popular forms of literature present a more accurate portrait of the actual response to the war than the usual anthology selections. The fact is that most poets endeavored to document the war as a recognizable narrative. Irish soldier poets, when they were not concerned with this narrative, tackled issues closer to home. The four soldier poets just discussed reveal distinctive variations on the same theme: with the exception of Weaving, each is preoccupied with his own reasons for fighting in the war. While Weaving's archaic language and penchant for classical myth illustrate a refusal to depart from the traditions of martial poetry, Ledwidge's war poetry unveils a gradual shift from standard escapist verse to Irish republican partisanship and experimentation with Irish literary sources. For Tom Kettle, self-doubts about his decision to enlist lead him to embrace the self-rationalization that he was fighting for an ideal rather than a cause. And finally, MacGill ventriloquizes popular British ideas about the war so faithfully that he annuls his own identity in favor of the dominant British prowar narrative. Taken as a whole, though, despite the fact that these soldier poets skim over many of the issues that the better-known war poets address, as personal responses to the war, they broaden our understanding of the kinds of literature that held an immediate appeal for those at home.

Above all, though, Irish soldier poets reveal the complexities of the Irish response to the war. The presence of pro- and antiwar rhetoric in their work indicates how Irish soldier poets did not shy away from using their poetry to broadcast their political convictions. But unlike English war poets, their work responded to the particular tensions of the Irish involvement, and their poems often attempt to reconstruct the nature of the Home Rule debate with the customary unionist and nationalist myths being trotted out to support the prevailing ideology. We also see—especially in the poetry of Ledwidge and Kettle—how the war shattered past confidences in political process and influenced the nature of the struggle for Irish autonomy by isolating Home Rulers like Kettle, thus providing an opportunity for more militant nationalists to play a bigger role in Ireland's political future. As we shall see later, perhaps the most important recurring motif of Irish war poetry is how this very debate about what and where is Ireland is carried on within the more easily recognizable dialogues about the war. For some of the soldier poets, their presence at the front was inextricably linked to the Irish conflict over political, cultural, religious, and linguistic heritages. While English war poets frequently look to the past, to a prewar idyll, in order to cope with the endless horror of the war, for Irish soldier poets like Ledwidge and Kettle, the past offers no such consolation. As writers who were deeply concerned about Ireland's future, the past only served to remind them of what Thomas Flanagan calls "that enormous colonizing empire that hovers, as fact or memory over every Irishman's shoulder" (1996, 6).

4

The Home Front

MOST OF THE POETRY WRITTEN BY BRITISH SOLDIERS DURING THE FIRST World War was destined for a short shelf life. While some "enjoyed massive sales, because they briefly caught a public mood" (Cecil 1996, 2), the slapdash technique and topicality of their work guaranteed that most of their war volumes inevitably wound up on bookshops' remainder shelves or were interred, row on row, in the lesser-traveled by-ways of the local public library. And deservedly so for most of this popular soldier verse is imaginatively sterile, stylistically third-rate, and thematically undistinguished. It delights in the simplest of pleasures, wallows in resignation, or entertains intermittent bouts of "fear and boredom," "homesickness," and "irritation at the army" (Stephen 1996, 136). Yet, as we have seen, what distinguished the poems written by Irish soldier poets from their English counterparts was the debate about Ireland's role in the war and the ongoing disputes over the country's political future. This preoccupation with constitutional issues and personal and political identity was also a predominant theme in the war poems written by other Irish men and women who sat out the war well behind the front lines. Like the soldier poets, though, the civilian response to the conflict is as equally tendentious precisely because it also exposes the political and cultural fault lines which crisscross Irish memory of the Great War. As with the soldiers' poetry, the quality of the war verse written by Irish noncombatants is equally uneven, but the range of perspectives is much broader as the binary voices of prowar imperialist and antiwar nationalist mingle with those of the elegist, the pacifist, the apathetic, and the ambivalent. Even more interesting are the apparent contradictions and shifting attitudes that we encounter in their work.

In the following survey of the war poetry written by Irish men and women on the home front, the virtually unknown, the decidedly minor, and the demonstrably great all respond to the defining historical event of their generation. While writers like F. S. Boas, Katharine Tynan, Winifred Letts, Eva Gore-Booth, and AE wrote patriotic, commemorative and pacifist verse, others like James Joyce and W. B. Yeats were more wary of the dangers of reacting to the latest atrocity yet felt compelled to respond in some manner to this heretofore unparalleled tragedy. Looked at collectively, the divergent viewpoints and ideologies found in these writers' war verse reflect the paradoxes and divisions in Irish political and cultural history during the first two decades of this century. Analyzing their war poetry for its commitment to imperialism, pacifism, political detachment, or nationalism illuminates our understanding of how Ireland's role in the Great War has been distorted and why the viewpoints of those who do not neatly fit into the binary categories (unionist/nationalist) were ignored during the War of Independence and the subsequent years of partition.

Perhaps the most strident Irish pro-imperialist war poet who elegized the Irish war dead was F. S. Boas (1862–1957). An Oxford-trained scholar who specialized in Shakespeare, Marlowe, and eighteenth-century drama, Boas actually only lived in Ireland for four years. In 1901, he was appointed "a Fellow of the Royal University of Ireland" and later served as "College Librarian" at Queen's College, Belfast, from 1903 to 1905 (White 1995, 22). After leaving Queen's, he spent the rest of an illustrious academic career in England where he made his reputation as a textual editor (26). As for poetry, Boas published one volume of poems during the war. In *Songs of Ulster and Balliol* (1917), only the first of the book's three sections, entitled "Ulster," directly addresses the Ulster-Irish contribution to the war effort. One of the current vogues in literary studies is the postcolonial perspective, where texts are analyzed for evidence of sociopolitical hierarchies, racist assumptions, and Anglo or Eurocentric ideologies. Inevitably texts predating our current period of supposed inclusion, enlightenment, and understanding are pared apart for their predictably irredentist and atavistic notions about race, nation, and empire. The result is a fairly predictable scenario where the colonized are portrayed as primitives in need of civilizing by altruistic imperialists who play their tutelary role with a deep sense of duty and moral rectitude. Of course today as "the Empire writes back" (to borrow Salman Rushdie's phrase), it is the formerly colonized who occupy the moral high ground, and it is the colonizers who are invariably depicted as racist, revanchist, and recidivist. Unfortunately, in the case of F. S. Boas, many of these imperialist stereotypes are too easily confirmed. If postcoloniality is all about exposing the essentializing schemas of a repressive empire, then Boas's war poetry loudly proclaims the colonizer's supremacist creed, which argues again and again for the "purity and essence of one's own racial group" (Cheng 1995, 54).

One poem that illustrates this brand of racial piety and faith in empire is "The Men of Ulster—September 1914" (1917, 13–14), a five stanza imperialist broadside that typifies the kind of patriotic verse popular during the early months of the Great War. The Kiplingesque rhythms and chivalric esprit reminiscent of the poetry of empire bards like William Watson certainly render Boas's blustery militarism ironic given the atrocities to follow, but from an historical point of view, the poem articulates some of the most fundamental beliefs of Ulster unionism and unionist mythography.

Throughout the poem, there is never any doubt that Ulster's loyalty is to the empire. In the third stanza, this fidelity is sanctified as a holy bond binding Ulster men to the mother country:

> But dearest to men of Ulster is the Empire's far-flung line,
> Where her sons have sped and toiled and bled, 'neath the
> Palm-tree and the pine.

In stanza four, Boas's Lambeg and sash-bedecked rhetoric celebrates Ulster's loyalty to king and empire despite the imminent threat of Home Rule:

> So, forward the men of Ulster for the Empire
>   and the King!
> Though their own fate be in debate, no
>   thought of wavering!
>
> The sword half-drawn in her own behoof,
>   in Ulster's red right hand
> Will leap from the scabbard and flash like fire,
>   for the common Motherland.

Despite the flag waving, Boas's portrayal of Ulster's role in defending the empire is also predicated on the contractual understanding that Ulster's sacrifices would be rewarded after the war with the shelving of Home Rule. In typically elevated and ceremonious language, he welds Ulster's regional identity to a greater sense of British nationhood. These lines also illustrate how unionism's sense of identity is local (the red hand of Ulster), British ("the common Motherland") and imperial ("Empire"). It is this complex mesh of loyalties that nationalists misunderstand as they regard Irishness and Britishness as mutually exclusive. Boas's rousing call to defend the empire carries other significant implications. In what Pamela Clayton describes as the process of "legitimisation" (1996, 120), the idea that Ulster unionists were fighting the war to preserve the Empire also "legimate[d] Ulster opposition to Home Rule" (118). As Boas's poem suggests, allegiance to empire provided Ulster's resistance to Home Rule with an imperial moral authority: far from being an act of betrayal, taking up arms to resist Home Rule legislation passed by the British government was actually an act of larger loyalty in that Ulster unionists were prepared to fight to preserve the unity of the United Kingdom and the empire. Consequently, Boas's pro-imperialism demonstrates how unionists saw the war as an opportunity to play what Clayton describes as the "empire card" (1996, 120) in order to resist Home Rule.

In the final stanza, Boas restates the widely-held belief that if Ulster played its part during England's hour of need then the union would be secure: "And wherever the fight is hottest, and the sorest task is set, / Ulster will strike for England— and England will not forget!" Despite a weakness for the stagy, grandiloquent phrase, the poem is particularly important for what it reveals about unionist attitudes toward the war during the early months of the conflict.

When Boas subscribes to this loyalist faith in a "chosen people" is where the poem portrays Ulster as an exclusively Protestant state, a locale identifiable only by its fairly clichéd images from Ulster Protestant folk mythology: the linen mills, the shipyards, and the well-tilled fields:

> Dear to the men of Ulster are her sunlit fields and bays,
> The whirr of the loom, and the hammer's ring, and the harvest of
>   toiling days;
> And dearer yet is the birthright, won by their sires of old,
> Their heritage forever, not to be bought or sold.

This is what the men of Ulster fight to protect: a homogenized narrative where loyalism becomes a synonym for hard work, thrift, and sacrifice. The history of loyalist resistance is celebrated and codified to brace future generations whose "birth-right" will be handed on. The last line with its covenanter's

resolve sounds a lot like the sort of rhetoric we hear from unionist scaremongers today who warn of Ulster's heritage being "sold
down the river." Yet self-aggrandizement is what this brand of
political essentialism is all about. Boas's mythologizing of the Ulster "volk" translates the Great War into another episode in the
ongoing struggle of the "chosen people," and with his exclusion
of any other form of Ulster identity, he reminds us how "forms
of national consciousness . . . reproduce the same binary, essentialist hierarchies inherited from Anglo-Saxonist racism" (Cheng
1995, 291).

Another of Boas's poems that deals directly with Ulster's war
experience is an elegy he wrote for one of his relatives who was
killed on the first day of the Somme offensive. In "Ulster on the
Somme" (1917, 15–16), the poet combines features of pastoral
elegy with nostalgic retrospect as he mourns the loss of his "kins-
man." Again the poem is fraught with the archaisms and commemorative affectations of the cenotaph:

> 'Twas two short years ago—they seem
>   Fate-laden aeons now—
> Faith saw the destined glory gleam
>   O'er Ulster's helmèd brow.

The descriptions of the battlefield seem more appropriate to the
Battle of Hastings than the first day of the Somme. The overall
effect transforms the dead soldier into a memorial for the glorious fallen as Boas buries the agony of his death under a welter
of splendid modifiers and noble personifications:

> "Gay as a lark"—the tribute he is
>   By chief and comrade penned—
> He sang his way to the Abyss,   ·
>   And smiled on Death as a friend.
>
> For him no sombre requiem,
>   No threnody of tears,
> Who bartered for Youth's diadem
>   The dross of After-Years.

Obviously Boas romanticizes the soldier's death, but the en-
thusiastic imperialist tone is rather more subdued here. While
he still cherishes the ideals that heroicize Ulster's sacrifice,
Boas's zeal for empire gives way to regional allegiances. In the
third, fourth, and fifth stanzas, we are reminded of these soldiers'
birthright, courage and loyalty:

From Antrim glens and hills of Down,
    And moaning Northern Sea,
From mill and mart and thronging town,
    Strode Ulster's chivalry.

Heroes re-born of the Red Branch,
    They leapt into the fray,
Whelmed by the steely avalanche,
    That long Midsummer day.

Life?—'twas a little thing to give:
    Death? — t'was a toy to try.
They knew that Ulster dared not live,
    Did they not dare to die.

Boas's selective geography creates the impression that only Ulster men supported the war effort. He makes reference only to Ulster counties despite the fact that southern Irish regiments were also involved in the Somme offensive. As a result, he exploits Ulster's war casualties to promote the "Unionist myth that between 1910 and 1921 there emerged in the north of Ireland a solid, united, self-reliant, and successful Ulster movement, which made good its claim to statehood, if not nationhood, and whose claim was sealed in blood: the blood of the men at the Somme" (Boyce 1993, 5).

Quite often, Irish war poetry relegates the Great War to the background in order to construct political and cultural identities. To achieve this, Boas exploits the cycle of tales associated with Ulster's pre-Christian Red Branch warriors to mythicize the deeds of these latter-day heroes. As a unionist, he celebrates the legendary warrior Cuchulain—the Red Hound of Ulster—who defended his homeland against the invading "Irish" forces of Connacht's Queen Maeve (as chronicled in the *Tàin*), and so the spirit of Ulster separatism emerges as the ancient warriors are linked with those on the Somme battlefield. This idea that "Cuchulain clearly personified the struggle of Ulster against the invading Gael" (Buckley 1991, 269) was resurrected during the 1970s by Ian Adamson whose books—*The Cruthin* (1974) and *The Identity of Ulster* (1982)—argue that "the earliest inhabitants of Ireland were not the Gaels, but the Cruthin" (269), the ancient forebears of Ulster Protestants. Adamson's speculative anthropology was later adopted for propaganda purposes by the Ulster Defense Association (UDA), and the "junior wing of the Ulster Unionist Party" published his views in their "Young

Unionists' pamphlet" in 1986 (269). (Today, some of the more impressive wall murals in Protestant areas in Belfast portray Cuchulain as a precursor of the loyalist paramilitaries who continue to defend Ulster from her enemies.) Of course, nationalists claim Cuchulain as a mythic forebear as well. Many commentators note Patrick Pearse's fascination with the legendary warrior's emblematic representation of a heroic Irish past, and the bronze frieze of Cuchulain that resides today in Dublin's General Post Office not only essentializes the Rising but reminds us of the power of art in creating myth. Ironically, these rival claims on Irish myth illustrate how even a common mythology can still prove to be a divisive force in the Irish imagination. Boas's mythic glorification of the Ulster Division may seem absurd considering the mass extermination at the Somme, but it also reveals how Irish legend continues to provide a narrative source for those determined to establish their tribal heritage.

Inevitably, Boas's elegy for his friend and all the other Ulster dead at the Somme demonstrates how the "unionist psyche chose to ignore . . . [the] exploitation and betrayal and turn the sacrifice of the Somme into something much more positive" (Dungan 1995, 126). As a result, "The Somme became an affirmation of Ulster Protestant loyalism" (126). Boas's celebration of empire reminds us how, in the hands of less gifted poets, poetry can be transparently exploited to serve the agendas of identity politics. As already noted, a long-term consequence of this kind of tribal tub-thumping was that after partition, memory of the Great War in Northern Ireland became exclusively associated with an Ulster loyalist sacrifice, a legacy that ignores the "claims of others to a share in the folk memory of the Somme offensive" (127). Inevitably, Boas's war poetry casts the conflict as another mythic saga in the loyalist narrative as the blood and horror of the Great War fabricate a regional identity that is both essentialist and separatist.

Like Boas, many women poets in the first two decades of the twentieth century were "still inspired by the mythology of the British Empire" (Tylee 1990, 252). Recent studies of women's war verse contest that war literature, with its privileging of the masculine experience, typically sublimated the female voice. Another conclusion postulated by these ongoing reappraisals of women's war poetry is that while it is not part of the official literary canon of the war, women's war verse does provide insight into the war experiences of other groups who also suffered.

The most prevalent themes of the war poetry written by Irish women between 1914 and 1918 closely resemble those that preoccupied English women's war verse. There is the struggle to cope with a sense of displacement as "the primary loss in war literature is inevitably death; mourning is secondary" (Higonnet 1987, 14). We also encounter plenty of prowar sentiment inspired by a naive faith in the invincibility of the empire as women poets openly encourage enlistment. As for antiwar statements in Irish women's war poetry, such criticism is seldom ideological in nature. With the notable exception of Eva Gore-Booth, pacifism holds little sway; deaths are simply mourned but the war is hardly ever condemned. Instead, attraction to the artifice of ceremony, the idealism and sentimentality of elegy, and the restorative properties of nature as an agent for change frequently predominate.

From a political perspective, Irish women poets rarely ever engage the complexities of Ireland's role in the war. Controversies or seeming contradictions are largely ignored. For the most part, the observations made about British women's war verse apply almost uniformly to the war poetry written by Irish women as their war verse is often "marred by the scars of haste, of hysteria, and of the melodramatic" (Khan 1988, 4), features that tend to portray these women poets as primarily "reporters, propagandists, interpreters, advocates, satirists, elegists, healers, and visionaries . . ." (4). For the many women who felt compelled to write war verse, the heavy influence of nineteenth-century idioms quite often led them to draw on the "perennial subjects of religion and nature to interpret war" (5, 7). Just as the war "starkly revealed Edwardian assumptions about women" (Marwick 1977, 12), their reductive image as "housewives, mothers, sisters or lovers" was also perpetuated by women poets whose themes predictably consist largely of "meeting, parting, separation, love, loss, death, and despair" (Khan 1988, 7). As we shall see, what is true of the war verse written by their mainland counterparts is equally true of Irish women's war poetry.

Of the three most notable Irish women writers who published collections of poetry during the Great War, certainly the most prolific was Katharine Tynan (1861–1931). Her career as a prominent figure of the Irish Literary Revival and friend of Yeats and AE has been well documented, and her overall reputation as a writer rests clearly on the collective significance of her considerable output as novelist, memoirist, reviewer, critic, and poet. As for her war poetry, while it can lay no claim to being her best work, it is significant for what it adds to our understanding of the Irish response to the Great War.

Between 1914 and 1918, Tynan published four volumes of war poetry: *The Flower of Youth: Poems in War Time* (1915); *The Holy War* (1916); *Late Songs* (1917); and *Herb O'Grace: Poems in War Time* (1918). Generally speaking, her war poems "cannot be seen apart from their context" (Fallon 1979, 94), but to be fair, Tynan never regarded her war poetry as anything other than a salve for the afflicted: "That even one person found consolation or a momentary appeasement of his or her grief through reading her poems was Tynan's only wish in the writing of them, and many people did find them a source of comfort" (95).

In her war poetry, Tynan appears to be drawn to the "heroism of the soldiers and the heroism of the families," and behind these portraitures of noble suffering lies the "unquestionable assumption that the war was just, and that the boys who died all died bravely, heroically, and gladly for a glorious cause" (Fallon 1979, 92). Of the chief features of her war poetry that warrant closer inspection, what is most interesting is what they reveal about the roles women played during the war and how Tynan, like many other war poets, seems incapable of divesting herself of the ready-to-hand imperialist myths when confronted with the need to locate a source of consolation for the bereaved. Perhaps the only overtly Irish character to some of her war poems is how they invoke Irish religious icons in an attempt to confer something of the spiritual and miraculous on the war dead. In fact, one would look hard to uncover any substantial references to Ireland's political tensions during the period, for Tynan "seems to have failed to recognize the significance of the Easter Rising of 1916 and the subsequent political events in Ireland" (111). Her years of exile in England meant that she was politically out of touch with the situation back home and had little understanding of the "political ambitions, the passions, [and] the hopes of her own people" (111). Perhaps one feature of her war poetry that can be linked to her Irish background is her preference for stylistic and thematic standards associated with the Irish Literary Revival: in many of her war poems, we see an "obsession with the past, the veneration of the primitive, and the rural, [and] the cults of the hero and of blood sacrifice" (T. Brown 1995, 32).

The most distinguishing feature of Tynan's war poems, though, is that the vast majority of them are "written on the occasion of the death of someone she did not know personally" (Fallon 1979, 95). There was a considerable audience for this kind of automatic elegy and "throughout the war she became what would now be called a 'grief counsellor' for countless correspondents" (Cecil 1996, 322). After looking over the several hundred war poems that Tynan wrote, it seems that no situation of bereavement escaped her treatment. Many of the poems are obviously written for grief-stricken mothers, and the casualties range from soldiers, airmen, and sailors to even those executed for dereliction of duty. The subjects of her elegies are always men, or "boys," while women usually occupy the roles of aggrieved housewives, bereaved mothers, or wistful lovers. If anything, Tynan's women resemble the standard stereotypes that we see in the poetry of some of the better known soldier poets of the war whose "women experience the war mainly through the loss of their lovers who will never return to gather flowers with them" (J. Breen 1990, 174). Redolent with conventional sentiment, Tynan's war verse is "chiefly consolatory," and because it never wavers from this eulogistic enthusiasm for glory and honor, the natural consequence of her fervor for the "heroic" and the "religious" inevitably "imparts a touch of banality to her poems" (Khan 1988, 14). Despite her rather formulaic approach to writing war verse, Tynan did not share the "popular fantasy" that the war resided in some "out-of-the-way chunk of the globe [designated] as a war zone" (Hanley 1991, 31). Instead, her elegies demonstrate that the effects of the front could be felt far from where the actual fighting took place.

Undoubtedly the most recurrent role allotted to women in Tynan's war poetry is that of mother. Of the hundreds of war poems she wrote, many are obsessed with the "universality of motherhood," a theme that dominates "British and German women's writing about the War," too (Cardinal 1993, 47). Perhaps the fact that she herself had two sons (Toby and Pat) at the front made her particularly sensitive to the fears and anxieties of all the mothers who lived in daily dread for their sons' lives. In "The Young Mother" (1915, 28), the innocence of the mother contrasts with the surrounding depravity "Of a mad world that slays and slays." Throughout the poem, Tynan describes the mother's cloistered existence as though she were the only inhabitant of an Edenic garden: "No rumour reaches her at all, / Beyond her safe encompassing wall." She leads the life of an earthly cherubim "Wrapped in mild tranquilities" and attended by "angels [who] bend to her / [in] A little secret garden-close." Totally removed from the horror of the war and its far-reaching tentacles of misery, the "Young Mother" symbolizes a nostalgic bygone innocence that counterbalances the war's savagery. Furthermore, these "Images of femininity, nurturance, and the family can be invoked to restore the balance and protect our faith in the social order" (Higonnet 1987, 1). The poem's escapist tone also gives it a specifically romantic inflection, but the message offers little in the way of coping with the war's realities; the sheltered dream world hearkens back not only to a remotely distant past but to a past that exists only in the imagination. Tynan's infatuation with dream worlds (a particularly nineteenth-century obsession) seems out of touch with the daily hardships of bereaved mothers and war widows who quite often had to cope with a "suddenly enforced independence . . . as breadwinner" (6).

Apart from this romantic conception of the maternal figure living in splendid isolation from the savagery of the war, Tynan repeatedly portrays women as passive sufferers whose very existence and happiness is exclusively defined by the presence or absence of men in their lives. Women rarely take on roles as nurses, munitions workers, or antiwar agitators; rather, they are continually typecast as forlorn lovers and deserted widows. Tynan is particularly fond of speculating on the lost possibilities for these women whose lives appear to have become purposeless now that they are deprived of male companionship.

In her depictions of women as gloomy lovers emotionally girdled to the memory of lost loves, Tynan's young women lament their losses and exist forever trapped in ironically beautiful pastoral landscapes. Their grief borders on the self-indulgent, and melodrama often prevails as descriptive associations with flowers in bloom contrast to the stony silence of their interred lovers. We see this juxtaposition between beauty and despair in "The Bride" (1915, 20–21) where the speaker announces, "I wear a red rose in my bosom; / To-morrow I shall wear the thorn." And in "A Girl's Song" (1915, 26) where "Some brown French girl the rose will wear" yet never "wonder why it is so red." Tynan's fondness for roses reminds us just how "indispensable [they were] to popular sentimental texts of the war" (Fussell 1975, 245).

Finally, Tynan implies that these young lovers whom the war has robbed of all happiness and expectation are also victims. In "The Vestal" (1930, 213–14) the joy of finding love is destroyed: the deprived lover "goes unwedded all her days" because "Her destined mate, has won his bays, / [and] Passed the low door of darkness through." Also dashed are the hopes for a generation of unborn children:

What of their children all unborn?
What of the house they should have built?
She wanders through her days forlorn,
The untasted cup of joy is spilt.

Traditional attitudes about women's roles dominate Tynan's depiction of grieving lovers as women's happiness seems largely contingent on whether they get married and have children. No other possibilities exist. This fairly circumscribed Victorian definition of women's roles naturally subscribes to the prevailing "archetypal female nurturing roles of mother" and lover (Higonnet 1987, 11). In "The Sad Spring" (1915, 75–76) only God's hand can help mothers raise fatherless children:

Tender nurslings born in pain,
Mother's comfort, mother's grief,
When her tears run down like rain,
Lord, bring Thou a handkerchief.

While Tynan provides religious consolation to help mitigate the terrible losses of fathers and husbands, in "The Bride" (1915, 20–21) she offers faith in honor and glory to bereaved lovers. The young female lover's despondency as her sweetheart leaves for the front and her moody resignation that she may never see him alive again are compensated by her faith in the glorious cause:

Go glad and gay to meet the foeman,
I love you to my latest breath;
Oh, love, there is no happier woman.
See, I am smiling! Love—till death!

For Tynan, the proper role for women was to stand steadfast and loyal behind their men despite the inevitability of loss and heartache. In many of her poems, Tynan's stereotypical portraits of women as meek and defenseless serve as reminders to men of what they are fighting to preserve: the timeless fabric of a society held together by a governing patriarchy.

Of course, the recurring images of motherhood throughout Tynan's war verse demonstrate just how popular was this image of women as symbols for homeland or empire "in the abstract" (Innes 1993, 17). Centuries of Irish writing crystallized the notion of an "ideal of Irish womanhood," but during the period between 1860 and 1914, the Irish and English press certainly played a key role in conflating nation and empire with a matri-

archal ideal (17). Tynan's war verse, then, was simply a barom-
eter of the popular feeling and patriotic sentiment of the time.
That it was also ideologically derivative goes without saying. The
sureties of Georgian society go unchallenged as Tynan reaffirms
Victorian platitudes about honor and violence while women remain creatures of passivity, limited to their assigned roles in a
world ruled by male militarism.

As Tynan's support of the war effort was inspired by her own
faith in "the ordered society that existed before the Great War"
(Fallon 1979, 47), it is not surprising that a significant number
of her war poems anoint the righteousness of the cause as a holy
crusade. In "The Call" (1915, 12–13), she has a vision of a huge
army converging from the corners of the globe to defend the cause
of freedom:

> Millions of men coming up from the edge of the world,
> The ring of unnumbered feet ever louder and louder
> Comes on and on like a mighty untameable tide,
> Steady, implacable, out of the North and the South,
> Out of the East and the West, they answer the call
> Of her who stands, her eyes towards God and the stars,
> Liberty, daughter of God, calling her men.

While she was no hawkish prowar propagandist, Tynan's reading of the war as a religious crusade against a barbarian foe
indicates just how widespread anti-German stereotypes were.
In "'What Turned the Germans Back?'" (1915, 24–25), she celebrates the stalled German advance on Paris during August and
September of 1914 as an omen of God's intervention on the side
of Britain and her allies. The war is reduced to an oversimplified struggle between good and evil rather than a battle between
rival empires:

> What turned the German myriads back
>   From Paris whither they had won?
> The sword dropped from their hold grown slack;
>   Children of Attila the Hun,
> Like Attila, went backward driven
> By a young shepherdess of Heaven.

Germanic brutality is repulsed by a messenger of God, this
"shepherdess" who "takes her golden crook and goes / And deals
destruction to its foes." The correlation between divine defender
and the British cause implies that the beauty and order of a

British pastoral world will overcome the alien threat. The danger in exploiting religious iconography to empower and justify one's cause, though, is that violence can be condoned without reservation if it serves a so-called lofty purpose.

In addition to her portrayal of the war as a Christian crusade, Tynan's war poems frequently imply that military sacrifice offers an opportunity for remission of past sins and a chance to earn eternal redemption. Sometimes her eagerness to locate a source of consolation results in her glorifying the soldiers' deaths rather than mourning them. On such occasions, her war poetry lends credence to the grossly oversimplified and inaccurate charge that during the war women, "inured as they were to domestic and public obedience, . . . retrogressively helped the government to foster the war, not only by actively encouraging young men to enlist but also by spreading the patriotic propaganda of the day" (J. Breen 1990, 169). The image that links these poems is that of a young man whose death in the war, rather than regarded as an obscenity, is actually celebrated as a moment of beauty. In "The Great Chance" (1915, 16–17), a young prodigal is offered an opportunity to redeem his past sins:

> Now strikes the hour upon the clock
> The black sheep may rebuild the years:
> May lift the father's pride he broke
> And wipe away the mother's tears.

Ironically, the war provides redemption, and the soldier's parents learn of his "baptism of blood" when they read the newspaper and "find his name among the dead, / Flower of the Army and the Fleet." The absurd assumption behind the poem (that glorious death atones for youthful prodigality) is summed up in the last stanza when, in a scene that has more in common with recruiting poster piety than the anguish and desolation of a lost life, the proud parents boast of their son's noble death:

> They tell, with proud and stricken face,
> Of his white boyhood far away—
> Who talked of trouble or disgrace?
> "Our splendid son is dead!" they say.

Again, in the absence of intentional irony, the sincerity of these lines rings hollow, and we are left to wonder at the lengths Tynan goes to provide solace.

Tynan also appropriates patriotic and religious rhetoric in order to offer consolation. In "The Summons" (1915, 31–32), an elegy for a young soldier cut down during the early months of the war, the message is that his death was ordained by God. The essential question—why did he leave to fight?—is asked repeatedly in the third and fourth stanzas:

> Why would he go so fast
> Out to the dead,
> All in a heavenly haste
> Not to be stayed?
>
> What did he see afar
> That drew him after?
> Light from a merry star,
> Singing and laughter?

In the final four stanzas, we learn what it was that inspired him to lay down his life:

> What was the voice before
> That lured him on?
> "Oh, thy long-hungered for,
> My son, my son!"

Christ-like in his martyrdom, the young soldier's death transcends life. Not for him the tragedy of a life cut short but rather the joy of eternity:

> Lo, he hath heard, hath seen,
> He hath slipped over
> Where the great days begin
> For friend and lover.

Once again Tynan carefully renders death as a part of a greater and more noble plan: the sense of destiny and the blessing of God's grace even make the nature of the soldier's death spiritually attractive. The war is God's cause, too, and the life lost is actually a life regained by its divine Creator. More important, however, is the yoking together once again of religious fervor with a patriotic high-mindedness. The soldier's death is not questioned; rather, it is seen as a sacrifice gladly given to a greater source of power and wisdom.

Likewise in "A Lament" (1915, 35–36) we see another casualty ennobled by the cause he chose to die for:

> Percy, golden-hearted boy,
> In the heyday of his joy
> Left his new-made bride and chose
> The steep way that Honour goes.

Tynan's allusion to Cavalier poet Richard Lovelace's "To Lucasta, Going to the Warres" becomes more apparent in the next stanza:

> Took for his the deathless song
> Of the love that knows no wrong:
> Could I love thee, dear, so true
> Were not Honour more than you?

It is the call of his country that Percy answers to: "Dear, I love thee best of all / When I go, at England's call." Tynan implies that duty and chivalry survive the ages, and though "Percy died for England," in the last stanza, we learn that he and his father reunite in

> The old loved companionship,
> And shine downward in one ray
> Where at Clouds they wait for day.

Again, happiness in the life hereafter provides consolation, but this faith in the spiritual compensations of religion is overshadowed by patriotic idealism and the imperial code of honor and duty.

Janet Montefiore believes that the reason why, for the most part, women played a role of "anguished complicity" in supporting the war is because they found the image of glorious death in combat so appealing in contrast to the "drably unheroic existence of wartime civilians" (1993, 53, 55). Perhaps in Tynan's most widely read war poem "The Flower of Youth" (1915, 54–55) we see her most blatant endorsement of the war: the poem's explicit assumption is that the war is a just one and that those who die in it are not only heroes but martyrs rewarded with eternal "happiness and peace in heaven" (Fallon 1979, 93):

> Now Heaven is by the young invaded;
>   Their laughter's in the House of God.
> Stainless and simple as He made it
>   God keeps the heart o' the boy unflawed.

In the last stanza Tynan's religious fervor descends into propaganda:

> Oh, if the sonless mothers weeping,
>   And widowed girls, could look inside
> The glory that hath them in keeping
>   Who went to the Great War and died,
> They would rise and put their mourning off,
>   And say: "Thank God, he has enough!"

The overall effect is that Christian consolation fosters a sense of national pride in the war dead, and Tynan's conjoining of religious piety with the "chivalrous myth" of national sacrifice for the motherland is typical of the "Victorian ideal of war, which has dominated the British imagination of the Great War ever since" (Tylee 1990, 252). Tynan herself could not have anticipated just how popular this mixture of piety and patriotism was to become. During the war, the Bishop of London quoted the poem extensively in his sermons and later on Tynan herself admitted that it "had an extraordinary vogue" (1919, 175–76). Yet like many others who saw the British cause as a Christian crusade, Tynan seems to have ignored any possibility that the Creator of mankind could have been "non-partisan" (Khan 1988, 37).

Furthermore, Tynan's reading of the war as a holy crusade reaffirms the correlation between British patriotism and Christianity: with their invocations of God and duty, many of her war poems celebrate the war as another glorious chapter in the history of the British Empire. Like F. S. Boas, a more overt unionist mythographer, Tynan's elegies for the war dead justify the sacrifices by implicitly accepting Ireland's subservient colonial role. Like the northern unionists, many Irish and Anglo-Irishmen and women supported the war because it was an opportunity to display their loyalty to the empire and thus "expiate some of the inferiority associated with peripheral origins" (Dooley 1995, 36). An interesting irony, then, to the construction of a unionist mythography predicated on a ethnic and sectarian superiority (the "chosen people") is that its more extreme manifestations (the bowler hats and other accentuated forms of Britishness) are attempts to mitigate what is ostensibly a cultural inferiority complex. The imperialist fervor that pervades F. S. Boas's and, to a lesser degree, Katharine Tynan's war poems typifies unionism's servitor imperialist (the imperialism of second-class citizens) mentality where self-definition and the propagation of the prevailing unionist mythography depend on public ritual and allegiance.

Tynan's mimicry of the "male idioms of patriotism" is also clearly the result of her dependency on the male-dominated canon of war and literary culture (Tylee 1990, 54). To the modern reader the presence of the Victorian ideal of chivalry alongside Tynan's sincere wish to alleviate the pain and anxiety of the suffering seems rather incongruous, for consolation is offered in the form of prowar propaganda: deaths are not so much lamented as they are exalted. The end result is that Tynan's war poetry responds to the immediate sentiments of a mass audience yet seems utterly unconscious of its crowding ironies and subsurface tensions.

Despite these traces of popular patriotism and Christian sermonics in her war poetry, some of Tynan's consolatory poems do avoid lapsing into imperial propaganda, especially when the recurring motif is her occasional reference to Irish hagiography and landscape. So far we have seen how her war poetry is largely indistinguishable in theme, language, and intent from the kind of war elegy popular in England, but where we see her war poetry assume a specific Irish focus is when she invokes the intercession of Irish saints to either help protect Irish soldiers or offer comfort to the dead and dying. In this respect, Tynan's predilection for depicting a world governed by the guiding hand of a divine presence seems to be a direct response to the prevailing sense of chaos and uncertainty of the war years.

In her poem "The Watchers" (1915, 18–19), the first five stanzas portray a quaint and orderly village scene where the "peace is builded sure and strong: / [and] No evil beast can creep inside." In stanza six, the protectors of this bucolic idyll are revealed:

> St Patrick and St Brigid hold
> The vale its little houses all,
> While men-at-arms in white and gold
> Glide swiftly by the outer wall.

The idealized peace and order of Irish rural life are preserved by attendant Irish saints, and even on the battlefield, St. Brendan, St. Kevin, and St. Colum "pluck / The robes of God that He may hear—" and " 'Keep the Irish flock / So that no shame or sin come near." In contrast, the destruction of Belgium and the suffering of its people are attributed to the neglect of that country's saints:

> What are her angels doing then,
> And are the Belgian saints asleep,

> That in this night of dule and pain
> The Belgians mourn, the Belgians weep?

The poem's prayerlike acknowledgment that Ireland is protected by her Christian saints is a fanciful attempt to secure a source of comfort for those whose sons were on active duty abroad, and Tynan links Ireland's rich Christian heritage to the desire for prayer in seeking God's intercession.

Another poem that exhibits Tynan's fondness for imploring Irish saints to intercede on behalf of Ireland's soldier sons is "A Woman Commends Her Little Son" (1930, 210–11). In the course of praying to all the angels and saints to aid her "little son" and protect him from all harm, the mother appeals to

> Patrick, Columcille, Bride—
> The Saints of the Irish nation;
> Keiran, Kevin beside,
> In the death and the desolation.

Tynan clearly had an Irish readership in mind here, and these poems illustrate how adept she was at writing war poetry for specific audiences, in this case Irish Catholic mothers. There is no grafting together of the religious piety and imperial idiom of the grand sacrifice: the simple message is a heart-felt human desire to cherish the lives of those in danger and to pray for their safe return.

One other war poem with a distinctly Irish flavor is "Wings in the Night" (1930, 208–9) where Tynan elegizes the Irish war dead by praying for the return of their souls to Ireland. This poem is especially preoccupied with the standard theme in Irish literature that Irish identity is wrapped up in the ideal of Irish landscape, but her language also seems typical of the Celtic Twilight with its "grey hills" and "grey weather" and the call of the "wild duck" on the rugged, watery, misty landscape. Invoking this standard nationalist trope of Irish soil as some sacred ossuary is as close as Tynan comes to filtering the war through a nationalist mythography. In the final stanza, mother Ireland welcomes her dead:

> Souls of the Irish dead,
> Flown from the fields of slaughter,
> Home to the mother's arms
> Over the wild grey water.

Like the mythical children of Lir, these soldiers' deaths are transcended by their spiritual transfiguration and subsequent return to Irish soil.

Taken as a whole, Tynan's war poetry never rises above its "immediate purpose of reaching and, perhaps, helping the readers with whom she shared the anxiety of wife and mother" (Fallon 1979, 95). But the hundreds of war poems she wrote during the terrible conflict reveal a "personal warmth, compassion, and love of people and her own continued trust in God" (95). As we have also seen, Tynan's war poetry contains quite an array of responses to the conflict. Caught up in the patriotic euphoria of the early stages of the war, she sounds a martial note that is later modified by a deep-felt grief at the human cost of fighting such a war. While she portrays what was essentially a struggle between rival imperial land grabbers as a holy war, she, in fact, "had few political opinions; she had a weak understanding of historical movements in Ireland or in any other country, no interest in political theory of any kind, and, after her initial involvement in the Ladies Land League which she saw as mainly social, she did not involve herself in any real political activity" (46). Her exploitation of the language of the crusade endorsed the war cause and justified casualties by offering the consolation of a Christian paradise, "unhindered by penitence or purgatory" (Khan 1988, 54) and cleansed of earthly sin.

Ultimately, Katharine Tynan's countless elegies for the war dead reflect not only her sincere empathy but also lament what she believed to be the demise of a highly ordered world where class distinctions, spiritual beliefs, political hierarchies, and social ceremonies were secure and collectively beneficial. As the old order was irrevocably fragmented by the concussive effects of the Great War and traditional values and absolutes were either undermined or overthrown, Tynan's war poetry offered a personal code of "spiritual courage and the setting up and veneration of new and unnamed heroes" (Fallon 1979, 95).

Though nowhere near as prolific or as self-consciously literary in her war poetry as Katharine Tynan, Winifred Letts (1882–1971) occasionally conveyed a greater awareness and responsiveness to the actual trauma caused by the war. Schooled at St. Anne's Abbots, Bromley, and at Alexandra College, Dublin, Letts published two volumes of poetry during the war years: *Hallowe'en and Poems of the War* in 1916 and *The Spires of Oxford and Other Poems* in 1917 (Feeney 1979, 375). While many of her war poems reveal little more than the borrowed patri-

otic rhetoric of countless other jingoistic versifiers, in several poems, Letts does challenge Horatian notions about the war and
undercuts the consolatory pieties offered as a form of spiritual
compensation.

While some of Letts's war poems feature the "optimism typical
of the early years of World War I" (Weekes 1993, 191), where
her war poetry is most limited in theme and perspective is when
she pays lip service to commonplace patriotic ideology. In this
context, many of her war poems illustrate how "Women's patriotic instincts were appealed to initially on two levels: they
were asked to keep calm and encourage their men folk to enlist"
(Cadogan and Craig 1978, 32). For her part, Letts embraces love
of country to instill a sense of racial pride in potential recruits.
In "Pro Patria" (1917, 15), she describes a group of office workers who willingly give up "Their one half-holiday" and resist the
temptations of home and the "theatres" and "The Picture Palace"
to practice military drill. Written before compulsory conscription
was introduced in England in 1916, Letts's poem honors the sacrifice and dedication of these volunteers united by "a Cause / Hid
deep at heart." The obvious intent, like all recruiting posters, is
to single out the special qualities of men who place their country
above their personal interests.

The first stanza contrasts the unalloyed patriotic spirit of these
sons of England with the frivolous pursuits of others who go to
"see the football heroes play." Letts's propaganda piece is clearly
meant to remind men of their military obligations and essential-
ize Victorian concepts of duty and honor. In the last line, she
implies that the sacrifices of these volunteers typify the kind of
spirit needed to be "Worthy of England's chivalry." This blatant
appeal to ethnic pride and commitment to the ideology of the
motherland was an integral part of recruitment psychology.

Another tactic Letts employs to ignite passion for the glorious
cause is her appeal to a sense of community—a community in
danger of being destroyed. In "The Call to Arms in Our Street"
(1917, 9–10), she devotes a separate stanza to describe the individual reactions of those who watch while the men folk march
away. In her depiction of a fearful wife, a crowd of impressionable
children, an anxious mother, and a young girl caught up in the
pageantry and excitement of the war, Letts encourages those left
behind to adopt a stoical attitude to their separations. Serving
as a reminder that women and children must play their part too
in the coming struggle, some stanzas conclude with the spirited
imprecation to keep the proverbial chins up ("Keep your tears

until they go"; "We must smile and cheer them so"). But the ultimate intent is to remind shirkers that this is what the war is being fought for: to protect the welfare of their wives, children, sweethearts, and mothers.

In some of her other patriotic poems, Letts honors those who died for king and country. Several reasons are offered to vindicate the price these men pay for such loyalty and sacrifice. In "July, 1916" (1917, 27–28), we are informed that those who "laid their splendid lives down, ungrudging of the cost" did so to protect "happy England." In the final stanza, Letts presents an exuberant picture postcard of an English Arcadia:

> The swallow-haunted streams meander at their
>   pleasure
> Through loosestrife and rushes and plumèd
>   meadow-sweet.
> Yet how shall we forget them, the young men, the
>   splendid,
> Who left this golden heritage, who put the
>   Summer by,
> Who kept for us our England inviolate, defended,
> But by their passing made for us December of
>   July?

As an eulogy for those who perished at the Somme, these lines epitomize how women's war poetry frequently dwelt on "transparently ideological assurances that the sacrifice of the dead was not in vain" (Montefiore 1993, 56). The elision of time between "December and July" also draws parallels between these heroes' Christian martyrdom and Christ's sacrifice for mankind. In this case, the passion that presumably inspired these men to give their lives so heroically is for the eternal and abiding beauty of England and English landscape. As in Edward Thomas's "Adlestrop," this wistfully nostalgic theme of a transient and disappearing England was a particularly popular one in Georgian poetry. There is no mention of grubby coal mining towns with grimy rows of terraced houses flanked by adjacent clotheslines and overshadowed by the ubiquitous slag heap. What Letts describes here is the rural England of a John Constable landscape.

This adulation of an England of the mind is repeated in Letts's most widely anthologized poem, "The Spires of Oxford" (1917, 3–4). First published in the *Westminister Gazette*, it was reprinted in Carrie Ellen Holmes's selection—*In the Day of Battle: Poems of the Great War*—a collection replete with standard war themes, images, and sentimental overtures. Letts's poem pays tribute to the Oxford men who "took the khaki and the gun / Instead of cap and gown." The poem is steeped in imperialist chivalry and esprit de corps as when the "boys at play" hear "the bugles [that] sounded—War! / They put their games away." But as we have seen before, Letts's simple message is that these sacrifices are not in vain:

> They left the peaceful river,
>   The cricket-field, the quad,
> The shaven lawns of Oxford
>   To seek a bloody sod.
> They gave their merry youth away
>   For country and for God.

Once again it is the defense of this restorative, serene and orderly homeland that inspires these noble sacrifices, and like Tynan, Letts endows the cause with the sublimity of a God-driven crusade.

Despite the excessive manipulation of imperial pride and nostalgia, Letts's war poetry does at times break free from the standard responses to the war. For her, experience was the great teacher. In 1915, she served with the Voluntary Aid Detachment (VAD) as a nurse before joining the "Almeric Paget Military Massage Corps," which provided massage therapy for wounded soldiers throughout the United Kingdom (Khan 1988, 123–24). This contact with the casualties of war liberated her poetry from its devotion to abstract ideals and lofty imperatives. As a result, her more convincing war poems are those that resist the temptation to deliver overarching encomiums and patriotic platitudes. It is when she describes scenes that reveal some kind of immediate contact with the war that she has something new and important to say. In "What Reward?" (1917, 23), she describes, in deliberately toned down language, the sufferings of one who blindly responded to "the ploy of the 'Great Sacrifice'" (Khan 1988, 124):

> *You* gave your life, boy,
>   And *you* gave a limb:
> But he who gave his precious wits,
>   Say, what reward for him?
> One has his glory,
>   One has found his rest.
> But what of this poor babbler here
>   With chin sunk on his breast?

> Flotsam of battle,
>> With brain bemused and dim,
> O God, for such a sacrifice
>> Say, what reward for him?

While the poem "shows that women were voicing criticism of the war well before the dominant male voices emerged on the scene," the description here of those that "Owen was later to label 'Mental Cases'" challenges the notion that war is a noble pursuit of glory (Khan 1988, 124–25). The questions that conclude each stanza ironically contrast the pseudo-solemnity of patriotic ideals with the psycho-babble of one of the war's victims. Along with this vivid depiction of the human wreckage of the war, Letts creates a situational irony of robust boys who set out to pursue glory with their heads held high and who wind up in grim hospital wards in a vegetative state. While the poem indicts the cruelty of the war, in the second stanza, Letts still holds faith with the idea that those who paid the ultimate sacrifice in battle or who survived but were horribly disfigured will receive their "glory" or their "rest." The war itself is not the subject of criticism; Letts only goes as far as to question the price paid by those rendered senseless by combat trauma.

A more complete and incisive critique of the war is found in "Screens" (1917, 21–22), a poem where Letts's honest portrayal of hospital procedures briefly liberates her war poetry from any presiding martial ideology. The poem successfully illustrates how the war not only condemned some soldiers to slow, lingering deaths in the antiseptic environment of a hospital ward but also how the conflict numbed the sensibilities of medical staff jaded by the unparalleled scale of death, suffering, and heartbreak. The first two stanzas detail the routines carried out by hospital staff when all hope for the wounded man's recovery is abandoned:

> They put the screens around his bed;
>> A crumpled heap I saw him lie,
> White counterpane and rough dark head,
>> Those screens—they showed that he would die.

> They put the screens about his bed;
>> We might not play the gramophone,
> And so we played at cards instead
>> And left him dying there alone.

In the second last stanza, one final preparatory detail is taken care of when the Union Jack is brought in "to spread / Upon him when he goes away." Draping the flag over the dead soldier "was an acknowledgment of the nation's indebtedness to her saviours" (Khan 1988, 125), and Letts's simple and unemotional description of these practices demonstrates how ceremony and procedure were used to cope with the apparently endless stream of emotionally draining situations. Death itself is compartmentalized, shut off behind "the screens." In the final stanza, the speaker notes how necessity takes precedence over civilized ritual and courtesy:

> He'll want those three red screens no more,
>   Another man will get his bed,
> We'll make the row we did before
>   But—Jove?—I'm sorry that he's dead.

The "light-hearted tone" of this last stanza "does not stem from any shallowness of emotion, but reflects the veneer of indifference assumed by those who tended the dying as a safeguard that enabled them to cope with such tragedies, which occurred all the time" (125). But the poem also highlights the ironic counterpoint between ceremony and reality. The placing of "the screens" around the dying soldier and the covering of his dead body with the flag signify the loss of his personal identity. Because he is a reminder of our own barbarity, he is isolated and hidden away, and when dead, he is transformed into an imperial icon—another flag-bedecked warrior-hero. Even the caregivers become victims of the war, for they, too, are stripped of their humanity. They suppress their instincts for human compassion, numbed as they are by the scale of the carnage and their strict adherence to cold, perfunctory routines.

Although Letts's criticisms of the war never come close to the vigorous antiwar stridency of Siegfried Sassoon, it is obvious that the generally bleaker vision in some of her war poems is a result of her closer contact with the war. Also interesting is how, like Tynan, Letts's war poetry submissively acknowledges the ascendancy of the governing culture. Many of her poems describe English landscapes and use the language of English pastoral. Apparently for many Irish writers, the whole act of creating literary texts was still very much dependent on Anglo cultural referents. Looking for evidence of an Irish perspective in Letts's war poetry is a futile search as she largely mimics the standard patriotic British sentiments of the time.

If Tynan's and Letts's war poetry generally belongs to that "species of poetry" that glorified "motherhood," "self-sacrifice," and "acceptance" of "inevitable tragedies" (Khan 1988, 152), there were other Irish writers who spoke out strongly against the war. Eva Gore-Booth (1870–1926) was certainly the most vociferous pacifistic voice among Irish writers of the period. At the outbreak of the war, she had been for some years an avid theosophist committed to nonviolent resistance; indeed, such was her distaste for violence that she and her life-long friend Esther Roper described themselves as "extreme pacifists" (Lewis 1988, 163). Prior to the war, Gore-Booth and Roper played key roles in the Irish suffrage movement, but when war came, "the nature of the suffrage movements in Ireland and Britain changed, with the English suffragists getting more involved in the war and the Irish suffragists becoming increasingly involved with the nationalist issue and at the same time pursuing a pacifist line as regards the war" (Murphy 1989, 196). Not surprisingly, Cumann na mBan (a nationalist women's organization) went so far as to discourage Irish Volunteers from enlisting in the British army (Sawyer 1993, 86).

For health reasons, Gore-Booth and Roper moved to London in late 1914 where they found the city's war fever terribly depressing (Lewis 1988, 137). This did not stop them from joining the Women's Peace Crusade and the No Conscription Fellowship (170). Part of their work involved travelling around the country "on speaking tours," doing "relief work among German prisoners of war" and attending tribunals on behalf of conscientious objectors (Wiltsher 1985, 189). Gore-Booth's pacifist activities were certainly not embraced by all suffragists back in Ireland: while many of them volunteered for various "'war-relief' works" (Owens 1984, 95), others, like Gore-Booth's sister Constance (Countess Markievicz), aligned themselves with the more extreme elements of Irish nationalism. As a result, the "small group of [Irish] peace advocates became increasingly unpopular both with the belligerent Imperialists and the militant Nationalists" (Fox 1958, 84).

Caught between the rival factions of Irish politics, pacifists like Gore-Booth also had to contend with the general climate of hostility toward all peace campaigners throughout Britain. Public fears were whipped up into such a hysteria of "anti-German feeling" that hatred of "the peace women and conscientious objectors knew no bounds," and it was quite common for antiwar protestors to be labeled as cowards and, worse, German sympathizers (Lewis 1988, 166). Yet amid all this public rancor, Gore-Booth continued to visit prisons and attend tribunals and courts-martial as a "watcher" or as a "prisoner's friend" (Khan 1988, 101). This close contact with prowar officialdom and with pacifists who resisted the wave of jingoistic ardor that convulsed most of the British Isles provided the subject matter for the few poems Gore-Booth wrote about the war.

The general tenor of the poems collected in her 1917 volume *Broken Glory* mark a temporary shift away from Gore-Booth's usual preoccupation with the mystical and the spiritual. Many of these poems are much more topical, written as they are in response to the immediate political crises that rocked Ireland and the global tragedy of the Great War itself. The predominant concerns here are for her sister Constance, still languishing in an English jail for her role in the Easter Rising, and for the death of Irish rebel Roger Casement whose court trial Gore-Booth attended throughout the summer of 1916. With the ascendancy of the gun and the bomb in world affairs, it is not surprising that most of the poetry that Gore-Booth wrote at this time should be "full of horror at militarism, the triumph of mindless violent aggression and the loss of Christ" (Lewis 1988, 143).

Generally speaking, her war poetry rejects partisanship in favor of the greater power of God. All the violence and the bloodshed confirm man as a Morlock-like figure who betrays his stewardship of God's creation. We also see traces of Gore-Booth's suffragist sympathies as her war poems reverberate with an underlying horror at man's abdication of his civic duties for greed and power. The war is read as further evidence not only of man's disregard for his fellow man but for the cosmic plan of his Creator. Ignorance and blind tradition may explain the war's escalation, but Gore-Booth suggests that all the death and destruction provide further proof of the excesses of a civilization dominated by brute force and the mindless will of a domineering patriarchy.

Unlike many other war poets who saw nothing wrong in conscripting God for the imperial cause, Gore-Booth viewed the war as a conflict that denied God's sovereignty. In her war poetry, God takes no sides. For instance, in the poem "Dreams" (1929, 516), she rejects the war apologists' notion that the conflict was a grand Christian crusade:

> Alas! our dreams are only of the dread
> Red fields of France where unreaped harvests rot,
> And the One Soul by all the world forgot
> Moves silently amid the hosts of dead.
>
> German or French or English, words most vain
> To that which knows not any nation's pride,
> Whose pity is as all men's sorrow wide,
> Folded about our broken world of pain.

Pacifist sentiment negates the adversarial component of the war as all are equally culpable in producing the global disaster.

That Gore-Booth associates fanatic militarism with masculinity run rampant is borne out in the poem's second last stanza:

> Men drench the green earth and defile her streams
> With blood, and blast her very fields and hills
> With the mechanic iron of their wills,
> Yet in her sad heart still the spirit dreams.

The gender politics here is fairly typical of Gore-Booth's war poetry. It is man's stubborn stupidity, his mechanized inflexibility, his robotic compulsion, which destroys God's "green earth"; on the other hand, the land and the "spirit" of God are associated with the feminine principle. Gore-Booth's reading of the war as another example of man's disregard for his fellow creatures and his Maker reveals how, unlike many other British suffragettes, she rejected the idea that by supporting the war she was fulfilling her patriotic duty. To do so was to endorse the patrilineal infrastructure with its outmoded notions about honor and its willingness to sacrifice lives for antiquated ideals. To repudiate the war was to hold firm to the suffragist conviction that gaining political rights was only a step along the way to creating truly representative democracies. Why support a war purporting to protect a regime that would inevitably become obsolete? For Gore-Booth, if the war, with its drum-beating call to arms and its sangfroid indulgence in "bloody frivolity," demonstrated anything, it was that man's abuse of power had irrevocable consequences for all of mankind. Instead of naked aggression, what was needed was a more inclusive political process which would temper the hothead politics of male militarism.

And yet despite the obvious tone of resignation throughout the poem, Gore-Booth concludes with a consolatory reminder:

True to all life, war-worn and battle-tossed
Doth the One Spirit, faithful to the end,
Live in that peace that shall be the world's friend,
The dream of God by men so lightly lost.

These lines ring with the religious euphoria characteristic of late Victorian devotional poetry: despite man's unworthiness and ghastly defilement of God's gift, the Creator's omnipotence transcends all. No matter how much we destroy, God's capacity for forgiveness and healing is limitless.

This kind of hastily appended glib moralizing is typical of some of the less than convincing resolutions to most of Gore-Booth's war poems. If the desire to strike a chord of hope diminishes the gravity of her themes, her war poetry also suffers from a fairly trite orchestration of the prevailing clichés of popular war verse where the war is synonymous with a cancerous growth spreading its poison from the horrors of the trenches to the once Arcadian serenities of the English countryside.

Convalescing from exhaustion brought on by stress and over-work, in 1916, Gore-Booth spent time at Pinehurst in Sussex where one of her friends ran a school (Roper 1929, 22). While there she wrote a short poem, "Pinehurst 1916" (1929, 517), which draws the customary lines between a peaceful rurality and the inescapable obscenity of the war:

Deep in the high-built fortress of the pines,
Lost to her stars dark night imprisoned lies,
Near my hushed soul in peace a white rose shines,
Like a new dream down flung from ancient skies.

Alas, the bugles on the distant plain—
The guns break forth with their insistent din,
The dews of noon-day leave a crimson stain
On grass, that all men's feet must wander in.

Even if the contrast between the front and home is typically reassuring, Gore-Booth reminds us that while there may be a disputed line of contention, the real front, the war between hope and despair, is nowhere and everywhere.

Like Letts, Gore-Booth's most interesting war poems are those that deal directly with her involvement with the war's victims. Some of these poems were not published during her lifetime but were later included in her collected poems (*Poems of Eva*

Gore-Booth), which appeared in 1929. As already noted, she traveled extensively in support of conscientious objectors, attending many of the tribunals and visiting those who had been imprisoned for their refusal to participate in Britain's war machine. In a couple of poems, she "portrays the humiliation undergone by the pacifists" as they tried to justify "the validity of their beliefs" at these tribunals (Khan 1988, 101). In "The Tribunal" (1929, 527–28), pacifistic doctrine is aligned with two of the world's great monotheistic creeds, Buddhism and Christianity:

> For the Hidden One in every heart,
> Lost star in the world's night,
> Fire that burns in the soul of art,
> The Light within the Light—
>
> For the gentleness of Buddha's dream
> And Christ's rejected truth,
> The treasure under the world's stream,
> Pearl of pity and ruth—
>
> Before six ignorant men and blind
> Reckless they rent aside
> The vail of Isis in the mind . . .
> Men say they shirked and lied.

Gore-Booth clearly saw these tribunals as nothing more than a violation of an individual's right to self-determination. But she also confronts the credo of duty to one's government. The list of theosophical tags for the Divine Being stand in counterpoint to this self-appointed jury of "six ignorant men" who pass judgment on those opposed to the war. Once again Gore-Booth attacks the war as the enemy of all that is sacred and eternal. By contrast, the benevolence of man's creators highlights the willful ignorance of those who play God on earth.

Taken as a whole, Gore-Booth's war poetry is an extension of her theosophist and suffragist sympathies as the war threatened the peace and universal suffrage she so vigorously campaigned for. Apart from the odd reference to the war itself, her war poems are written in much the same style as many of her other poems: they show a flair for mystical opacity, a fondness for the grandiloquent phrase, an obsession with the derivative language of a stale romanticism, a weakness for forced and facile rhyme and a penchant for abstract personifications. Yet her heartfelt

condemnation of the war, her refusal to be drawn into the preda-
tory games of super patriotism, and her devotion to nonviolence
(unlike many of her British suffragist counterparts) makes her
a refreshing voice amid the throng of militant poetasters and
empire apologists.

One other Irish writer who adopted a pacifist view of the war
quite early on was AE. He privately published a volume of war
poems (*The Gods of War*) in 1915 that condemned man's primordial passion for bloodletting, but subsequently suppressed
all of his war poetry from the early editions of his *Collected Poems* because he felt they were too strident in tone.[1] Later, in a
separately published war poem, he venerated Irish sacrifices on
different fields of conflict in an attempt to reconcile the rival
factions of Irish nationalism. However, AE's brand of inclusive
nationalism (with its conciliatory endorsement of Irish sacrifices
in the war and the Easter Rising) represents, at best, the evolution of his nationalist sympathies. To come to an accurate understanding of his response to the greater European conflict, we
need to review his initial reaction to the war and his critique of
its purported aims in his early war poetry.

In the year preceding the outbreak of hostilities, AE warned of
an imminent crisis that could destroy Europe. As editor of *The
Irish Homestead*, he had a convenient forum from which to publi-
cize his misgivings about the state of current affairs, and several
of his articles expressed his faith in nonviolence. These pacifistic
leanings confirmed his belief that "a resort to violence was always a sign of intellectual failure" (Summerfield 1975, 167). If
war was unethical, AE was convinced that it would be an unparalleled economic disaster for all involved as well. In 1911, he
professed his wholehearted belief in the argument advanced by
Norman Angell in his book *The Great Illusion* "that peoples and
governments must be taught to recognize that war under modern
conditions would ruin the victors as well as the vanquished by
destroying international credit" (168). Despite his abhorrence of
violence, when the war began, AE "sympathized with the British
revulsion against the German invasion of small, neutral Belgium, and unlike some of his fellow Nationalists, [he] was firmly
on the side of the allies" (169). As soon as war was declared,
AE also "started a series of campaigns in the *Homestead* to urge
farmers to do their duty by their country" and "produce the max-
imum quantity of food for the Irish people" (171). He was care-
ful enough never to specify what Ireland's duty was during the
war, and as the conflict intensified, he continued to denounce the

violence and gloomily forecast that the present hostilities would resolve nothing, for there would continue to be "outbreaks of barbarous violence to shatter the peace they [warring foes] had not rightly earned" (173).

This dual role as pacifist critic of the war and active supporter of the allied cause is given full voice in the *Gods of War* published in September 1915. Though stereotypical phrases occasionally weaken his criticism of the prevailing war fever, "the rhetorical clarity of these denunciations of bloodshed lends them a distinction denied to much of AE's verse" (Summerfield, 1975, 174). The themes of these poems are presented through a range of antiwar perspectives. Attempts are made to parcel out blame for the current catastrophe, mockery is made of greedy autocrats who exploit the helpless masses for their own gain, resignation is expressed at man's seemingly eternal capacity for savagery, and an unfathomable faith is professed in the Creator's design for a new civilization born out of the ruins of the old.

In the title poem "Gods of War" (1935, 236–38)[2] comparisons between modern and ancient warfare suggest that "the war is still the old battle between good and evil which no one wins but the Devil" (Davis 1977, 67). As a result of the news of German atrocities in Belgium, popular feeling in Britain had been gripped by a mood of extreme militarism, and it was this primordial bloodlust that disgusted AE. He felt that the present age ignored the Christian message of peace, love, and understanding; instead, the martial zealotry of antiquity represented by these gods of war was now in vogue (67):

> Choose ye your rightful gods, nor pay
> Lip reverence that the heart denies.
> O Nations, is not Zeus to-day,
> The thunderer from the epic skies,
> More than the Prince of Peace? Is Thor
> Not nobler for a world at war?

In "A European Litany," another poem taken from *The Gods of War* (1915),[3] he resumes his ironic diatribe against those "whose true god is power" (Summerfield 1975, 174):

> You, who now wield by earthly right
> The sceptres God-conferred of old.
> Who know no law above your might,
> No sceptre higher than you hold:
> Have pity on the people, lords!

By questioning our propensity to adulate earthly rulers and then by mingling phrases from Our Lord's Prayer with his own plaintive appeal, AE questions the human cost of the faith devoted to these "lords" "whom the nations have taken for their gods" (174):

> You take the father and the son,
> The brother and the kin away.
> We can but cry "thy will be done,"
> As to the gods of yesterday.
> When childhood is bereft of all,
> Will you be Father at its call?

His indictment of those who reject God in pursuit of immediate political gain also anticipates the consequences of the war and its handing on of a legacy of misery to future generations. But his war poetry does not place the blame entirely on these self-appointed saviors.

In another broadside against European governments called "Statesmen" (1935, 254–55), he suggests that mankind has a long history of ambitious conquest, and it is excessive pride that is responsible for the present crisis:

> The pride that builded Babylon of Egypt was
>   the mighty child:
> The beauty of the Attic soul in many a lovely
>   city smiled.
> The empire that is built in pride shall call
>   imperial pride to birth,
> And with that shadow of itself must fight for
>   empire of the earth.

As pride propels man's instinct for violent acquisition, his ancient impulse for bloody aggression makes us all victims of history:

> Fight where ye will on earth or sea, beneath
>   the wave, above the hills,
> The foe ye meet is still yourselves, the blade
>   ye forged the sword that kills.

Not all of the poems in *Gods of War* roundly criticize the war or seek to attribute responsibility for the breakdown of civilized society. At times, AE expresses a faith in the birth of a new society emerging from beneath the debris of a dead world. We see these optimistic expectations in "Apocalyptic" (1935, 251–52) and "Continuity" (240) where a hope in the world's inherent ability to survive and reinvigorate itself is accompanied by a faith "in the perpetual guardianship of the Creator" (Summerfield 1975, 175).

"Apocalyptic" draws its governing symbolism from the description of the four horsemen of the Apocalypse in the sixth chapter of Revelations "whose horses are white, bright red, black, and the last a pale horse whose rider is Death" (Davis 1977, 68):

> If the black horse's rider reign,
> Or the pale horse's rider fire
> His burning arrows, with disdain
> Laugh. You have come to your desire,
> To the last test which yields the right
> To walk amid the halls of light.

If the war signals the onset of the Apocalypse, rather than simply the collapse of a corrupt society, it also offers to the worthy an opportunity for immortality in the "halls of light." This notion resembles the common consolation Katharine Tynan offered to the relatives of the war dead—that their beloved now enjoy eternal comfort and blessing in God's heaven—except that here this quest for immortality is a "test" rather than a guarantee of redemption. In the next stanza, the criteria for those adjudged to be worthy of immortality is established:

> You, who have made of earth your star,
> Cry out, indeed, for hopes made vain:
> For only those can laugh who are
> The strong Initiates of Pain,
> Who know that mighty god to be
> Sculptor of immortality.

Those who the war will truly claim as victims lead self-absorbed existences, loving life too much; the survivors are those men who are "courageous in the presence of pain and death and have the will to be reborn as immortals" (1977, 69).

An abiding awareness that all earthly experience is transcended by the guiding hand of the Creator is also the underlying theme of "Continuity." "Despite the atrocities of World War I, AE often retained a cosmic detachment" (Kain and O'Brien 1976, 82) toward the war, and in this lyric he echoes G. M. Hopkins's Christian faith ("Spring") in a world rejuvenated by the eternal and restorative power of God:

> Though the crushed jewels droop and fade
> The Artist's labours will not cease,
> And of the ruins shall be made
> Some yet more lovely masterpiece.

In essence, "'Continuity' holds that empires pass away but flowers and stars remain" (82). Considering his previously expressed resignation at man's habitual capacity for greed and savagery, though, AE labors to sound a note of optimism. Expectation appears to overlook the intervening scale of human suffering. The desire is sincere, but the poet's frail device—this lyric—cannot transcend the war's terrible cost.

If AE's war poetry sometimes suffers from the excesses of the autodidact, some poems do depart from the customary antiwar commentaries. In "Battle Ardour" (1935, 239), a poem Robert Davis believes to be "a companion piece to Yeats's 'An Irish Airman Foresees His Death,'" AE describes the "ecstasy" of a fighter pilot as he dies in aerial combat (Kain and O'Brien 1976, 67):

> Not now it battles for the rights of kings.
> This ecstasy is all its own; to be
> Quit of itself, mounted upon the power
> That, like Leviathan, breaks from the deep
> Primeval and all conquering. He dies!
> Yet has he conquered in that very hour.
> He and his foeman the same tryst do keep.
> His foemen are his brothers in the skies.

In terms of theme, the poem offers a refreshing departure from the admirable yet heavy-handed platitudes of AE's other war poems. The pilot's motives for fighting are liberated from ideological burdens and parochial allegiances. Up above the clouds, he experiences the thrill, the "ecstasy," of battle; like Yeats's airman's "lonely impulse," he discovers a "power" that is "Primeval and all conquering," his identity annulled by the exhilaration of the experience. The last two lines also identify an ancient bond between adversaries in combat, for it is only in union that they have meaning. Reminiscent of Owen's dead soldiers in "Strange Meeting," these "foemen" become "brothers": separated in life but ironically united in death.

Perhaps AE's most enduring tribute to the Irish war dead is a poem that never appeared in any of his published volumes. In his study of Irish literature, *Inventing Ireland*, Declan Kiberd argues that "George Russell wrote the only significant poem of the time to lament the Irishmen who died in both conflicts [the war and the Easter Rebellion]" (1995, 240). Kiberd refers to the poem "To The Memory of Some I Knew Who Are Dead and Who Loved Ireland" that appeared in the 19 December 1917 issue of *The Irish Times*.[4] The poem was accompanied by a letter that attempted to defuse the "increasing bitterness between those who risked their lives fighting for independence at home and those whose equal sense of duty impelled them to fight for Ireland and the Empire in the Great War" (Summerfield 1975, 186). AE wrote:

> I myself am Anglo-Irish, with the blood of both races in me and when the rising of Easter Week took place all that was Irish in me was profoundly stirred, and out of that mood I wrote commemorating the dead. And then later there rose in memory of the faces of others I knew who loved their country, but had died in other battles. They fought in those because they believed. They fought in those because they believed they could serve Ireland, and I felt these were no less my people. I could hold them also in my heart and pay tribute to them.

Besides honoring the patriotism that inspired the sacrifices of both groups, AE's letter tries to render the tribal animosities of unionism and nationalism obsolete by arguing that Irish racial identity cuts across convenient ethnic and sectarian divides. Citing "Flinders Petrie's argument in *The Revolutions of Civilisation* that only the blood and culture of an invader revived a decaying society," AE argues in his letter "that the modern Irish nation was not Celtic or Norman or Saxon but an inextricable mixture with a new racial identity" (Summerfield 1975, 186):

> We have been told that there are two nations in Ireland. That may have been so in the past, but it is not to-day. The union of Norman and Dane and Saxon and Celt which has been going on through the centuries is now completed, and there is but one powerful Irish character—not Celtic or Norman-Saxon, but a new race.... The modern Irish are a race built up from many races who have to prove themselves for the future.

This notion that the existing political divisions in Ireland were fueled by naive notions about racial purity may have held little appeal to those committed to ethnic separatism: on the one hand, Patrick Pearse's advocacy of a Celtic state seems totally at odds with AE's point about Ireland's racial diversity while to the outsider, Ulster unionism's inherent sectarianism could be largely attributed to what Freud would diagnose as the exaggerated "narcissism of minor differences."

The presence of these arguments in "To the Memory of Some I Knew Who are Dead and Who Loved Ireland" imply that posterity will view "the martyrs of [these] two causes" as heroes fighting for "the same ideal" (Summerfield 1975, 186). The poem is an extended version of "Salutation, A Poem on the Irish Rebellion of 1916," which AE published in January 1917 (Davis 1977, 152). In the course of its seven stanzas, the poem cross-cuts between tributes to the heroic dead of Easter Week (Pearse, MacDonagh, and Connolly) and the Great War (Anderson, Kettle, and Willie Redmond) before concluding with a moving eulogy to all the exalted dead:

> Their dream had left me numb and cold,
>   But yet my spirit rose in pride,
> Refashioning in burnished gold
>   The images of those who died,
> Or were shut in the penal cell.
>   Here's to you, Pearse, your dream, not mine,
> But yet the thought, for this you fell,
>   Has turned life's waters into wine.
>
> *You who have died on Eastern hills*
>   *Or fields of France as undismayed,*
> *Who lit with interlinked wills*
>   *The long heroic barricade,*
> *You, too, in all the dreams you had,*
>   *Thought of some thing for Ireland done.*
> *Was it not so, Oh, shining lad,*
>   *What lured you, Alan Anderson?*
>
> I listened to high talk from you,
>   Thomas McDonagh, and it seemed
> The words were idle, but they grew
>   To nobleness by death redeemed.
> Life cannot utter words more great
>   Than life may meet by sacrifice,
> High words were equalled by high fate,
>   You paid the price. You paid the price.
>
> *You who have fought on fields afar,*
>   *That other Ireland did you wrong*
> *Who said you shadowed Ireland's star,*
>   *Nor gave you laurel wreath nor song.*
> *You proved by death as true as they,*

In mightier conflicts played your part,
Equal your sacrifice may weigh,
  Dear Kettle, of the generous heart.

The hope lives on age after age,
  Earth with its beauty might be won
For labour as a heritage,
  For this has Ireland lost a son.
This hope unto a flame to fan
  Men have put life by with a smile,
Here's to you, Connolly, my man,
  Who cast the last torch on the pile.

You, too, had Ireland in your care,
  Who watched o'er pits of blood and mire,
From iron roots leap up in air
  Wild forests, magical, of fire;
Yet while the Nuts of Death were shed
  Your memory would ever stray
To your own isle, Oh, gallant dead—
  This wreath, Will Redmond, on your clay.

Here's to you, men I never met,
  Yet hope to meet behind the veil,
Thronged on some starry parapet;
  That looks down upon Innisfail,
And sees the confluence of dreams
  That clashed together in our night,
One river, born from many streams,
  Roll in one blaze of blinding light.

Stylistically, we still see traces of AE's dependence on literary forms synonymous with the poetry of the Irish Revival as the poem is marked by its reiterated motifs (the "wreath" of commemoration and the "dream" of nationhood), conventional descriptions of heroic *personae* (the "nobleness" of the "shining," "gallant" dead), and a self-conscious interlacing narrative typical of oral story-telling. The poem also features a strange mix of elegiac euphemisms ("clay" for grave and "veil" for death) intermingled with romantic motifs (the rising "spirit" and "flame" of hope and inspiration) and the military parlance of the trenches ("barricade," "parapet").

Despite these incongruities, the poem's interweaving of two heroic narratives achieves in its totality an eloquent and poignant effect. As a Rebellion poem, it pays homage to the executed leaders of the Rising by valorizing their noble dedication and subsequent sacrifice to the ideal of nationhood. The favored images of nationalist mythography are also employed: *"the long, heroic barricade"* subscribes to the myth of a centuries-old tradition of unified Irish resistance to British rule while the usual touchstones of martyrdom, sacrifice and symbolic ritual are ably orchestrated in the appropriately heightened language of classical icon and euphemism ("laurel wreath" and "high fate"). AE achieves that rare accomplishment of combining images from nationalist and unionist mythographies in the same poem. Of course many of these images and ideals are shared by both traditions (especially the lofty idealisms of blood sacrifice and noble death for a sacred cause), but the recurring images associate both causes with a religious fervor reminiscent of the sort of triumphalist piety we see in traditional unionism and nationalism. And, of course, only in an Irish context could that last image of a river, that "one river," be an ironically ambiguous symbol for reconciliation.

As a Great War poem, the work reveals a shift in the dominant viewpoint expressed in AE's earlier war poems. He still displays his revulsion toward blood sacrifice ("Their dream had left me numb and cold"), but the advent of Easter Week has retrospectively altered his apprehension about the violent act of martyrdom. Like Yeats, he now sees the "terrible beauty" of patriotic sacrifice.

In terms of what the poem says about the Great War and Ireland's role in it, AE moves beyond the antiwar rhetoric of his earlier war poems to celebrate the war as the birth place of an inestimable Irish will that lights a *"long heroic barricade"* of Irish solidarity. The fourth and sixth stanzas vindicate the dreams and aspirations of those Irish nationalists who, though they died in British uniforms, *"played"* their *"part"* for their *"own isle."* Consequently, AE sees the war as the launching ground of a resurgent and indomitable Irish heroism.

The final stanza's poetic tribute to the legacy of the dead expresses the hope that though these men gave their lives in different conflicts, their noble sacrifice and common love for their country will result in the emergence of a new Ireland, one characterized by a consciousness of its different heritages yet united by the acceptance of a new identity and spirit of inclusivity—"One river, born from many streams." This image signifies "AE's attempt to remind his fellow Irishmen that no single culture could claim a monopoly of Irishness" (Lyons 1979, 107).

This spirited evocation of a future freed from the debilitating encroachments of sectarianism and tribalism also reveals AE's very real fear that memory of the Great War in Ireland would further divide Irish unionists and nationalists. By commemorating the war and the Rising, he hoped to demonstrate that the sacrifices in Dublin and on the Somme were reconcilable with his ideal of a new Ireland. He later protested the introduction of conscription in Ireland not only because of its catastrophic impact on Ireland's economy but also because its effect would be to remind the Irish that they were "a subject people" and thus galvanize the heretofore fringe elements of Irish nationalism (Summerfield 1975, 189).

As it turned out, AE's fears that memory of the Great War in Ireland would actually reinforce existing sectarian animosities were to be confirmed: "For decades after independence, the 150,000 Irish who fought in the Great War (for the rights of small nations and for Home Rule after the cessation of hostilities, as many of them believed) had been officially extirpated from the record" (Kiberd 1995, 239). AE's vision of a new state formed from the various strands of Irish identity and inspired by the heroic spirit manifested in the war and the Rebellion was to be extinguished by the emergence of "a State anxious to repudiate its own origins" and which "—after a predictable period of post-independence purism—" failed to "evolve a joint ceremony which celebrated the men who served in either army" (240).

On the whole, AE's response to the Great War, from his initial denunciation of the violence to his subsequent admiration for those who fought, illustrates how political events in Ireland could alter ambivalence toward the war. There were others who at first felt equally compelled to ignore the whole nasty business of the war. While AE regarded the war as further evidence of man's intellectual decline, Joyce and Yeats's views of the conflict oscillated from apathy and disgust to denunciation. Yeats would eventually view the war as a sideshow to Ireland's ongoing domestic disputes, and his artistic and political perspectives led him to question the distinctions between Irish political and cultural identity. For Joyce, though, no violent conflict could be justified. For him, "all wars were unholy, and destructive of culture and civilisation" (Manganiello 1980, 153).

Unlike AE and Yeats, Joyce spent the entire war in exile. Up until June of 1915, he resided in Trieste, when, "to avoid internment, he went to Switzerland" (Joyce 1959, 246) and remained officially neutral there. It was in Zurich that he worked briefly as a translator for Siegmund Feilbogen's *International Review*, a journal devoted "chiefly to proving that the atrocity stories on both sides were groundless" (Ellmann 1959, 410). Joyce's motives for working for Feilbogen were primarily monetary despite the fact that he shared Feilbogen's neutralist politics and contempt for the war. The job was short-lived, however, as the *Review* was forced to cease publication less than a year after its first issue due to pressure from English and American authorities who regarded the periodical as propagandistic (410).

Judging by Richard Ellmann's account of Joyce's years in Zurich and the extant letters Joyce wrote during the period, it would appear at first glance that the war was a distant rumble that sporadically intruded into his affairs. Preoccupied as he was with *Ulysses* and the ongoing complications over the publication of *Dubliners*, Joyce continued his daily routines almost as though there was no war going on. And yet before his removal from Trieste, some of his letters written in 1915 do make mention of his brother Stanislaus's internment, the "military congestion" in Trieste and of an 1915 air raid by Italian airships that occurred not far from his home (Callow 1990, 193). Later, in Zurich, Joyce wrote a letter of condolence to Mary Sheehy, the wife of his former college friend Tom Kettle, but apart from this expression of grief, he rarely discussed the war with his correspondents. There were the odd outbursts of irritation at being deprived of the company of good friends who were conscripted and his disgust with war profiteers and their "inflated prices" (193). Otherwise, the general impression is that Joyce largely lived out the war as an inconvenienced refugee separated from his books and furniture.

Ellmann's descriptions of Joyce's affairs in Zurich do, however, shed some light on the complexities of his political viewpoints. While critics have noted Joyce's "deep-seated pacifism" (Fairhall 1993, 48), there appears to be some disagreement over his attitude toward the war. One view is that he "steered clear of politics and said little about the war" (102) while others believe that Joyce was not "indifferent to politics during the war" at all (Manganiello 1980, 102). Dominic Manganiello makes a convincing case for the latter view, arguing that "Joyce's perspective on the war was equally paradoxical"; while he could cherish his "neutrality," he could still praise the most recent "German offensive" (150). Paradoxical Joyce may have been but certainly not apathetic, for the war not only disrupted his Triestine domicile but also affected his family and acquaintances. As already noted, Kettle's death and Stanislaus's imprisonment in Austria certainly ensured that Joyce's Zurich exile was not a total refuge from the war's horrors (Fairhall 1993, 163). And while he rejected any notion of volunteering for active service, his involvement in Zurich with the theatrical group The English Players, which he helped form, was initially seen as a subtle attempt at pro-British cultural propaganda. Yet his subsequent confrontations with British consular officials was to result in his stirring up some "anti-British propaganda" (Ellmann 1959, 436).

In the course of his promotional work for the theater company, Joyce's apparent indifference toward the outcome of the war, his previous work with the *International Review*, his failure to "offer his services in wartime," and his lawsuit over acting fees against one of his actors—Henry Carr, an invalided English soldier—earned him the enmity of the British consul, A. Percy Bennett (Ellmann 1959, 436–40). Joyce apparently enjoyed this legal wrangle immensely, and the subsequent success with The Players' production of Wilde's *The Importance of Being Earnest* seems to have aroused some degree of nationalist pride (410, 439). But his desperate financial situation and the ongoing fiasco over the Irish publication of *Dubliners* revived his bitterness toward Ireland: his mood swings from nostalgia to outrage typified his shifting political viewpoints and confirmed his resolve to stay out of Irish and European conflicts.

The only poem Joyce wrote that addresses the war extensively is his rumbuntious 1916 broadside "Dooleysprudence" (Joyce 1991, 120–22), which "reflects his pacifist irritations with both sides," defends the nonpartisanship of the "isolated exile," and mocks the epidemic of foolhardy heroism that swept Europe early in the war (Joyce 1959, 246). His initial enthusiasm for "socialism as an antidote to war" (Manganiello 1980, 102) quickly waned after he saw the sickening waves of Europe's working classes join the rush to don uniforms and chase glory. But he still lent his support to other notable pacifists such as Bertrand Russell who appealed to European intellectuals to help end the war (152), and such expressions of intellectual solidarity no doubt reinforced Joyce's belief that it was ultimately the artist who "represents the common man" (154). In this regard, Mr. Dooley is Joyce's attempt to represent the ordinary Everyman caught up in this fratricidal march to annihilation.

In technique and structure, Joyce's pasquinade combines the rollicking end rhymes of dance hall recital with a scabrous disregard for institutional authority. The poem consists of six stanzas of ten lines each, with the first four lines posing a question and the final six providing the answer. Mr. Dooley—the subject of the poem—is depicted as a detached cynic who freely dispenses telling japes and mocking jibes at the hypocrisy and duplicity of those who govern Europe's affairs. The poem also reveals Joyce's talent for the bon mot, the cutting pun, and the ironic rejoinder, and the bathetic shifts from talk of European politics to Mr. Dooley's banal quotidian details intensify the lampoon's satirical edge.

As Joyce's intent is to mock Europe's sacred cows, he takes aim with a range of satirical devices. Bathos frames the second stanza where Joyce ridicules the churches' complicity in promoting the war. His fondness for punning is evidenced in the poem's title which mockingly contrasts Mr. Dooley's good sense with the moral bankruptcy of statutory law while the comic play with literary reference ("The curse of Moses / On both your houses" as a risible misquote of Mercutio's belated declaration of non serviam in *Romeo and Juliet)* highlights Mr. Dooley's repudiation of the war. Then there is the irreverent citation of so-called "holy" texts like "the pandect, penal code, and Doomsday Book" that signifies Mr. Dooley's contempt for civil law, religious conformity, and property rights.

All jokes aside, though, the poem is unyielding in its raillery against the prowar fever that gripped Europe. In the first line, Joyce parodies the veneer of chivalry associated with the war effort; these "gallant" nations' noble battle is nothing more than an atavistic scramble for power, wealth, and prestige:

> "They are out to collar
> The dime and dollar"
> Says Mr. Dooley-ooley-ooley-oo.

In stanza two, the church comes in for some brutal excoriation for its part in whipping up prowar fervor under the guise of a holy crusade:

> Who is the funny fellow who declines to go to church
> Since pope and priest and parson left the poor man in the
>   lurch
> And taught their flocks the only way to save all human souls
> Was piercing human bodies through with dumdum
>   bulletholes?

In the subsequent refrain, Mr. Dooley offers up a solemn prayer that mankind be spared the intrigues of self-appointed arbiters of morality:

> "Who will release us
> From Jingo Jesus?"
> Prays Mr. Dooley-ooley-ooley-oo.

In these lines, Joyce indicts "both Church and governments" as those responsible for the "bloodshed" (Manganiello 1980, 153).

In the next stanza Mr. Dooley sustains his general hostility toward all existing political and religious hierarchies with his dismissal of the equally specious British and German political doxologies:

> Who is the meek philosopher who doesn't care a damn
> About the yellow peril or the problem of Siam
> And disbelieves that British Tar is water from life's fount
> And will not gulp the gospel of the German on the Mount?

Joyce's cynicism about the expansionist ambitions of rival imperial powers was not recently acquired. In one of his early essays "Ireland, Island of Saints and Sages," he condemned the pseudo-solemn Christian high-mindedness put forth by colonial apologists to legitimize their territorial acquisitions. Joyce wrote, "no one who is not deceived by self-interest or ingenuousness will believe, in this day and age, that a colonial country is motivated by purely Christian motives" (1959, 163).

In the final two stanzas, constitutional monarchs and imperial heads of state are also routinely castigated. We see the general contempt for royalty when Mr. Dooley becomes nauseous after licking the backside of a postage stamp featuring the unsavory image of some autocrat. The last stanza completes the wholesale condemnation of the powers-that-be:

> Who is the tranquil gentleman who won't salute the State
> Or serve Nabuchodonosor or proletariat
> But thinks that every son of man has quite enough to do
> To paddle down the stream of life his personal canoe?

As he ladles out the blame to those forces who have brought European society to the brink, Mr. Dooley displays his anarchic hostility toward democracy, monarchy, and socialism: "'Poor Europe ambles / Like sheep to shambles!' / Sighs Mr. Dooley-ooley-ooley-oo."

Like Swift before him, Joyce despaired at man's self-destructive propensities and chaotic departures from rational and cultured thought. To say that Joyce's attitude toward the war was that of a bored neutral is inaccurate. To a certain extent, Mr. Dooley is Joyce's misanthropic alter ego, but Joyce was also wary that his declared indifference toward the war may be interpreted as narcissistic self-regard and ignorance. Again, in "Ireland, Island of Saints and Sages," he notes that quite often "impartiality can easily be confused with a convenient disregard of facts" (1959, 163). Yet throughout "Dooleysprudence," we clearly see evidence of his informed opinions about the various determinants that brought European culture to such a nadir of depravity. The poem's breezy tone belies its vigilance against the simplifying structures of self-deception and the prepossessing nonchalance of political and clerical doctrinaires.

Joyce's behavior throughout the war reveals just how complicated his personal politics were. Certainly his political views were secondary to his desire to forge a new aesthetic and cultural identity, but his acceptance of a grant from the Civil List in 1915 demonstrates how economic necessity often took precedence over personally held political beliefs. His litigious activity against British consular officials in Zurich also illustrates his readiness to play adversary against the old colonial nemesis. Expatriate sentiment triggered uncharacteristic outbursts of ethnic pride: it was no accident that most of The English Players' repertoire consisted of Irish plays.

Ultimately, for Joyce, the war left European "culture eroded rather than ratified by the battles to protect it" (Kiberd 1995, 241). But perhaps his shifting moods of ambivalence, pacifism and outright hostility toward the war could be regarded as a political acts in themselves. His sense of a broader Europeanism hoisted him above parochial politics, and like Ezra Pound, his faith in a new form of literary expression was a bold attempt to sever himself from the traditions of a disintegrative culture. The dissentient note sounded in Joyce's only substantive war poem and his conflicts with British authorities in Zurich can also be read as a minor note in a larger political score, for *Ulysses*, *the* major modernist work that consumed most of Joyce's energies during the war years, has come to be regarded by many "as a specifically Irish response to British and Anglo-Irish cultural imperialism" (Platt 1995, 3). Charting Joyce's reaction to the war reveals that far from occupying a position of political disengagement, he embarked on a project that was to challenge all previous notions of novelistic and historical narrativity and by doing so we can see how his antiwar, anti-imperialist, anticlerical, and anti-establishment poses cohere: to reach self-determination, Mr. Dooley's "personal canoe" is the ordinary man's mode of transport through the entrapping currents of outmoded ideologies.

Like AE and Joyce, Yeats's attitude toward the war was also complicated by the passions of the Irish conflict. Up until very recently, most major Yeats scholars had little to say about the poet's attitude toward the war, preferring, instead, to interpret his famously dismissive remarks about the kind of poetry produced by that bitter, bloody conflict as evidence of his general disinterest. In his introduction to the *Oxford Book of Modern Verse*, Yeats defends his omission of some of the best-known war poems by arguing that "passive suffering is not a theme for poetry" (1936, xxxiv). Essentially, his objections to Great War poetry were threefold: the quality of the poetry was weakened by the war poets' self-imposed obligation to "plead the sufferings of their own men"; their obsession with "passive suffering" was not a suitable "theme for poetry"; and they "were too close to their experience to write properly about it—they reflected what they underwent, but did not illuminate" (Carter 1988, 15).

Looked at collectively, these objections are ironic as we find examples in Yeats's own poetry of some of the very qualities he condemns as excessive in, for instance, the poetry of Wilfred Owen. If Owen's war poetry is allegedly marred by its self-absorbed replay of the common soldier's pain and distress, aren't Yeats's Easter Rebellion poems basically an attempt to "plead the sufferings" of his fellow Irishmen? On the second point, that "passive suffering is not a theme for poetry," Yeats appears to express a self-arrogating and heavily prescriptive attitude about what subjects are suitable for poetry. Furthermore, critics like Jon Stallworthy question the validity of Yeats's charge that Owen's work suffers from an excessive preoccupation with "passive suffering." In the essay "W. B. Yeats and Wilfred Owen," Stallworthy contends that "'passive suffering' was . . . no theme of Owen's" either (1969, 209), for the poet "who turns [his] . . . suffering into such a passionate indictment of a false creed" can hardly be accused of "passivity" (208). These arguments form the basis of Stallworthy's point that Owen's war poetry, far from violating Yeats's prescriptive criteria, actually conforms to many of Yeats's theoretical strictures concerning the form and content of poetry.

As for Yeats's third point about the war poets being too close to their subject to be able to write about it, his own practice once again contradicts his reservations about Owen and war poetry in general. In fact critics like James Longenbach believe that Yeats, like Ezra Pound, "wrote war poems that express a sensibility close to that of the poets who suffered in the trenches" (1988, xi). While many of Yeats's best poems respond to deeply felt personal experiences, like Owen, he was not afraid to "accept contemporary history as a subject, and to respond to it as a poet" (J. Johnston 1964, 22). Yeats's attempt to distinguish between the poet as "a public figure who speaks for the people" (Dawe 1988, 191) and someone who uses poetry "for purposes more proper to the politician, the social reformer, and the revolutionary than to the artist" (Carter 1988, 16) seems, at best, a dubious and transparent distinction. Perhaps the crux of Yeats's distaste for Owen's poetry is that while Yeats was still preoccupied with "reinterpreting the heroic figures of the past" (Stallworthy 1969, 213), Owen realized that looking for mythic parallels between the past and the present was rendered obsolete by the unparalleled carnage of the front. Evidence that Yeats's omission of Owen from his Oxford anthology was more likely due to Owen's treatment of the war rather than the subject of war itself can be gauged by the fact that Yeats did include Julian Grenfell's war poem "Into Battle," which, with its epiphanic visions of glory and its devotion to the idea of an heroic narrative linking the ages, was much more compatible with Yeats's view of war and history. As Fran Brearton points out, Yeats's dismissive attitude toward war poets like Owen may explain why Yeats has not been regarded as a war poet. As his "illiberal views" do not echo the pacifist sentiments of the major soldier poets, the critical consensus has been that such views must be ideologically unsound (2000, 82). However, as we shall see later, there is plenty of evidence to illustrate how Yeats's own war poems violate his lofty prescription that a poet's art should not be conscripted to serve a cause.

As already noted, Yeats's critics say little about his response to the war. Two of his most distinguished critics, Richard Ellmann and Norman Jeffares, devote little more than a few sentences to the Great War in their numerous studies. Ellmann, in particular, goes so far as to maintain that Yeats "had little to say about the First World War, its issues being too abstract and international for his mind, but he [Yeats] shared in the feeling that 'many ingenious lovely things are gone'" (1948, 232). While others, like Jon Stallworthy, argue that Yeats wrote only "two war poems during the First World War" (1969, 211), more recent commentators like David Pierce contend that every poem Yeats wrote between 1914 and 1918 was a war poem (1995, 177–85).

Any understanding of Yeats's shifting and complex attitudes about the war and his war verse must begin by examining his personal circumstances during the war. By following his activities between 1914 and 1918, we can construct a narrative that demonstrates how his attitudes about the war and Ireland's role in it evolved. For this purpose, we can assemble a more scaled back chronology than the one offered by David Pierce of poems which either address the war through direct reference to the conflict or whose themes, tone, and language reveal the war's intrusive presence:

November 1914: "A Meditation in Time of War"
January 1915: "Her Praise"
February 1915: "On Being Asked for a War Poem"
October 1915: "Ego Dominus Tuus"
May-September 1916: "Easter, 1916"
December 1916: "Sixteen Dead Men"
February 1918: "Shepherd and Goatherd"
June 1918: "In Memory of Major Robert Gregory"
1918: "An Irish Airman Foresees his Death"
January 1919: "The Second Coming"
November 1920: "Reprisals"

Despite the range of styles and expressed emotions found in these war poems, they all reveal that the traditional view that Yeats was largely indifferent to the war is completely inaccurate. In the first volume of his ongoing biography of Yeats (*W. B. Yeats: A Life, The Apprentice Mage, 1865–1914*) Roy Foster argues that by late 1914, Yeats saw the war "as a conflict between the ideas of the New and Old Testament (Germany representing the latter)" (1997, 523), but the poet still took a "detached approach" to the unraveling of European civilization (523), speaking out only when the welfare of personal friends was in jeopardy. As we shall see, this notion that Yeats's response to the war was "personal" (522) is only partially accurate, for as the war dragged on, his feelings toward it were to change significantly.

Certainly the "war years were among the most productive of Yeats's career as a writer" (Pierce 1995, 198), and the fact that he resided mostly in England during this period meant that he was more exposed to the daily talk of the war's escalation. His witnessing of some of the sporadic Zeppelin attacks on London (Gregory 1974, 524) opened his eyes to the close proximity of the violence much more so than if he had remained in Dublin. It was true that he felt marginalized by a conflict that sidelined all other activities.[5] His work with the Abbey Theater was especially disrupted. He confessed in a letter to John Quinn in June 1915 that "the war has hit us hard" and later in September of the same year, in a letter to Ernest Boyd, he again admitted that "the Abbey has been hard hit" and that "The anxiety of the war and the many deaths reduced our audience both in Dublin (where we could play only the more popular pieces and those at a loss) and in England till we were losing heavily" (Yeats 1955, 594, 601).

During the first two years of the war, Yeats's behavior and attitude toward the conflict could perhaps be best described as a haphazard oscillation between private withdrawal and tacit support. While the war's economic repercussions gave cause for complaint, by the third month of hostilities, in letters to Florence Farr and John Quinn, Yeats admitted that he was already tired of the daily round of rumors and scraps of information about the war that dominated all conversation. By January 1915, this tone of war weariness creeps into his work. In "Her Praise" (1983, 150), he proclaims that he "will talk no more of books or the long war" but pay tribute to Maud Gonne's enduring beauty so that "her praise should be the uppermost theme." As David Pierce notes, the poem's "desolate landscapes seemed to chime with news from the front" (1995, 177). But the "war obtruded and needed, as was later the case with the War of Independence and the Civil War, to be distanced somehow" (179).

Written in early November 1914, the title of his first "war poem," "A Meditation in Time of War" (1983, 190), reaffirms Yeats's faith in the infinitely greater importance of private vision over public event. John Unterecker points out that the poem's symbolism ("tree," "wind," and "stone") rehearses one of the essential ideas later fully fleshed out in *A Vision*—that of an impending apocalypse and the seer's gift of seeing "the pattern of all things" (1959, 168). However, read as a war poem, we encounter, on the one hand, "the unreality of war and mankind beside the oneness of life" (Pierce 1995, 179) with an overwhelming sense of trepidation as though the poet had a fearful vision of imminent ruin:

> For one throb of the artery,
> While on that old grey stone I sat
> Under the old wind-broken tree,
> I knew that One is animate,
> Mankind inanimate phantasy.

The poem reveals this disturbing awareness of impending destruction through its condensed images of temporality and fragility. In a fleeting moment of insight, the speaker sits on an "old grey stone" underneath an "old wind-broken tree." These images of superannuated decay depict a self-contained wasteland that seems particularly appropriate given the contemporary scenes across the channel in Flanders, but they also highlight the poet-seer's predicament. Conscious of the eternal inconsequence of man's mortality (the "inanimate phantasy"), he is rendered helplessly passive as he sits in the afterglow of perception; all he can do is know and record. On one level, the poem expresses the resignation of a middle-aged observer of the war who, burdened as he is by a flashing memory of the past, can only watch Europe's slow, torturous decline; on another level, we have a powerful image of modern man: a deracinated, self-conscious, and pathetically incapable Prufrock figure.

In the poem's five lines, Yeats presents us with one of the war's earliest apocalyptic visions: a despairing meditation on the imminent collapse of civilization. The overriding sense of despondency contrasts with the popular stridency or escapism of other contemporary verse. Also, the poem's location near the end of his volume *Michael Robartes and the Dancer* (1921) seems consistent with that collection's preoccupation with "impending social chaos" and the counterpoint between a "personal joy set against a background of irrational destructive violence" (Unterecker 1959, 157).

Another way Yeats tried to counter the war was "by fashioning his 'habitual memories'" (Pierce 1995, 180). *Reveries* was finished at Christmas 1914, and in contrast to Tom Kettle's "experience of camaraderie in the trenches," Francis Ledwidge's "sweet understanding of a soldier's heart," and Katharine Tynan's "devotion to those who suffered in the 'holy war,'" Yeats retreated into "his childhood inheritance of solitude and remoteness" (180). But if he tried, as he later described Joyce's response to the war in August 1915, to "become absorbed in some piece of work till the evil hour is passed" (Yeats 1955, 601), he also expressed concern for the welfare of friends who were directly involved in the conflict.

In a letter to Lady Gregory dated 31 August 1914, he mentions how Richard Aldington had "difficulty in enlisting" (Pierce 1995, 176), and later, in November of the same year, he made his first public pronouncement about the war when he told the audience at the Thomas Davis Centenary Conference in Dublin that "'I have friends fighting in Flanders, I had one in the trenches at Antwerp, and I have a very dear friend [Maud Gonne] nursing the wounded in a French hospital. How can I help but feeling as they feel and desiring a German defeat?'" (Pierce 1995, 177; Cullingford 1981, 87). This spirit of alliance with the British war effort may have been initially stirred by a concern for the welfare of friends, but there is evidence that Yeats also actively participated in a number of fund-raising schemes in support of the war like the "'Poets' Reading'" he attended on Tuesday 11 April 1916, two weeks or so before the Easter Rebellion, when he was one of ten featured poets who read from their work at Baroness D'Erlanger's house in London in "aid of the Star and Garter Fund" (Asquith 1968, 152).

The picture emerges here of a man who, though disillusioned by the prevailing militarist fervor, gave his tacit support to a war personified for him by the participation of a few of his closest friends. The suspension of the Home Rule Bill and the ensuing propaganda battle between the pro-enlistment advocates of Redmond's Irish Parliamentary Party and the antirecruiting faction led by Patrick Pearse and Sinn Fein complicated Ireland's involvement in the war. When Yeats received a request from Henry James to submit some verses for Edith Wharton's *The Book of the Homeless* early in 1915, his response, while it rejected political commitment to the European war, was a carefully measured statement of his political position. Written in February 1915 and originally entitled "To a friend who has asked me to sign his manifesto to the neutral nations," Yeats later retitled the poem "A Reason for Keeping Silent" before sending it on to James in August of that year (Jeffares 1968, 189). Of course the poem, as we now know it, was later included in *The Wild Swans at Coole* (1919) under the title, "On being asked for a War Poem" (1983, 155–56), but the alteration of the original title and the version Yeats sent James is indicative of how the poet began to view the war from a distinctly politicized Irish perspective.

The poem's original title suggests a toysome evasiveness as its salutary nature and reference to the reason for the poem being commissioned in the first place closets any suggestion that it was written for propaganda purposes. While Peter McDonald argues that the poem's title changes indicate how Yeats adapted the poem for various "occasions to suit itself" (1996, 179), the renamed title ironically reveals, despite its more compressed circumspection, a subtle shift in Yeats's attitude toward the war.

"A Reason for Keeping Silent" may declare his belief that the art of poetry should be placed above the "chaos of contemporary concerns" (Carter 1988, 14), but it also insinuates other reasons for "Keeping Silent."

In *Yeats, Ireland, and Fascism*, Elizabeth Cullingford argues that the poem's "disingenuous" nature is purposefully designed as a deftly-balanced political high-wire act (1981, 86). Rather than merely adopt a nonpartisan attitude toward the war, Yeats responded to the politically delicate state of affairs in Ireland. Far from being indifferent to the war's unparalleled scale of butchery, he was actually looking to "the larger historical frame and the war's possible outcome" (Pierce 1995, 176). Thus, his refusal to write a poem that actively endorsed the war demonstrates his dissatisfaction with both the pro- and antiwar factions in Ireland: "he had no desire to act as propagandist for the Irish Parliamentary Party. Nor, however, did he identify himself with the anti-recruiting and pro-German stance of Pearse" (Cullingford 1981, 86).

Yeats spent the first few winters of the war in residence with Ezra Pound (who had agreed to be his secretary) at Stone Cottage in Sussex, and perhaps the spirit of his American friend's attitude toward the war mingled with Yeats's lukewarm affiliations. Pound quickly tired of the facile war poetry that filled the daily newspapers, and he declared as much in one of his own unpublished war poems ("War Verse"): "O two penny poets, be still . . . give the soldiers their turn" (Longenbach 1988, 115). The text of "A Reason for Keeping Silent" does appear to reaffirm the poet's obligation to his art. James Longenbach contends that the poem resembles Pound's "War Verse" in that it keeps faith with the belief that "a poet should confine himself to traditional lyric subjects, [thus] leaving the war to soldiers and statesmen" (118). However, such a reading ignores the poem's coy restraint:

> I think it better that in times like these
> A poet's mouth be silent, for in truth
> We have no gift to set a statesman right;
> He has had enough of meddling who can please
> A young girl in the indolence of her youth,
> Or an old man upon a winter's night.

In addition to altering the title, as Jon Stallworthy points out, Yeats also rewrote the first two lines: the original version's harsh, admonitory and "colloquial" tone ("I think it better that at times like these / We poets keep our mouths shut") being replaced by a heightened "language" that illustrates Yeats's subsequent disapproval of Sassoon's trench vernacular (1969, 199). But how serious do we take his avowal of complete political disengagement? Any examination of his career up to this point reveals a willingness to play a vocal part in politics. For example, in the month preceding and during Queen Victoria's visit to Dublin in April 1900, Yeats wrote letters to friends and the press alike to register his protest against the Union, and as Elizabeth Cullingford points out, "setting the statesman right had always been, and would continue to be, one of Yeats's favourite pastimes in Ireland" (1981, 86). But like many other Irishmen, Yeats, while he was not pro-German, certainly did not share Redmond's belief that fighting Britain's wars was in Ireland's best interest. The idea popular among some of the Volunteers that "England's difficulty was Ireland's opportunity . . . was [also] far from Yeats's thoughts" (Pierce 1995, 176). The simple fact is that Pound and Yeats could not escape the war anymore than they could remain silent about it. On the one hand, while Yeats's first war poem "codified the remote attitude . . . about the war" (Longenbach 1988, 118), it also illustrated the impossibility of adopting "an aristocratic indifference" toward the conflict (108). While at Stone Cottage, troop maneuvers on the nearby heath and letters from their friend Henri Gaudier-Brzeska who was on active service helped "Yeats and Pound to picture the daily life of the soldiery"; the two modernist ascetics could imagine the "smoke and noise that shook the French countryside across the channel" (117–18). Essentially, Yeats's poem about keeping silent about the war had ironically broken that silence: the war was to continue to cast its shadow over many of the subsequent poems he was to write.

During the rest of 1915, Yeats worked on his Nóh-inspired play *At the Hawk's Well*, canvassed for a grant for Joyce from the Royal Literary Fund, and lobbied diligently but unsuccessfully to secure the Irish claim for the Hugh Lane collection. Splitting his time between London and Coole Park, he continued to do his best to ignore the war, or, when mention of it proved unavoidable, adopted a cynical and pessimistic anticipation of its outcome. In a letter to his father dated 12 September 1914, but which David Pierce claims is "in fact from 1915" (1988, 175), Yeats states, "The war will end I suppose in a draw and everybody too poor to fight for another hundred years, though not too poor to spend what is left of their substance preparing for it" (1955, 588).

In his public affairs, he proved to be anything but an obedient servant of the crown. He bristled at the notion that Joyce's pension hinged on whether he (Joyce) could produce an "expression of solidarity with the Allies" (Cullingford 1981, 87), and he was quick to respond to Edmund Gosse's suspicions (which he expressed in a letter to Yeats dated 25 August 1915) that Joyce "was in sympathy with the Austrian enemy" (Pierce 1995, 178). That the year ended with Yeats's refusal of a knighthood confirmed his increasing sense of alienation from the British establishment: earning distinction was one thing, passive acceptance of the existing status quo quite another.

In the context of these events, Yeats completed another poem that engages in a direct dialogue with the war. In October 1915 he completed "Ego Dominus Tuus" (1983, 160–62), a poem that combines some of Yeats's more recondite thinking on the nature of being with a debate, made especially topical by the ongoing war, about the true role of the modern artist. In retrospect, the poem's structure, with its contentious dialogue between two opposing mindsets ("Hic" & "Ille"), seems appropriate given the adversarial spirit of the times. The essential debate conducted throughout the poem—the quest for one's true identity—also reflects the thematic concerns of emergent modernism where the artist must cope with the dehumanizing forces of expansionism and industrialism. The poem's aesthetic self-consciousness is also a response to the Great War's mass uniformity and negation of the human will:

> *Ille*. That is our modern hope and by its light
>   We have lit upon the gentle, sensitive mind
>   And lost the old nonchalance of the hand;
>   Whether we have chosen chisel, pen or brush,
>   We are but critics, or but half create, . . .

The other theme that appears to have grown out of a refusal to be coerced by the monologic discourses of the war era concerns the relationships "of art to the world, [and] of poetry to rhetoric" (Pierce 1995, 183). As in "On being asked for a War Poem," Yeats resumes the debate here about the role of the artist during times of public tumult. This time he draws distinctions between men of "action" and artists within the context of a "tragic war":

> *Hic*. Yet surely there are men who have made their art
>   Out of no tragic war, lovers of life,
>   Impulsive men that look for happiness
>   And sing when they have found it.

Ille.   No, not sing,
For those that love the world serve it in action,
Grow rich, popular and full of influence,
And should they paint or write, still it is action:
The struggle of the fly in marmalade.
The rhetorician would deceive his neighbours,
The sentimentalist himself; while art
Is but a vision of reality.

In a time when art became the desperate handmaiden of propaganda and when men of action were hailed as prophets and heroes, Yeats reminds us that "a vision of reality" can not be gleaned from a "common dream"; only those who abjure all sentiment and immediate acclaim can present realities as they are for they are "men that in their writings are most wise [and] / Own nothing but their blind, stupefied hearts."

The poem's rejection of propaganda is a timely reminder to artists who cave in to public sentiment. The language also bears traces of the war's imprint: " 'The struggle of the fly in marmalade,' preceded by references to serving the world 'in action,' quickly conjures up the stalemate along the Maginot Line . . . [while] [w]aking from a dream also acquires greater urgency because of the war" (Pierce 1995, 183). Other phrases ring with war-induced irony. The description of things past—"the unconquerable delusion" and "the old nonchalance"—are reminders of how, despite the war's modern terror, archaic ideals and outmoded notions of chivalry and militarist bluster died slowly in the trenches. And few veterans of the Great War could read the poem's penultimate line without reviving some repressed memory of the front line where the dying exhale "Their momentary cries before it is dawn."

Emotionally, the year 1916 was to prove to be Yeats's annus horribilis. Maud Gonne's umpteenth rejection of his proposal of marriage was one suffering blow, but the events of Easter Week were to shatter his preconceived notions about the Irish situation and force him to reevaluate his attitude toward the national cause. In his celebrated war poem "Easter, 1916" (1983, 180–82), completed in September of that year, he not only struggles with his own response to that "terrible beauty" but also adopts a new stance toward the larger drama of the Great War. As David Pierce remarks, "for everyone at the time, insurgents, soldiers, politicians, journalists alike, the Easter Rising and the Great War were theatres of the same war. Only later did the poem become detached from one of its historical orbits" (1995, 183).

Pierce goes on to list some of the contextual parallels between the war and the Rising that were noted by prominent figures of the day: chief among these were Patrick Pearse who, prior to the Rebellion, was energized by the return of "Heroism" during the previous sixteen months of the war; G. B. Shaw who, after the executions, argued that the insurgents were "prisoners of war" and that "the relation of Ireland to Dublin Castle was precisely that of Belgium to the Kaiser"; and Maud Gonne, who recounted to Yeats her vision of Dublin's streets in darkness and ruin (184).

To read "Easter, 1916" as a Great War poem as well as the most famous utterance about the Easter Rising is hardly contentious. The indisputable fact is that the war provided the opportunity for Pearse and his fellow republicans to carry out their plans for an armed insurrection. They "rose in the conviction that further involvement by Irish people in the Great War would lead to far more bloodshed than their Rising, which they hoped would take Ireland out of the war altogether" (Kiberd 1995, 199). In fact as early as September 1914, "the Irish Republican Brotherhood had appointed a military committee" to begin making plans for an armed offensive (Pierce 1995, 176). Like the majority of Irish people, though, Yeats was totally surprised by the ensuing revolt, and in his subsequent elegy for the executed leaders of the Rebellion, his attempts to come to terms with their act and its "excess of love" reveals his own ambivalence about the Great War, too.

First of all, we detect a change in Yeats's attitude about responding to episodic violence. His previously announced conviction that it was "better to keep silent" in times like these is now replaced with the new self-assured stridency of "I write it out in a verse—"; where he formerly advocated circumspection, he now declares that "our part / [is] To murmur name upon name. . . ." Apparently the course of events in Dublin were more politically significant to Yeats than the war, but in light of his prior refusal to compose a poem that subscribed to popular war ideals, we now see further proof of his changing attitude toward the war, for "Easter, 1916" furnishes another example of his willingness to enlist literature in support of an Irish rather than a British or international cause.

In addition to what it reveals about Yeats's attitudes about literature and nationalism, the poem also critiques the Great War. Critics generally agree that the controlling metaphor of the third stanza contrasts the politically constricted doctrines of the revolutionaries ("Enchanted to a stone") with the fluid current of life in the "living stream." Shackled as they are to the old Anglo/Celt antagonisms, the insurgents shared an obsession common throughout Europe: the Rising like the Great War was fought in the spirit of the purifying sacrifice. While ancestral myopia makes stones of the hearts, Yeats questions the price of a militant fanaticism that swept across Europe and asks when "may it suffice?"

The poem's pacifist protest against sacrificial slaughter is followed by another criticism of the Great War as in the final stanza when Yeats asks "Was it needless death after all?" The question is "not so much a criticism of the patriots, as a comment on the political situation" (Cullingford 1981, 85). The Great War intrudes again here, for without its occurrence, there may never have been an English "hour of difficulty." These lines also refer to the war's impact on Irish affairs, for it momentarily defused a thorny dilemma for the British government. The postponement of the Home Rule Bill for the duration of the war deferred the likelihood of an Irish civil war, but it also introduced a contractual motivation for nationalists and unionists to enlist in the British army with the idea that their contributions would be rewarded at war's end with the implementation of Home Rule or the preservation of the unionist veto. Yeats can only wonder whether England may "keep faith" with Ireland's show of good faith in supporting the empire in her hour of need.

Inevitably, the Great War lingers in the margins of the poem in such a way that we see the Rising as another skirmish in the bigger conflict. Those "that dreamed and are dead" are casualties of the Great War also; in a period of national alert, their deeds are regarded as acts of treason against the state and so they are executed as collaborators. If the war effectively created the conditions for the revolt and, through the subsequent executions, rendered the dead leaders as martyr-heroes, it also galvanized extreme nationalist sentiment, destroyed the credibility of the Irish Parliamentary Party, and indirectly contributed to subsequent Irish independence. But these inseverable links between the Rising and the war also force Yeats to reevaluate his political position. In the first stanza, the description of his interaction with these political zealots reveals as much about his political identity as theirs:

> I have met them at close of day
> Coming with vivid faces
> From counter or desk among grey
> Eighteenth-century houses.

I have passed with a nod of the head
Or polite meaningless words,
Or have lingered awhile and said
Polite meaningless words, . . .

If Yeats had no idea that he could be so deeply moved by "any public event," he did not shrink from committing himself to self-scrutiny. The events in Dublin evolved in direct response to the state of emergency that existed across Europe, so in a way, the ongoing stalemate on the Western Front and the ensuing Irish conflict forced him to conduct a political reassessment. In this first stanza, he juxtaposes the vigor of these "vivid faces" full of revolutionary zeal with the "grey / Eighteenth-century houses"—those stultifying monuments to Ascendancy privilege. Ireland's new heroes are dwarfed by reminders of their colonial status in the geopolitical landscape. Later, Yeats retreats to "the fire at the club," another symbol of Ascendancy exclusivity. These carefully arranged political subtexts suggest his uneasiness with his own position in Irish affairs. In effect, the advent of the Rising and the Great War forced him to recognize the tensions within his own Anglo-Irish identity.

Ultimately, the Rising unmasks Yeats's pose of indifference toward the mounting crisis in Europe. The threat of defeat in the war provoked the British to use strong-arm tactics in Ireland to crush any domestic dispute, and it is not surprising now to see him identify the war more and more as a British cause. In a letter to Lady Gregory a few weeks after the Rising, he does not try very hard to conceal his contempt for the British High Command's ineptitude in France and links this general dereliction of honor to the ongoing spate of executions in Ireland where he says: "I see therefore no reason to believe that the delicate instrument of Justice is being worked with precision in Dublin" (1955, 613).

"Easter, 1916" marks a general shift in Yeats's attitude toward the war. If in the past, he vacillated between polite indifference and a halfhearted expression of neutrality or struck the pose of the isolated artist, he also engaged in intermittent bouts of partisanship for the cause his friends took up. But now, the war is seen through its Irish context. In "Sixteen Dead Men" (1983, 182), he elides the narrative of Irish history by celebrating the company the recent Easter dead keep now with those Irish heroes of another century like Wolfe Tone and Lord Edward Fitzgerald. In the second stanza, Yeats strikes a new note of dissent with the cause against Germany:

You say that we should still the land
Till Germany's overcome;
But who is there to argue that
Now Pearse is deaf and dumb?

For Yeats, the executions demonstrated British insensitivity to
the Irish situation and made it clear to him that any promise
to "keep faith" was highly unlikely. His question also challenges
the view that Ireland's interests were best served by supporting
the British war effort. Yet in his public life, he apparently saw
nothing incongruous between his nationalist sympathies and his
acceptance of membership in the male-only Savile Club in London in January 1917. Such behavior typifies the "cultural dependency and antagonism" of a colonized people (Said 1994, 220).

While the Rising and its aftermath aroused Yeats's nationalist
sympathies, his letters reveal that his attitude toward the war
still wavered between passing interest and war weariness. He
was not above using the war as a political expedient to benefit his
own causes. During his and Lady Gregory's vigorous campaign
for the return of the Hugh Lane paintings to Ireland, he wrote
a long letter to the editor of *The Observer* in January 1917 supporting the Irish claim to the Lane collection. In the course of his
argument, he assumes a tone of incredulity at the fact that the
trustees of the National Gallery would take advantage of Lane's
death aboard the ill-fated *Lusitania*. Yeats wrote: "I cannot believe that a great English institution would wish to benefit by
a German act of war" (1955, 621). Obviously, Yeats was eager
to manipulate British patriotic sentiment and arouse feelings of
war guilt if needed to further his own brand of cultural politics.

Throughout 1917, though, he continued to express a deep resignation at the war's seemingly interminable duration; any hope
for peace grew more out of a sense of despondency than optimism. In the early summer of 1917, he wrote to Olivia Shake-
spear from his refuge at Coole Park: "I do not mean to be in any
town for more than a few days till September or October when
I hope and almost believe the war will be over" (1955, 626). But
his attitude toward the war would be changed irreparably by a
"late death" that would take all his "heart for speech."

The death of Lady Gregory's only son Robert (shot down mistakenly by an Italian pilot on the Italian front in January 1918)
inspired Yeats to write a series of elegies for the young airman
over the next two to three years, and it is in these four poems
that we see the final development of Yeats's attitude toward the

war and its relationship to Ireland as he moves beyond simple elegiac consolation to bitter political condemnation.

The first poem Yeats wrote to commemorate Gregory—"Shepherd and Goatherd" (1983, 141–45)—was written in February and March 1918. Yeats had also published an essay-long tribute in *The Times*, and his actions show that he was equally concerned for the welfare of the heartbroken mother as he was for the loss of her son. That Yeats chose to write a pastoral based on what he described as Virgilian and Spenserian models seems somewhat anachronistic in the twentieth-century context. Perhaps, as James Longenbach suggests, Yeats chose this "artificial pastoral form because he doubted his ability to convey the real emotion of the tragedy" (1988, 128). Furthermore, the yoking together of "Gregory's character and Yeats's occult ideas" tends to cloud the poem's intent (Archibald 1983, 64).

As an ostensibly cheerful pastoral elegy, "Shepherd and Goatherd" derives much of its antiwar tenor from its character and setting. Throughout the dialogue between these two innocent rustics who meet while out tending their flocks, the serenity of their pastoral world is contrasted to this faraway war that claimed the life of one of their own:

> *Shepherd.* He that was best in every country sport
> And every country craft, and of us all
> Most courteous to slow age and hasty youth,
> Is dead.

And in the Goatherd's song near the end of the poem, the war is denied its place in folk memory, for while "The outrageous war shall fade," only the memory of the dead hero will be cherished. By distancing the war from the peaceful climes of home, the poet subordinates the cause for which Gregory died in order to celebrate his life.

If the war is seen as antipastoral (foreign and deadly), the elegy also portrays the traditional profile of the Renaissance soldier-courtier. Gregory leaves the charms of a simple life behind to seek glory and adventure and dies on foreign soil much like his chivalric forebear Sidney:

> Shepherd.   He had thrown the crook away
> And died in the great war beyond the sea.

This romantic portrait of the dead pilot does not endorse the cause for which he died. The noble impulse is extolled, but his absence is not wrapped in euphemism, for "There's nothing of him left but half a score / Of sorrowful, austere, sweet, lofty pipe tunes." If consolation is the chief chord struck throughout the poem, the war is accorded little respect. Even that quintessential icon of the Great War—the poppy—is denied its privileged place in the grieving process for the dead war hero:

> Goatherd.   They have brought me from that ridge
> Seed-pods and flowers that are not all wild poppy.

In between this first elegy for Robert Gregory and the completion of his next tribute to him, Yeats became more actively involved in the war and its consequences for Ireland. He now began to play the self-styled role of Irish elder statesman, and in May 1918, he put his signature to a public protest against a recently passed bill that called for the implementation of conscription in Ireland:

> We, the undersigned writers, feel compelled to appeal and protest against the enforcement of conscription in our country, believing, as we do, that such action will destroy all hope of peace and goodwill towards England in our lifetime. A. Gregory, W. B. Yeats, James Stephens, George Russell ("AE"), Douglas Hyde ("An Craobhin").[6]

Yeats felt that the situation was becoming so tense in Ireland that he canceled plans he had made for a lecture in Dublin "on recent poetry including war poetry" (Yeats 1955, 648). In a letter to Clement Shorter in May, he acknowledged the very real dangers at present of politicizing literature:

> I have had to postpone my lecture. Your wife's poems would have been my chief effect; and times are too dangerous for me to encourage men to risks I am not prepared to share or approve. If the Government go on with conscription there may soon be disastrous outbreaks—I doubt the priests and the leaders being able to keep the wild bloods to passive resistance. . . . [T]he old historical passion is at its greatest intensity. (649)

The following month, Yeats completed arguably his most accomplished commemorative poem, "In Memory of Major Robert Gregory" (1983, 132–35). (It was published that August in *The English Review*.) Roughly six months had passed between Gregory's death and the writing of this elegy, and as Frank Kermode, among others, points out, the poem is more concerned with Gregory's image as "an artist" who had mastered "both action and

contemplation" (Kermode 1961, 32). Of course Yeats's naming of
friends "that cannot sup with us" is also about cultural loss, too.
Lionel Johnson, J. M. Synge, and George Pollexfen represent a
past that seems no more alive than a print in "some old picture-
book." Others have noted that by "incorporating Gregory's death
into his private mythology . . . Yeats evaded the brutal reality
of the war" (Longenbach 1988, 128), yet by listing these names
along with the recently deceased Robert Gregory, Yeats was simply holding true to an archaic martial tradition. Like Malory's
heroic lists of gallant knights, the utterance of these names preserves the past in the present. The poem also subscribes to the
myth that only the best and the brightest perished:

> Soldier, scholar, horseman, he,
> And all he did done perfectly
> As though he had but that one trade alone.

Yeats's subscription to this myth, though, does not share the
spirit of more orthodox war elegies that elevate the war to the
status of epic combat; in this case, the war is reduced to "an
occasion" (Unterecker 1959, 134). But if the immediate business
of the poem is to canonize a hero, we again see the consequences
of an intrusive war that disturbs Yeats's memory like that bitter
"wind / That shakes the shutter." Gregory, "Our Sidney and our
perfect man," is not only a war casualty but a man whose "death
becomes the final sign of Yeats's own generation's unmanning"
(Gilbert and Gubar 1988, 2: 310). In the Irish context, Gregory
personifies the noble qualities of the Anglo-Irish gentry, and his
death marks the decline of his class. The war's culpability in
Gregory's death is not addressed here, though. Yeats's concerns
lie more with the "moral and political complexities of an Anglo-
Irishman serving in the Royal Air Force, a problem Yeats mutes
here but fully, and grimly faces in the last Robert Gregory poem
["Reprisals"]" (Archibald 1983, 66).

In "An Irish Airman Foresees his Death" (1983, 135), Yeats begins to explore the political complications of an Irishman dying in
British uniform. Declan Kiberd argues that the poem reflects the
"difficulties faced by one Irish gentleman in working up enthusiasm for a British imperial war" (1995, 482). No longer concerned
with providing consolation or ruminating on the cultural repercussions of Gregory's death, Yeats's dramatic monologue lets the
dead man speak for himself. David Pierce believes that the "stillness" of this poem (and its predecessor) "reflects Yeats's distaste

for the kerfuffle of war poetry" (1995, 182). The poem's conceit certainly eliminates the rhetorical distance between speaker and audience. Gone is the pastoral affectation and heroic cataloguing as Gregory makes it abundantly clear that he is no "Empire loyalist" (Cullingford 1981, 107): "Those that I fight I do not hate, / Those that I guard I do not love." If Yeats's airman rejects the notion that British patriotism motivated him to fight, he also dismisses civic duty, political conviction, or egotistical desire for publicity:

> Nor law, nor duty bade me fight,
> Nor public men, nor cheering crowds. . . .

Yeats essentially negates the customary martial pieties: causes are rejected; ideologies spurned; public platitudes ignored. The hero's death is recognized, but unlike the previous two tributes to Robert Gregory, the consolatory tone is replaced by a bittersweet remembrance of this "perfect" man who died in a meaningless war. The poem also demonstrates how many of Yeats's responses to the war are triggered by the war's impact on his life and the lives of his friends; the greater drama is largely ignored as the poet examines its "local effect" (Gerstenberger 1990, 82).

Yet it should be noted that while the poem illustrates Yeats's view of the war as a British conflict, he does not condemn war itself. Gregory's "lonely impulse of delight" suggests the allure of combat as a self-actualizing experience where immediate danger reinforces the urgency of life. Speaking of Robert Gregory's death in a condolence letter written to Lady Gregory, George Bernard Shaw noted how war for all its horror crystallizes existence down to a defining moment of infinite purpose: "war must have intensified his life as nothing else could; he got a grip of it that he could not through art or love. I suppose that is what makes the soldier" (Gregory 1974, 558). Like Shaw, Yeats's elegy subscribes to this idea of war as the ultimate form of theater, a liberation of the individual will over the nugatory routines of family expectation and domestic obligation.

While the war is rejected, Yeats exploits its larger drama to express Gregory's Irish patriotism (thus reinforcing the idea that Irish Protestants can be Irish patriots, too) and dissolves class antagonisms between the Anglo-Irish gentry and their tenantry: "My country is Kiltartan Cross, / My countrymen Kiltartan's poor." In fact, "Yeats frequently insisted that 'An Irish Airman' was written to express Protestant patriotism towards Ireland"

(Cullingford 1981, 107). However, D. G. Boyce contends that the poem is really "about the Anglo-Irish predicament in the twentieth century" (1993, 22). Certainly the image of Gregory—Yeats's personification of the Anglo-Irish—lost "somewhere among the clouds above" is an appropriate symbol for a class caught between the exclusive and rival hegemonies of a gaelicized independence movement and Ulster unionism. Gregory's declared alliance with his "country" conveys Yeats's desire to create a cohesive Irish identity that transcends class and sectarian divides. Seamus Deane's point that Gregory the man has been transformed into an "infinite symbol" (1989, 38) implies that given the sectarian realities, particularly in Ulster, Yeats's conscription of Gregory as one of many "central images around which the nation could cohere" (D. Johnston 1985, 18) appears, in retrospect, to be pure political fantasy. Certainly, Gregory was always secure in his identity as an Irish unionist, but the poem continues to address its major theme: that the Great War was not Ireland's fight, for "No likely end could bring them loss / Or leave them happier than before."

Douglas Archibald reads the poem as evidence of Yeats's fascination with "the relationship between action and contemplation, the burdens of subjectivity . . . , [and] the death as a willed refusal to plunge 'into the abyss' of the self" (1983, 68–69). But Gregory's death in the Great War was for Yeats not only a foretaste of the many future predicaments his class and culture would face but also of the uncertainties of Ireland's political future. With bitter prescience, the dead airman sees no future in the "years to come" while the colonial past—"the years behind"— is equally scorned. Perhaps these lines share James Connolly's "sad prediction" that "the worship of the past really was a way of reconciling people to the mediocrity of the present" (Kiberd 1995, 247).

Ironically, the sacrifices of the Anglo-Irish elite in the Rising and the Great War contributed to the demise of their own class, a decline Yeats later described as inevitable in "In Memory of Eva Gore-Booth and Con Markievicz" (1983, 233):

> We the great gazebo built,
> They convicted us of guilt;
> Bid me strike a match and blow.

The impact of the Great War on Irish affairs was immeasurable. It brought about the conditions conducive to a rising and thus

helped galvanize Irish republican sympathies. Yeats's elegy for
Gregory anticipates the marginalization of Anglo-Irish culture
as one of the inevitable consequences of such an upheaval. For
Yeats, the war not only hastened the political isolation of most
southern Protestants, but it also indirectly shaped the politics of
his last years as he searched for an alternative sense of "Irishry"
than the one sponsored by the new state. His romantic retrospect for Ascendancy Ireland and brief flirtation with fascism
were in some ways attempts to preserve an Anglo-Irish identity
whose demise had been accelerated by the Great War and the
Easter Rising: the Irish Free State's "lack of attention to Protestant liberties" no doubt heightened his sense of internal exile,
but the "continuing Protestant emigration and the gradual dis-
appearance of Yeats's cultural world" were also attributable to
the political fallout of the Great War (E. Longley 1991, 205).
As a result, in postpartition Ireland, many of Yeats's class, and
certainly most southern unionists, found themselves as "lonely
as some banished Roman in a land where the eagles had de-
parted" (Finneran, Harper, and Murphy 1977, 2:512). New economic forces in Ireland would also be in ascendancy, as men
like Gregory and "Kiltartan's poor" would become "victims of
the pushy new elite, the Catholic farming middle class" (Kiberd
1995, 482–83).

Unlike its predecessors, "Reprisals" (1957, 791), Yeats's final
poem in the Robert Gregory sequence, directly engages the political ramifications of Gregory's military service by calling into
question the cause that Gregory gave his life for and contrasting
the airman's wartime heroics with the present atrocities committed by the British army during the War of Independence. By now
the details surrounding the origin and publication of the poem
are fairly well known. In the autumn of 1920, Yeats was living
in London, but his correspondence with Lady Gregory and her
articles in *The Nation* kept him apprised of the outrages committed by the British army's auxiliary forces and Black and Tans in
their daily operations against Irish republicans. One such atrocity inspired Yeats to write his most bitter indictment of the Great
War and the British army. In her journal for 5 November, Lady
Gregory recorded her disgust at the murder the previous day of
Eileen Quinn, the wife of Malachi, one of her tenants, who was
gunned down in the doorway of her home in Kiltartan "with her
child in her arms" by "a lorry of passing military" (1995, 444).

This episode spurred Yeats to write "Reprisals," which he originally entitled "To Major Robert Gregory, airman" (Pierce 1995,

210). He sent it to Lady Gregory with the intent of submitting it for publication first in *The Times* (a combative gesture given that paper's unionist sympathies) and later *The Nation*, but she did not like it and asked that it not be published; later in her journals, she confessed: "I cannot bear the dragging of R. from his grave to make what I think a not very sincere poem—for Yeats only knows by hearsay while our troubles go on—" (1978, 1: 207). Another objection to the poem was that it would "distress Robert Gregory's pro-English widow" (Cullingford 1981, 108). Consequently, the poem was never published in their lifetimes. *Rann/An Ulster Quarterly of Poetry* finally printed it in its autumn 1948 issue, almost ten years after Yeats's death. Obviously the dredging up of painful memories about her son proved distasteful to Lady Gregory. The memory of Robert Gregory remained with her throughout her last years at Coole. On the occasion of her grandson Richard's sixteenth birthday party, she noticed "Robert's shadowy portrait on the wall" and wondered "what a birthday it would have been could he have been here" (1995, 495). Despite her own nationalist sympathies, she had suffered and lost too much during the Great War to allow Robert's death to be used to further some passing political agenda.[7]

As for Yeats, he felt satisfied with the poem and its chief purpose, which was to shame current British policy in Ireland by contrasting the debauched blood-letting of the Black and Tans with the gallantry of an Irish hero. Ironically, the poem also shares "the same disillusionment with patriotism and heroism that one finds in the war poems of Owen or Sassoon" (Longenbach 1988, 129), two poets Yeats excluded from his *Oxford Book of Modern Verse*. But while eminent critics like Richard Ellmann believe that the poem's chief purpose is to express the "poet's rage over the Black and Tans" (1954, 231), as a war poem, "Reprisals" is much more than a hastily written salvo against the British army's injustices and excesses.

In his brief analysis of the poem, Frank Kermode describes "Reprisals" as "an angry little poem" (he oddly neglects to give its title) that he feels narrows "down the significance" of Robert Gregory's death (1961, 41). In that the poem seems less preoccupied with addressing Gregory as a symbol for Yeats's "Unity of Being," Kermode is certainly right, but "Reprisals" transcends Yeats's fixation with working out the details of a private philosophy in order to make a political statement about the apparently pointless sacrifice of Robert Gregory and many other Irishmen who died fighting for Britain in what Yeats came to believe was a dubious cause. Yeats wastes no time in conducting a historical reevaluation of Ireland's role in the Great War, and the verdict is uncompromising:[8]

> Some nineteen German planes, they say,
> You had brought down before you died.
> We called it a good death. Today
> Can ghost or man be satisfied?

Again, Gregory is portrayed as the "typical generous aristocrat" (41), and the poem begins as a rather orthodox commemorative piece acknowledging his past heroism. But Anglo-Irish pieties aside, the tone shifts quickly to one of recrimination: the oxymoronic "good death" communicates especially well the speaker's complicity in the myth-making process that made Gregory a hero. This indictment of the war continues in the next lines where Yeats attacks the pursuit of glory and honor, for their appeal is so strong that they curtail awareness and lead to self-deception:

> Although your last exciting year
> Outweighed all other years, you said,
> Though battle joy may be so dear
> A memory, even to the dead,
> It chases other thought away, . . .

There appears to be a tradition in Irish poetry where the poet calls on the dead as part of a process of retrieving them from the oblivion of Irish history. Eileen O'Leary's eighteenth-century poem "The Lament for Art O'Leary" and more recently Seamus Heaney's "A Postcard from North Antrim" are two notable examples of these spiritual exorcisms of murdered friends and loved ones. In "Reprisals," Yeats conducts his own political exorcism as he calls on the ghost of Robert Gregory to return to Ireland to witness the scenes of murder and devastation there:

> Yet rise from your Italian tomb,
> Flit to Kiltartan cross and stay
> Till certain second thoughts have come
> Upon the cause you served, that we
> Imagined such a fine affair:
> Half-drunk or whole-mad soldiery
> Are murdering your tenants there. . . .
> Armed men
> May murder them in passing by

Nor law nor parliament take heed.
Then close your ears with dust and lie
Among the other cheated dead.

Tensions only hinted at in the other three Gregory poems about the dead airman's war service are paraded out in full view here. There are no veiled reservations: simply put, Robert Gregory "threw his life away mistakenly in supporting the English" (Cullingford 1981, 107). Yeats's use of ironic contrast coalesces these "second thoughts" about "the cause"; the dead hero who shot down "nineteen German planes" now witnesses the atrocities committed by the same army he served. Black and Tan outrages blight Gregory's memory as a war pilot. While Gregory died fighting for the very government that authorized these criminal reprisals, Yeats's scathing critique of the Great War—that "grand affair"—implies that Ireland's tragedy is compounded by the absence of many Irishmen who died in the war and whose reward is the destruction of their homes and communities. The "cheated dead" have been betrayed by "English bad faith" (Archibald 1983, 70).

Yeats's portrayal of the Great War as a pointless venture that destroyed Ireland's best young men and stained their memory with political treachery is intensified by the poem's more subtle antiwar statements. Irish soil is again connected to Irish identity for Gregory's ghost can only learn the truth about its place in Irish history when it returns to "Kiltartan Cross." British soldiers not only victimize the Irish poor, but they also slander the memory of Robert Gregory's father, for it is his and Robert's tenants who are slaughtered there while "law nor parliament take heed." All strands of Irish identity come under assault, including the Anglo-Irish. These lines are also a "direct indictment of specific actions that recently occurred in the government," for the British administration had refused to open an inquiry into the death of Mrs. Quinn (Krimm 1981, 48).

The poem's last lines where Gregory is interred again into the "dust" with the other "cheated dead" is a far cry from the elegiac pastoralism of "Shepherd and Goatherd," yet Yeats's use of the war to prick "the British conscience" was especially effective given that "all England's attention [had been] turned towards that event" (Krimm 1981, 49). Also significant is how Gregory's interment with the "other cheated dead" recalls the memory of Ireland's other heroes who were defeated by betrayal. In this sense, for Yeats, "Reprisals" restores "to his people the heroic spirit and fierce integrity of earlier heroes" (D. Johnston 1985, 18). Despite the poem's specific concern with the Irish situation, it reveals how Yeats saw the violence and chaos in Ireland as part of a "wider phenomenon of disruption" (Bushrui 1982, 119).

Shortly after the war (January 1919), Yeats wrote what could be described as the most comprehensive war poem of the period—"The Second Coming" (1983, 187). Much has been written about how he conjoins his cyclical theories of history with an apocalyptic vision of the future. In terms of the war, the poem represents the poet's collective impressions of an era when nothing held together. The Great War threatened his all-encompassing myth (the "Unity of Being") of a "vibrant society . . . grounded in a racial and cultural tradition" (Kelly 1990, 110). Its spin-off dramas like the Russian revolution marked the nadir of a civilization whose collective intellect had failed to prevent it from committing self-annihilation. The Irish situation was only a microcosm of the global upheaval. As a poem that undoubtedly grew out of Yeats's residual war despair, it braces with images that only a postwar mind could vividly visualize: centers "fall apart," "anarchy" and "blood-dimmed" tides are "loosed," "innocence is drowned," and fanatics "full of passionate intensity" reign. But Yeats did not need to visit the front to confirm his worst fears about his generation; all these excesses were acted out on a smaller scale on the Irish stage between 1916 and 1923. Lady Gregory's reports of mindless violence and human cruelty in the Gort area of Galway were only part of a greater civilizational decline. The slouching beast was a postwar Europe that had expended so much in a war that was supposed to rescue it from complacency and decadence yet delivered nothing. The cost of learning that war was not a "heroic alternative" to the past was obscene; only meaninglessness prevailed (Kiberd 1995, 330). The reality was that "the Great War and the waves of revolution which passed over Europe in its wake, as now-defiant soldiers returned home impatient with the discredited rhetoric of the upper classes, had served further to erode all forms of authority" (489).

Looked at chronologically, Yeats's war poems certainly became more militant in tone and theme as the war dragged on. Generalizations about his war poetry have to be measured and circumspect, for, as we have seen, his responses to the war, like Pound's, were often "idiosyncratic" at best (Longenbach 1988, 130). With regards to the war itself, closer contact with it and the escalation of events in Ireland spurred him to move from

initial apathy to outright denunciation. Most of his antipathy
toward the war was due to the fact that he clearly identified it
as a British/English cause, so for someone who repeatedly defined "the Irish spirit by contrasting it with English influences"
(Kelly 1990, 124), it is not surprising that he would regard the
war as a threat to Irish political and cultural autonomy. As Fran
Brearton notes, Yeats saw "the Great War on the English side of
an English-Irish opposition" (2000, 45). The subsequent heavy-
handedness of the British army in its war with Irish insurgents
and the British government's insensitivity to Irish affairs in general inflamed Yeats's sense of fair play. As his war poetry largely
responds to the war through the interpretative lens of Irish history, in a sense then, Yeats contributes to the postwar politicization of Ireland's Great War memory. Years later (1936), he would
acknowledge that "established things were [so] shaken by the
Great War" that "now influential young men began to wonder if
anything could last or if anything were worth fighting for" (1961,
499). Events in Europe during the 1930s certainly exacerbated
his retrospective note of resignation about the Great War's futility, but his general air of historical detachment from that global
catastrophe was, as we have seen, fueled by both his nostalgia
for a prewar prelapserian world and his nationalist sympathies.
Irish politicians were to follow his example and adopt a more
partisan view of the war. The Irish statelets formed after partition quickly institutionalized factionalist readings of the war
like Yeats's, and the Rising and the Somme became the respective and exclusive icons of republican and unionist myth.

5

Postwar Reflections

$\mathbf{F}$ OR SOME OF THE WAR'S MAJOR PROTAGONISTS, THE ARMISTICE IN NOVEMBER 1918 only signaled the end of international hostilities, as domestic crises and internecine conflicts continued to flare up throughout Europe in the political fallout of the war. Though Ireland was to suffer through the bloody "reprisals" of the War of Independence and the subsequent Civil War that followed partition, Ireland's role in the Great War continued to be disputed during the decade or so after the negotiated peace. Like the boundary line that divided the two new Irish states after the 1922 Treaty, a line of demarcation was drawn through Irish memory of the war. In the Free State, eagerness to assert a new identity distinct from its former colonial master led to a flurry of political and cultural reinterpretations of the past: "Not only was the record of parliamentary nationalism more or less dismissed, [but] the real nature of pre-1916 Irish society had to be glossed over, including, among much else, the hundreds of thousands of Irish who had volunteered in the Great War" (R. Foster 1988, 535). As Micheál Ó huanacháin relates, in the south most of the returning Irish war veterans were "treated with silence if not contempt . . . [,and] [t]heir answer was an equal silence" (1984, 159). Meanwhile in the new Northern Irish state, the siege mentality of Ulster unionists saw to it that memory of the war would be processed through loyalist and imperialist ritual. Consequently, the Irish soldier of the Great War became a pariah in one state and an imperial icon in the other.

For Irish poets, the uncertainty and mutual distrust that dominated cross-border affairs in the 1920s made it almost impossible to respond to the war free from the insidious influence of local politics. Trapped in a retrospective malaise, some poets wrote war poetry in a stylistic and political vacuum as though there had never been a war, while other poets, particularly those ex-

184

servicemen living in the Free State, soon discovered that their place in history was gradually being erased by the new establishment's efforts to discard all vestiges of its colonial past. Some poets even used their poetry as a way to preserve the memory of the Irish war dead by either glorifying their sacrifice or by defending their political ideals amid a climate where "self-definition against Britain—cultural or political"—became an all-consuming passion (R. Foster 1988, 516). Obsession with national identity still dominated Irish war poetry also; so much so, that the myth-making process about the war was already well underway during the 1920s. For some of these war poets, the historical significance of their part in the Great War ended when the war ended, but in their belated war poetry, they fought a desperate rearguard action against those forces that strove to consign their memory to historical oblivion. To ensure that the war would be remembered, some Irish poets undertook the task of preserving *their* versions of the war by emphasizing selective narratives to support their sectionalist politics. Others whose verse was predictably sentimental were drawn by the war's exhaustless capacity to evoke nostalgia and pathos while a third response was more concerned with examining the war's impact on Irish society and culture.

In Britain during the late 1920s and early 1930s, the first major historical and literary reevaluations of the war were published with the result that some of the war's most enduring myths were forever embedded in the popular imagination. British folk memory was actually bound by the common belief that not only were the best men of an entire generation killed, but that they were also squandered by the incompetence of the military top brass. In Ireland, though, there was "no consensus about the war"; instead, Irish war memory was not only "divisive," it was also the "subject of controversy" (Boyce 1993, 3).

Given the gradual deterioration in the relationship between the Free State government and the newly convened Northern Irish parliament, it was perhaps inevitable that remembering the war would provoke political and cultural antagonism. The breakdown in any meaningful cooperation was accelerated by paranoid unionist extremists who feared cross-border power sharing and by IRA militants whose ongoing campaign of violence in Northern Ireland was motivated by their view that the Northern Irish state was "temporary and illegitimate" (Hughes 1994, 70–71). For many Ulster unionists, the war became "a key symbolic event in their emergence as a distinct people with a special history, one almost guided by providence" (Boyce 1993, 4). Inevitably, as mutual political distrust between both regimes became more entrenched, so did the need to reinterpret the past: as a result, the recent losses of the Great War were quickly seized upon by propagandists from both camps in order to further their political agendas.

Throughout the 1920s commemorating the Great War in Northern Ireland became a carefully calculated political act as "Celebrating the loyalist tradition in Ireland also, inevitably, meant celebrating the contribution of Irish soldiers to the British war effort" (Jackson 1994, 255). While an Easter Rising hagiography provided the Free State with its own revolutionary mythology, in Northern Ireland, as we have already seen, the Somme became a defining moment in Protestant Ulster's allegiance to empire. The upshot of these rival mythic narratives was that the war "simultaneously united and divided the Irish people . . . [as] 1916 came to represent a different sort of 'magic number' to different types of Irishmen" (255).

As Irish war memory became increasingly politicized after partition, most postwar Irish verse appeared impervious to cultural and political change. A number of Irish poets continued to publish war verse that was in theme and style almost indistinguishable from the sincere yet sentimental lyrics popular during the war years. Reading the poetry written by most of these retrospective war poets reminds us that the predominant styles of the Irish Revival did not simply disappear after the advent of the war and the emergence of modernism. Among the outstanding features of revivalist poetry were its chiefly romantic conceptions of Irish peasantry and Irish landscape and a concomitant "catalog of vague imagery and pale impressions" (Garratt 1986, 54). Two theories have been put forth to explain why the literary standards of the Irish Revival remained popular: first of all, there was a continuing faith in the rich potential of Celtic materials, and secondly, as a result of domestic and global political crises, there existed a willingness to engage in the ongoing disputes over "national identity" (45).

Considering the fact that throughout the 1920s the regimes on either side of the border engaged in creating their own political narratives, it is not surprising that debates over Irish political and cultural identities should seep into retrospective Irish war verse. The politicizing of Irish war memory was to have a disastrous effect on community relationships across the political and sectarian divide. While in England ceremonies of remembrance provided a forum for the expression of a shared, national grief, in both Irish states, war memory not only widened the existing political and sectarian divisions between unionists and nationalists but also provided another clash point that to this day still triggers bouts of raw tribal emotion and confrontation.

Evidence of how Ulster memory of the war has been appropriated by loyalist ideology can be found in Samuel McCurry's *The Ballads of Ballytumulty* (1922)—a volume that contains a few war poems among its mostly demotic collection of local color, rural anecdote, and Ulster dialect. While McCurry's use of Ulster dialect is reminiscent of revivalism's excessively self-conscious attempt to effect an air of "peasant realism" (Loftus 1964, 15), his handling of the local vernacular clearly privileges an Ulster, as opposed to an Irish, war memory. In the sentimental ballad "The Brothers: A Tale of the Ulster Division" (1922, 104–9), McCurry combines cliché, stereotype, and historical inaccuracy in order to mythologize the heroic sacrifice of Ulster's sons, but the facile rhymes, mawkish melodrama and maudlin caricatures ensure that the poem succeeds only as a fairly trite polemic.

In the first stanza, the goal of fixing a historical event as a defining moment in the tribe's narrative is achieved by establishing a link between the oral storyteller—the tribal bard—and his audience in the typical declamatory style of public oratory:

> Hear my story, men, and wonder at a scene
>   that once befell
> On a battle-field in Flanders, place your memory
>   knows so well;
> 'Tis no fiction false and foolish, 'tis no fairy song
>   I sing,
> But a tale of truth and valour in the service of the
>   King.

In keeping with the most popular of unionist myths, McCurry's stentorian delivery instantly enshrines the Somme as the latest in a series of battles to preserve Ulster's liberty. This fairly conventional rhetorical style is accompanied by a glut of trite images and themes common in sentimental war verse. Two "noblehearted brothers" answer the call in the time of "England's danger," and on a foreign battlefield, under a "waning moon," one brother rescues his badly wounded sibling and kisses his "pallid brow," only to be killed himself by a "sniper's bullet" and taken "away to be / with God." In the poem's conclusion, we encounter the customary offering of Christian condolence:

Praise the Lord! the strife is ended, there is nothing
    more to tell,
Yet remains the moral splendid, which to learn,
    it would be well,
When in sorrow for a season, tho' our prayer
    should vain appear,
Cry aloud, nor wait to reason, God will come, for
    God is near.

We have seen these sentiments before as McCurry's glib moralizing and stock characterization resurrect the popular wartime notion that a woman's role was to suffer her losses stoically and encourage enlistment. In stanza four, the brothers' "grey-haired widowed mother" is portrayed as nothing more than a mouthpiece for imperialist imperatives:

But that darlin' little woman knew the time had
    come to part,
Silently she stilled her anguish and the beating of
    her heart,
With a hand upon each shoulder she exclaimed,
    'Tis time to show
To the world what stuff you're made of, and in
    God's name, up and go!

Standard racial stereotypes predominate, too: the Kaiser is "that son of hell" and his army a "host of / hated Huns." And like many wartime propagandists, McCurry defines the war as a holy crusade.

Despite the promilitarist clichés and stereotypes, in terms of the Irish context, perhaps the most important and controversial theme in the poem is how the Irish experience in the war is distorted to promote a unionist mythography. As previously noted, some unionists were keen to circulate the falsehood that Catholics sat back while their Protestant neighbors enlisted to a man. McCurry does not conceal whose side he is on. In stanza five, the little widower associates Irish nationalism with cowardice and treason while appropriating for her own community the much more admirable qualities of unyielding loyalty and sacrifice:

Let the Fenians and Sinn Feiners and that poor
    unworthy crowd
Stay at home and help the Kaiser, every shirker
    makes him proud,

> If I had, this blessed minute, thirteen sons instead
> of two,
> Every son should be a sojer, and be keen to go
> like you.

Of course historical truth gets lost in McCurry's rush to create a Protestant myth out of the Great War. By parading the customary sectarian smear in linking all Catholics ("Fenians") with the more extreme elements of Irish nationalism ("Sinn Fein"), he conveniently overlooks the fact that the Ulster Volunteer Force had been quite amicable with the Kaiser's Germany shortly before the war started. "Loyal" Ulster Volunteers had smuggled in large shipments of German-made firearms with the Kaiser's blessing just months before war was declared as part of a carefully planned act of resistance against any attempt to implement the Home Rule Bill. In this instance, McCurry's pedaling of historical untruths reaffirms Edna Longley's point that there appears to be a symbiotic relationship between "bad literature" and "bad politics" (1985, 26).

We see another exercise in unionist propaganda in "August Fourth, Nineteen Fourteen" (1922, 64–65). The poem's title suggests that Ulster's loyalty to empire and to the war effort was absolute even from very outset of the conflict, but this is simply untrue. In the first stanza, McCurry secures the holy bond between Ulster and England:

> Up boys of Ballytumulty,
>   The loyal and the true,
> The eyes of all your countrymen
>   Are proudly fixed on you.
> The day of the sword has dawned at last,
>   The day foreseen for years,
> But you are strong to face the wrong,
>   And England has no fears.

Though the "loyal" and "true" stand steadfast in "England's hour of need," the situation in Ireland at the outbreak of the war was much more complicated. Like many nationalists, unionists were initially cautious in their response to the British army's call for recruits. As a matter of fact, Sir Edward Carson "would only send his UVF to fight for Britain if the British Government played fair with the Unionists," but like Redmond, he soon realized that his political agenda could be furthered by an act of unqualified patriotism and thus the UVF was delivered en masse into the service of the British army (Boyce 1993, 6–7).

Another sacred unionist belief espoused in the poem is the image of a nurturing mother-empire defended by a loyal commonwealth:

> Whilst fast from far Colonial skies,
>   O'er fields of shining foam,
> They come, they come, to the roll of the drum,
>   To the help of the host at home.

Historical links to a tradition of imperial service also codify Ulster's right to retain its membership in the colonial family:

> Far out on the brine in a far-flung line
>   Our mighty warships ride,
> And our sea dogs wait with resolve as great
>   As the day when Nelson died.

The rest of the poem endorses England's cause against the "savage legions" of the "tyrant" Kaiser. Imperialist supremacy ("England rules the wave") and religious piety ("in God alone we trust") combine to create a flagrant piece of propaganda untouched by the war's misery or complexity. Like most of McCurry's war verse, the poem is not really concerned with the war itself but with the task of creating an Ulster myth of imperial sacrifice diametrically opposed to the emergent nationalist myths of the Free State. The complexities of the Irish involvement in the war are excised in order to serve the exigencies of the political present. Evidently, like nationalism's encoding myth of the Easter Rising, unionist ideology "does not demand a complex vision of its own past" either (Jackson 1994, 253).

These simplified historical readings of Ulster's war experience helped define Northern Ireland's sense of separateness from the Free State. Just as the south's newly-won independence encouraged it to develop "its own recognizable identity, so too in the north we find a growing consciousness of an Ulster, [or] if you like a 'regional' personality," which begins to emerge in the years after partition (Lyons 1994, 102). In the course of his discussion of the unique qualities of the Ulster dialect in his introduction to McCurry's ballads, Sir John Byers notes that the region's linguistic peculiarities are "due to the fact that in no similarly sized portion of the British Empire have there been so many different racial strains at various periods as in the Northern province of Ireland" (McCurry 1922, xxi). Among the political subtexts of this statement is the assumption that Ulster's membership in the British Empire is non-negotiable, while nationalist claims to a homogeneous and exclusively gaelic/Celtic Irish identity are historically naïve. (As empire apologist, Byers's point here about Ulster's racial diversity also appears to muddy Ian Adamson's theory that Ulster Protestants are the unalloyed descendants of the pre-Celtic Cruthin.) As for Byers's argument that the Ulster dialect has clear and strong links to Elizabethan English (xxvi), his intent here is not simply to point out the diversity of Ulster's linguistic heritage but rather to disaffiliate Ulster's ethnic and cultural identity from other strands of Irishness. We see this nascent sense of regional identity in some of McCurry's ballads where his use of local dialect appropriates the war as an exclusively Ulster experience. This dialect is Ulster-Scots (McCurry supplies a glossary of terms with their English meanings), a language which contemporary poets like Michael Longley and Tom Paulin periodically employ in their poetry.

In "Betty's Sympathy" (1922, 42–43), the combination of dialect and caricature produces a comic yet concerted attempt to promote Ulster nationalism. The poem recounts the martial ardor of an old Ulster woman whose maternal concern for the soldiers is matched by her naive assumptions about the horrors of killing and dying. McCurry again raises the issue of women's wartime complicity in encouraging young men to enlist:

> She had heard of the soldiers marching
>   And the miles they had to go,
> Of their terrible time in the trenches
>   In the sleet and the driving snow,
> She thought of the villainous Germans,
>   And she cried as she clenched her fist
> "I declare this day I 'cud up an' away—
>   Och, och if a woman 'cud list!"

Betty's subsequent fantasy about being at the front envisions the war as a game interspersed by frequent tea breaks. Such a view suggests the gulf between the soldiers' experiences and the home front's often naive and cheery impression of the war:

> And after the shootin' was over,
>   And the Germans had gone for the day,
> I wud hurry and boil up the kettle

And make them a cup o' tay,
Then do wee turns for the craythers,
And clean off the clabber and dirt,
And bathe their feet at the hearth in the heat,
Or mend their sock or their shirt.

McCurry's comic portrait of a heroic granny darning the troops'
socks amid the horrors of gas and piled up corpses modifies to
a certain extent the poem's obvious absurdities. But the Ulster-
speak is too much; it lacks the value of irony. It is the caricature
equivalent of Ulster comedian Jimmy Young garbed in granny
drag and singing behind the barricades in bomb-blasted Belfast,
except that, unlike McCurry, who essentializes Ulster memory of
the war as a narrative of selfless heroism, imperial devotion, and
folksy pluck, Young's mock send-up of the absurdities of Ulster
violence transcends the ideological posturing and sectarian cant
of Northern Irish politics. Consequently, McCurry's war poetry
resembles the more rancorous loyalist songs, whose "most common themes are still fear of attack, tales of battles won, and most
frighteningly of all, sectarian viciousness" (Rolston 1999, 52).

Another strain of postwar commemorative poetry was Irish
pastoral, and one particularly adept exponent of flowery romantic ruralism was Michael Walsh (1897–1938) whose few retrospective war poems create a wistful Irish Arcadia. In his heyday,
Walsh's poetry received lavish praise from his fellow poets and
critics. One reviewer, in the *Times Literary Supplement* no less,
noted that even in the "agony of battlefields" Walsh "preserves
the simplicity and quiet of the Irish countryside" (Walsh 1929,
45). Once celebrated as a "new Irish poet . . . who cannot fail to
win a way . . . to the heart of every lover of good poetry" (45),
Walsh is largely forgotten today as none of the major dictionaries
devoted to Irish literary biography (including the *Dictionary of
Irish Literature* and *The Oxford Companion to Irish Literature*)
even acknowledge his existence. His critical neglect may be due
in part to his imitative revivalist style.

In "The Marne 1914" (1929, 19), taken from the volume *Brown
Earth and Green*, Walsh, like Ledwidge before him, mediates
between the trench horrors in France and the Irish countryside's
leafy pastoral:

Ah! could it be, my brother, in that hour
When you were dying on the battle plain,
You saw the crab trees breaking into flower—
Young summer in the lane?

The ironic juxtaposition of the soldier's death and the trees' sprouting buds recalls the common war motif of nature as the restorative agent of change. However, Walsh's desire to locate for the dying soldier a romantic consolation through recollected images of Irish landscape seems forced: the speaker's fanciful reconstruction of his dead brother's final moments betrays his dependence on an inherited idiom that does not actively engage the true complexities of his grief. In the final stanza, generalized physical details and romantic views of rural Irish life produce a prophylactic effect:

> Perchance you saw the big bog field in meadow,
>> Your father mowing by the river side,
> Or what fond face came clearest through the shadow,
>> The hour before you died?

Death is not confronted; only a nostalgic landscape from the poet's memory remains.

In another poem "After Ypres—The Mother," taken from Walsh's second collection *The Heart Remembers Morning* (1931, 27), the trite image of a soothing mother figure and the memory of her dead "golden boy" reveal not only how romanticized impressions about the casualties of the war persisted but also how for some poets, the war as a subject for poetry seemed to require a specific poetic style. Romantic exclamations enclose a stale personification and refulgent light typical of watery Irish twilight landscapes:

> O Glimmer soft on his cold head to-night
>> Far-travelled moon; white wanderer through the mist,
> His fair gold hair like a cloudless summer light
>> That oft of old a smiling mother kissed.

Only in the second stanza, when Walsh drops the second-rate Keatsian mimicry briefly, does he have something more important to say:

> Parchment and trophies—honours that he has won;
>> Tribute of kings—valour in bronze that gleams!
> Ah! but those eyes where all things precious shone,
>> Morning and innocence and blue of dreams!

Walsh's ironic comparison between the "cold pastoral" permanence of the dead soldier's military decorations and the fleeting memory of his physical beauty underlines the artificiality of a man-made aesthetic when contrasted to the miracle of life. But this passage is a rare departure from the general contours of Walsh's retrospective war poems, which betray a desire to write about the war but have little new to say. The war gradually became fixed in popular memory as a grand crusade: in only a few short years, myth became memory. As Walsh's press reviews indicate, there was a growing audience for this sort of romantic euphemizing a decade or so after the war, and his brief success reminds us that the general public's taste in poetry rarely reflects the views and attitudes of the canonical writers who we quite often presume to be the spokesmen of their age.

Equally enraptured by this sentimental commemorative mode was Randal McDonnell, or MacDonnell (1870?-1930?), who was better known for his historical novels (McDonnell 1996, 334). It is not clear when his war poems were first written, but in his presumably posthumous 1932 collection, *Songs of Seaside Places and Other Verses*, he recycles conventional, pietistic sentiments in his glorification of Irish soldiers and their forlorn sweethearts. One poem, "The Irish Brigade" (1932, 63), rehashes the usual militarist fervor and swinging rhythms of a marching song. The result is nothing more than propaganda. It is only in the third and final stanza that McDonnell's febrile war chant reveals its retrospective sanitizing of the contradictions surrounding Irish participation in the war:

> They have marched to the tune of a spirited chant
> 　And together will conquer or fall;
> They are free from the curse of sectarian cant,
> 　They are brothers and Irishmen all.

This desire to portray the Irish war effort as a cross-sectarian collaboration seems more an act of political wishfulness. We have already seen how remote was the likelihood that the war would reconcile tribal differences, and by the early 1930s, memory of the war had become an instrument of division in Ireland, not one of reconciliation. One only had to look at the war memorials erected to commemorate the memory of the war dead. At Thiepval, the feats of the Ulster Division on the Somme were heroicized according to tribal protocol. One Ulster monument's marble obelisk still bears the inscription: "Commemorating the men and women of the Orange Institution who have been killed in many fields of conflict" (Stedman 1995, 136). The same memorial also features a cross with the phrase "In God Our Trust" etched with a crown on the stem and the emotively triumphalist "Boyne" inscribed at the base of the cenotaph (136).[1] Even though by 1926, "three Celtic crosses" had been erected to honor the Tenth and Sixteenth Divisions at Messines, Guillemont, and in Salonika (Harris 1968, 210), southern Irish soldiers would have to wait another seventy-two years for a monument to be erected to their memory in Belgium.

If McDonnell eagerly sponsored the idea of a committed and collaborative Irish effort during the war years—a golden moment that could perhaps be revived somehow—he was also keen to celebrate Irish heroism. In "Michael O'Leary, V.C." (1932, 66), McDonnell pays tribute to Ireland's glorious tradition for producing fighting heroes:

> Yours is the gallant breed, O'Leary,
> History recalls,
> Rolled back the tide of fierce attack
> From Limerick's shattered walls—
> Who broke the line of Fontenoy,
> Undaunted, undismayed—
> In the list of lonely triumphs
> Of the glorious Brigade—

The subject of the poem, a sergeant in the Irish Guards, won Ireland's first Victoria Cross during the war, and "his rapturous reception in Dublin was only surpassed by that in the British newspapers, with such statements as 'How Michael O'Leary VC kills eight Germans and takes two barricades'" (Boyce 1993, 7). O'Leary's bravery was quickly exploited to boost enlistment figures, and his face soon adorned recruiting posters throughout Ireland. Obviously McDonnell still finds the image of an Irish hero irresistible as the poem does not commemorate the war so much as it celebrates the supposed ethnic superiority of Irish soldiers. Such racial stereotypes—remember the Irish were regarded as the empire's finest "missile troops"—apparently still gripped the popular imagination after the war ended.

McDonnell also reminds us of other casualties. In "Maureen" (1932, 64), he recounts, in typically lachrymose fashion, the endless sorrow of a young woman whose lover never returns from the front. The desire to provide consolation for the bereaved results in the usual display of wartime simulacra and ceremony. The cliché-ridden last stanza is ample illustration:

> O blue eyes dull with weeping for your English lover
> sleeping,
> And those flowers of dear remembrance that you
> wore whilst kneeling there;
> Death has ended all forgiving, but because he loved
> them, living,
> A rose was on your bosom—a blossom in your hair!

Heavily reliant on borrowed themes and images and similar in style and theme to Kettle's marching songs and Tynan's laments, McDonnell's war verse is like a long-lost postcard that finally arrives in the mail.

Like McDonnell, Seumas O'Sullivan (1879–1958) also felt compelled to address a conflict that his retrospectively romantic style seemed ill equipped to accommodate. A pharmacist by trade, O'Sullivan, whose real name was James Starkey, is chiefly remembered for his "sustained editorship of the *Dublin Magazine* from 1923 to 1958" (J. Russell 1987, 9). Announced as a fresh talent in George Russell's anthology *New Songs* (1904), his poetry usually sounded like "old songs, especially like Yeats's Celtic Twilight poetry of the 1890s" (Garratt 1986, 51). Regarded as the "archetypal Celtic poet and incurable idealist" (Burnham 1979, 547), O'Sullivan was frequently criticized for his inability to shake off "the Revival's grip" on his imagination (Garratt 1986, 53). Yet his preference for the revivalist mode also garnered critical praise from Thomas MacDonagh who cited O'Sullivan as one of several promising Irish poets in his study *Literature in Ireland* (1916, 124). Like the previously discussed poets who wrote in the revivalist tradition, O'Sullivan's interest in the war seems to have been largely limited to regarding it as a source for occasional poetry. When his *Collected Poems* appeared in 1940, only a couple of war poems were included, but unlike McDonnell, O'Sullivan avoids the worst excesses of political propaganda and emotional affectation that we find in most commemorative verse. If anything, O'Sullivan's war poems engage in historical reevaluations of war and its continuing impact on Irish culture. In "The Miracle" (1940, 195), for instance, the poet recalls an encounter on a deserted street with a young girl:

> And yet as she passed me I swear to you
> somebody coughed
> No merely civilian, inadequate, meaning-
> less cough.

> But a soldier's cough, chesty, profound,
> And female-attention-compelling.
> Yet the road was quite empty
> Save only for me, who went silent,
> And the lovely demure-stepping maid,
> And the statue of Gough on his horse,
> With his field-marshal's baton.

The reference to General Hugh Gough, commander of British forces during the Opium War (1839–1842) and subsequent commander-in-chief during the Indian campaign in the 1840s, recalls Ireland's illustrious tradition of producing military leaders who served with distinction in Her Majesty's armed forces. O'Sullivan's reference here to this servant of the empire who, frozen in bronze, keeps vigil now over a deserted Irish road, illustrates how Ireland's past is littered with heroes who are reduced to marmorealized passivity. O'Sullivan may not have intended to represent Gough here as a convenient symbol of unionist intransigence, but the cold, militaristic pose of the ever vigilant general on horseback holding the authoritarian symbol of his rank—the baton—suggests how in Irish history, the past is never really past. Irish landscape is dotted with reminders of its complicated and troubled history, and Gough's statue's imperious presence serves as a reminder of the country's colonial past. The speaker's brief encounter with the "demure-stepping maid" (an ironic stand-in for Kathleen ni Houlihan?) is spoiled by war's intrusiveness (the statue); apparently the desire for a new national identity cannot escape the omnipresence of a colonial past whose icons demand recognition and interpretation.

One other poem that takes a rather unconventional look at war is "Collectors—1915," a period piece presumably written during the last year of the Great War (1940, 172–173). First published in *The Rosses and Other Poems* in 1918, the poem is a caustic rejection of wartime recruitment as O'Sullivan's archaisms create an Old-Testament-like indictment of those who sold the war:

> Pass by with your fluttering flags,
> And your tinsel guns,
> O dainty beggars, pass by, for I know you
>   not.

If war recruiters are villainous and duplicitous, the poor—the potential cannon fodder—are the helpless victims of urban decay:

But they came to us not like these, with
  the glories of war,
And pennons waving, and all the lure-
  ments of far
Romantic places, gay fields, th' Argonne's
  fair valleys,
But dark with the shadow of death and
  disease,
Wild-eyed with hunger and shivering in
  fluttering rags
From their sunless alleys,
Where were ye then, O dainty ones?

A close friend of Arthur Griffith (Burnham 1979, 548), O'Sullivan's distrust of those who peddled war aims and other induce-
ments to encourage enlistment can be partly attributed to his
nationalist sympathies.

But there were other poets who did not shy away from addressing the consequences of the war and its impact on the national psyche. Indeed, the more interesting war poems published
during the immediate postwar years were those written by ex-
servicemen who, though they had remained largely silent during
the conflict, reflected on their experiences in order to come to
terms with the war's legacy and its ongoing influence on their
personal and public lives.

Described by a critic for the *Irish Independent* as belonging to
"'the Kipling-Service-MacGill school'" (Gray 1994, 28), Thomas
Carnduff's roots (1886–1956), like Patrick MacGill before him,
were working-class, and like MacGill, an impoverished upbring-
ing, lack of a formal education, and frequent periods of unemployment did not prevent him from enjoying some success as
a published poet and playwright. Politically, though, Carnduff
came from a "staunch Orange background" (17). Raised in Belfast's Sandy Row, he witnessed many of the city's worst sectarian and labor disputes during the first decade of this century.
By 1912, he had joined the Young Citizen Volunteers and later
played a part in the UVF's successful gunrunning enterprise in
Larne in 1914. At the outbreak of the war, he worked as a hand
driller in the Belfast shipyards up until 1916 when he enlisted in
the Royal Engineers and served in France for three years before
demobilization in 1919 (7–21).

During his lifetime, Carnduff published only two volumes of
poetry: *Songs from the Shipyards* (1924) and *Songs of an Out-*

of-Work (1932). In 1993, Lapwing, a Belfast press, issued what appears to be a collected edition of his poetry entitled *Poverty Street and Other Belfast Poems*. In the following year, autobiographical chapters under the title *Thomas Carnduff: His Life and Writings* (1994) was published by the Lagan Press. Unfortunately, Carnduff's memoirs contain little or nothing about his war experiences and only a handful of poems provide any kind of a direct response to the war itself.

Of his five poems that do address the war, several general observations can be made. Unlike MacGill, to whom he has been compared, or Samuel McCurry, Carnduff did not adopt any cockney or local vernacular, but his war poems do feature the customary paleo-romantic stylistic tics we come to associate with a belated Victorian/Edwardian public verse. Carnduff had no grand illusions about the quality of his poetry as he himself admitted to a "fondness" for "'writing doggerel'" (Gray 1994, 23). Certainly his war verse is riddled with facile rhymes, studied archaisms, heightened chivalric idioms, and figurative clichés, and his themes seldom depart from sounding out the customary elegiac or jingoistic platitudes one finds in thousands of other glibly written war poems. At certain junctures where Carnduff's commemorative verse does depart from the well-traveled thoroughfares of received sentimentality, we discover a brooding outrage at the human cost of the war accompanied by a martial celebration of the war dead in terms that range from pride in empire to a more regional sense of political and cultural identity.

In "Ypres, September, 1917" (1993, 70), an otherwise trite, florid and undistinguished description of the battlefield, Carnduff predictably observes how the beauty of the natural scene has been despoiled by the war:

> Below the ramparts lie the plain
> As far as eye can see,
> Its beauty scarred with gory stain,
> Of man's artillery.

In the last stanza, however, a dissentient chord is appended to this retrospective catalogue of generalized impressions of the battlefield:

> 'Neath Zillebeke's green fossilled lake
> Pale ghostly faces gleam,

> And round its slimy bottom rake,
> The embers of their dream.

These lines are as close as Carnduff comes to indicting the war as an orchestrated exercise in pointless savagery. Whether it was the dream of fighting for glory, freedom, or the promise of youth, he suggests that commemoration should not be a simple gesture of retrospective glorification but an act of emotional contrition, a taking stock, an acknowledgment of the cost of peace. A trace of postwar dejection also pervades this final stanza. For Carnduff the working-class activist, the notion of victory is mitigated by his current situation; perhaps the dream that lay at the bottom of that "fossilled lake" was that of returning to a "land fit for heroes," an irony not lost on Carnduff, the unemployed Belfast shipyard worker.

Like many of the war poets we have encountered so far, Carnduff's war poetry articulates no consistent ideology. The poet who could register his bitterness about those who died is equally capable of writing a sword-rattling broadside replete with all the usual demonizing of the enemy. In "Graves of Gallipoli" (1993, 32), the war is described as though it were another chapter in an ongoing epochal dispute between Islam and Christendom. In this case, the holy ground of the British graves at Gallipoli provides the pretext for Carnduff's crusade against the heathen hordes of the Saracen:

> You can wave your arms in triumph,
> You can yell until you choke,
> You can scheme of ridding Turkey
> Of a galling Christian yoke;
> While your warlike spirits rising,
> And your crescent banners wave,
> Don't forget the lion's watching
> O'er Gallipoli's graves.
>
> No heathen hand shall sacrilege
> The Graves of Britain's dead,
> No Turkish mob or Kamel horde
> On Christian bones be fed.
> You numbered us in thousands—
> We'll come in countless waves,
> If you claim our silent brothers,
> In Gallipoli's graves.

Such jingoistic posturing is not as evident in "The Graves of the Unknown" (1993, 74) where Carnduff's elegy for the "Unknown Warrior" presents a pleasing and cathartic image of the war dead. Though the dead soldier is buried in foreign soil, Carnduff makes grand use of the requisite euphemisms to enshrine him in a place that is forever home:

> O cold and damp the earthen bed
> Which holds his mangled form,
> Yet peaceful lies the pillowed head
> Immune from wind and storm;
> And often when the twilight fades
> Across the sea from home,
> A gentle breeze will stir the grass,
> Above the brave unknown.

The scene in the poem's last stanza shifts to a wreath-laying Remembrance Day service:

> The scene is changed—I see a throng
> Within a city square,
> A grave and solemn multitude
> In deep and earnest prayer;
> A cenotaph, bedecked with flowers,
> A flag half-mast is flown—
> A nation's thought in glory crowns
> The Graves of the unknown.

Presumably Carnduff's poem describes memorial observances in Belfast and mention of the war memorial, the flowers, and the flag at half-mast reveal the extent to which such occasions were quickly staged with imperial pageantry. However, a more overt rendering of the war's ideological appropriation by one side of the community in Northern Ireland is evidenced in two other war poems.

In these poems, any authentic recollection of the training camps and battlefields is paralyzed by Carnduff's archaic language. Like the chivalric idioms with which F. S. Boas mythologizes the unionist war dead, Carnduff's work in the same vein also comes across as a very third-rate imitation of some medieval romance, yet like Boas, Carnduff's reading of the war privileges regional and ideological allegiances before king and empire. For Carnduff, duty and patriotism are structured hierarchically, with God and Ulster coming before king and empire.

In "Messines, 17th June, 1917. A Memory" (1993, 42), Carnduff portrays Ulster's troops on the battlefield in terms compatible with the spirit and rhetoric of Ulster loyalism:

> It seems but yesterday since we,
> With flashing eye and naked sword
> Uncowed by hell's artillery
> Kept faith with country and with God.

The last line of this first stanza would not be out of place on the banner of any local Orange lodge, and the fact that Carnduff was a member of the Independent Orange Order indicates his familiarity with this kind of religious fraternity rhetoric. Of course when he describes keeping the "faith with country and with God," it is Ulster, Britain and a Protestant God to which he refers. This sentiment forms a sacred component of unionist mythology as all battles are essentially struggles to preserve the Ulster Protestant's civil and religious liberties. The favored image is one of resilience against great odds: once again, Ulster is under siege. Regional loyalties are reaffirmed on the battlefield as the soldiers think of "home—the hills of Down" and "Slieve Donard's crown." In the final stanza, the idea that Ulstermen fought for a local cause more than out of any real sense of servitor imperialism is established:

> Beyond Messines our vision swept
> O'er white-foamed sea and golden strand,
> And silently each spirit kept
> A tryst beneath the crimson hand.

Like Boas, Carnduff reads the war as another critical moment in the narrative of a besieged Ulster Protestant people. The "crimson hand" of battle (the Red Hand of Ulster) obviously renders the war as a fight for Ulster, and while Ulster's customary enemies are not mentioned, the rather special and secretive relationship between the troops (the "tryst") and the "crimson hand" evokes other popular images from loyalist mythology, most notably the notion of blood sacrifice and the signing of the Ulster Covenant (1912), an act of defiance against Home Rule which some signatories famously made all the more sacred by inscribing their names in their own blood and sealing their loyalty to Ulster with more bloody hands.

Another poem, "The Ghosts of Clandeboye" (1993, 48–49), also commemorates the bravery of Ulster's soldiers by drawing connections between the war dead and their warrior ancestors. Clandeboye in County Down was one of the camps where the Thirty-sixth Ulster Division went through basic training prior to embarkation for France in 1916. Throughout the poem, the speaker links the "clansmen of O'Neill" to the "khaki figures" who represent Ulster's most recent band of heroes. Despite all the overtures to men in arms, the last stanza honors the war dead by acknowledging that eternal peace will be theirs only when war becomes a distant memory:

> When days of strife and warfare change
> To years of peace and joy,
> Their silent wraiths will cease to roam
> The fields of Clandeboye.

Again the emblematic power of the Red Hand is evoked in the poem, but instead of the image being exclusively associated with one particular tradition, Carnduff's image of these "khaki figures" standing steadfastly beside the "red hand of O'Neill" hints at the symbol's more complicated history, harking back to Ulster's gaelic past when the red hand was the family crest of the rebel O'Neil. Once again, the battle over whether the province is Irish or British involves a struggle over emblems, too.

Unlike Boas or McCurry, Carnduff's war poems cannot be easily labeled as the work of an empire apologist or an Ulster separatist. We do find the usual propagandistic banalities evident in his few war poems, and the language and imagery he employs to commemorate the war dead certainly portray the war as another defining moment in Ulster Protestant culture. However, at times his war poems evince the sort of shared grievance at the cost of victory and a willingness to question the validity of the sacrifice given the state of postwar Europe—a place where he himself was a firsthand witness to the general climate of social dissension and unemployment.

On the other side of the recently drawn Irish border, other ex-soldiers were to register a more ambivalent response to the war. One such ex-serviceman was Oxford graduate Stephen Gwynn (1864–1950), an active politician, man of letters and close friend of Tom Kettle's, who enlisted as a private at the beginning of the war, "was promoted to captain, [and] served in France until 1917" (Hogan 1979, 280). Apart from his collaborative work at the outset of the war with Kettle when they published a collection of traditional marching songs for the Irish brigades, it was not until 1923 that Gwynn's own war poetry first appeared in his *Collected Poems*. As a former nationalist member of parliament, he played an active role in Irish politics from 1906 to 1918, so it is not surprising to find him still struggling with the political ramifications of the Great War in his verse (280).

Like other former soldiers, Gywnn was concerned with the legacy of the Irish war dead and how they would be remembered. Certainly the new state's preoccupation with "enforcing public modes of 'Irishness'" would have made ex-British officers like Gwynn particularly uneasy about their place in the new Ireland (R. Foster 1988, 518). Memory of the Irish war dead was threatened by the prevailing climate of political and cultural irredentism, and in Gwynn's best war poems, we see him trying not only to preserve the memory of the war dead but also, like AE before him, reminding his countrymen of the role those dead played in the formation of the new state.

In an "Inscription for a Fountain Erected in Memory of Mabel Dearmer Who Died in Serbia and of Christopher Dearmer killed at Suvla Bay" (1924, 103), Gywnn commemorates the deaths of a mother and son on separate battle fronts. Mabel Dearmer had been a fairly successful author of children's fiction before she died of fever in Serbia, and Gwynn wrote a prefatory essay for her memoir *Letters from a Field Hospital* published in 1916. This two-stanza poem is a sincere tribute to a woman who believed that all wars were "unrighteous" (Dearmer 1916, 2). The poem contains some of the usual features of memorial plaques with its odd archaism and valedictory tone, but there is no attempt to glorify the mother and son's deaths; those who drink from the fountain are asked only to remember them:

> Proud of the war, all glorious went the son:
> Loathing the war, all mournful went the mother.
> Each had the same wage when the day was done:
> Tell me, was either braver than the other?
>
> They lay in mire, who went so comely ever:
> Here, when you wash, let thought of them abide.
> They knew the parching thirst of wound and
>   fever:
> Here, when you drink, remember them who died.

Gwynn consciously avoids political platitude and Christian piety. The question that comprises the first stanza suggests how pointless it is to measure bravery when the only "wage" of war is death. In the second stanza, jolting contrasts intensify our empathy for the war dead. The ironic note in the first line contrasts the obscenity of the mother and son's deaths with their prewar unspoiled beauty, and the cleansing ritual in the last three lines recalls, by contrast, their suffering.

Perhaps Gwynn's most important war poem, though, is one he entitled "A Song of Victory" (1924, 39–47), a far-ranging exposé of the poet's distilled memories of the war. In the course of its eighteen stanzas, Gwynn threads together a series of associated images and impressions of the front. After several descriptions that communicate the desolation, destruction, and blood horror of the trenches, the focus shifts to describing the camaraderie of Irish troops before the final twelve stanzas examine the political fallout of the war in Ireland. At the end, Gwynn takes up the issue of locating a place in Irish history for those Irishmen who died on foreign fields in British uniforms.

The poem begins with visual description and ironic understatement:

> Ditches of mud
> Where the boot clung till it tore,
> Snow-cold water thigh-deep,
> Holes in the ground for shelter:
> It was not well to be there.

The impersonal tone and unembellished detail are sustained in the second stanza where the speaker recalls that the "German line and the space behind . . . [were] so remote and mysterious that actually to see any of its occupants . . . [was] a shock" (Fussell 1975, 76). But Gwynn also communicates the political ambivalence some Irishmen experienced in fighting a war whose aims seemed distant and ambiguous:

> Something glimpsed in the dark:
> What did you fire at?
> Seldom a form clear-seen,
> Never the face of a foeman.
> Strange, impersonal war,
> No heat in it, no hate.

This first section of the poem concludes with an account of a search party. The graphic horror of the scene is conveyed again in cold understatement:

> Then in the grey dank dawn
> Search for one missing.
> There in a tangle of wire,
> Posts fallen, ruin of sandbags,
> What is that darkness?
> Wedged in, frost-bound:
> Lift him, you, by the head—
> —There is no head, sir.—

The next sequence of stanzas explores the camaraderie at the front between Irish troops from various political and sectarian persuasions. Gwynn's account echoes Willie Redmond's hope that a new spirit of Irish unity would emerge from the trenches:

> Yonder behind the line,
> We met while we rested,
> Other men of our country
> Who had not counted us friends.
> There at ease for a moment,
> With the common danger behind us,
> . . . .
> And from the ditches of mud,
> From the pit of destruction,
> Word went back to Ireland:
> We have met, we have spoken,
> Who at home would never have spoken,
> Strange to think of it.

Again, the war is relegated to the background as Irish political divisions are explored and examined. But any likelihood of reconciliation between these political adversaries is dashed by news of the Easter Rising:

> Suddenly flashed to us there
> Word from Ireland:
> Ditches of blood in Ireland,
> Widening chasms.

After the war, the "widening chasms" of extremism were to render Gwynn and many other returning Irish veterans historically obsolete:

> We trod our way to the end;
> We were part of victory:
> And in the face of the world
> Ireland disowned us.

While some veterans like Tom Barry played an active role in the War of Independence, some ex-servicemen were shot by IRA extremists as traitors, and the vast majority of returning soldiers learned to keep quiet about their war service. Gwynn himself was a victim of IRA violence as republicans burned down his home in Kimmage, County Dublin in 1923 (Pierce 1995, 325). It is the despair of those who feel that their part in the "wider battle" was all for nought that Gwynn gives voice to:

> Was it for nothing, my comrade?
> Is there atonement of healing? Is there reward?
> Not yet.
> . . . .
> Rather, O loyal heart,
> It may be your time of purgation,
> Idle, powerless, apart,
> To look upon Ireland.

Acknowledging the historical displacement of men like himself, Gwynn can only hope that the passage of time will bring recognition and reconciliation for those caught between the warring ideologies of unionist and nationalist extremism:

> It may be, O comrade, that Ireland
> Casting a backward glance on the road she has
> travelled,
> Beyond the descent into victory,
> Past the ditches of blood,
> Will turn and yearn in her heart for the valour
> she once rejected,
> For the wisdom she cast aside . . .
> Will cry to her own sick heart,
> *My faithful, my children,*
> *My lovers who never hurt me,*
> *You also are Ireland.*
> *And it may be that Ireland*
> *Crying it so, will take courage*
> *To tread on the forward track.*

Gwynn foresaw that a narrowly-defined Irish nationalism threatened to erase the memory of Ireland's Great War soldiers, and his worst fears were to be confirmed. In 1929, the foundations for the National Memorial were laid at Islandbridge, even though a stir was caused by the fact that an Englishman, Sir Edward Lutyens, designed it. When work began on the monument in December 1931, half the workforce consisted of ex-servicemen, yet by April 1937, the memorial still had not been completed (Leonard 1988, 60). By the mid-1980s, "the bleak granite, decapitated columns, broken-down hedges, rotting pergolas, damaged fountains and empty pavilions . . . [were] aptly evocative of a long neglected battlefield" (67).

There were other ex-servicemen like Gwynn who saw their identity slowly extirpated from the historical record after partition. For many Anglo-Irish men and women, the reality of life under the new Free State regime meant further isolation and ultimately emigration: "A sense of bitterness and betrayal accompanied these men and women into exile, together with a conviction that the new Ireland was, sadly, no place for them" (T. Brown 1985, 91). Others have argued that the murder of Irish Great War veterans was no doubt due in part to the way in which the British government "prosecuted the War of Independence" (read Black and Tan and Auxiliary atrocities) (Dungan 1997, 41), but no reasoning can atone for the political killings that claimed the lives of quite a number of ex-servicemen, nationalist and unionist alike.

One writer who felt particularly displaced by postwar political realities was Lord Dunsany (1878–1957), an Irish peer who was "neither of old Celtic stock, Irish Catholic peasantry, or Protestant ascendancy-turned-Irish-nationalist. He was a loyal British subject who fought for the crown in Africa, France, and Dublin" (Hogan 1979, 217). In fact, Dunsany was wounded during the Easter Rising after returning home on leave from the front in order to "see how he might help quell the rebellion" (218).

When the war began, Dunsany, who had served with the Coldstream Guards and had seen action during the Boer war, was eager to reenlist (Amory 1972, 113). According to his biographer, Mark Amory, he was "unswervingly loyal to his King and Country, but also deeply attached to his home and lands around it [in County Meath] and fond of the local people" (116). He joined the Royal Inniskilling Fusiliers, the same regiment as Ledwidge, in September 1914 and was assigned the rank of captain (Joshi 1995, 183). After spending the first years of the war in Ireland and England training troops for the front, he was posted to France in January 1917 (Amory 1972, 133).

As a prolific producer of dramas and fantasies, Dunsany's large literary output contains little or no reference to Irish myth, history, or politics. During the war he helped edit and publish Ledwidge's verse but wrote little about the war himself. In fact, he rarely ever criticized "the stance of neutrality that many in Ireland adopted during World War I, and he never refers to the bungled German attempt to aid the Easter Rebellion" either (Joshi 1995, 183). Except for a collection of thirty-two short stories published in 1918 under the title *Tales of War,* he wrote only a handful of what could be called war poems. To label his *Tales of War* short stories may be too much of a generalization; anecdote, elegiac essay, pastoral evocation, or anti-German panegyric may be more appropriate. In one particular story, "The Road" (1918, 24), Dunsany imagines a dream-like allegory where he envisions a group of dead British soldiers building a road leading to some kind of celestial city where among the ranks of the victorious allied nations march the "ghosts of the working-party" (1918, 24). What makes this fantasy of more than passing interest is that it is an elegy for Ledwidge. Apparently Ledwidge "had written that year [1917] to say that he could no longer bear the army and Dunsany always regretted that he had not tried to find some way to get him out" (Amory 1972, 140). Perhaps "The Road" indirectly expresses Dunsany's sense of guilt at not acting sooner to campaign for Ledwidge's military release. At the story's end, one of the soldier ghosts tells the lance corporal (Ledwidge) in charge of the working party, "That is a fine road that we made, Frank!" (Dunsany 1918, 24).

This brief reference to his dead soldier-poet friend is as close as Dunsany comes to writing any kind of direct statement about personal loss during the war. After the war, he experienced a growing sense of political displacement and artistic isolation. In a letter written to Yeats in July 1924, Dunsany confessed that "my work counts as less in Ireland than the work of almost every Irishman who does any of the things I do" (Finneran, Harper, and Murphy 1977, 458). As for any poetic response to the Great War, with a couple of noteworthy exceptions, his first significant war poems do not appear until 1929 when he published *Fifty Poems.*

One of the two poems Dunsany published during the war was "Song from an Evil Wood" (1929, 11–13). The poem was written in France, probably in January 1917 shortly after he was posted there. In a letter home to his wife, Beatrice, he described the stars in the night sky during a barrage, noting that the "contrast" between the sky overhead and the "troubled and scarlet" color of the immediate horizon was "so amazing that it almost made the poem itself" (Amory 1972, 133). Dunsany's found poem was published shortly after in the *Saturday Review* in February 1917 and later reprinted in several wartime anthologies. Divided into two sections, it demonstrates Dunsany's predilection for "the exotic wonder of fantasy and fairy tales" (Hogan 1979, 219). We also see him take up his most common war theme of a world in anguish and turmoil (Littlefield 1959, 97–98). "Song from an Evil Wood" features a dark, foreboding forest where a mighty giant destroys the landscape and a demonic dwarf rages all through the long, cold night. Throughout this thinly-veiled allegory, the speaker marvels "most at the birds, / At their chirp and their quietude." But the serenity is short lived as phantasmagoric creatures terrorize the landscape:

> And the giant with his club,
>   And the dwarf with rage in his breath,
> And the elder giants from far,
>   They are all the children of Death.
>
> They are all abroad to-night
>   And are breaking the hills with their brood,
> And the birds are all asleep,
>   Even in Plugstreet Wood.

The Tolkienesque scene obviously allegorizes the destruction that Germany and her allies (the giants) unleashed on Europe, and all life ultimately falls silent in this inverse pastoral. The choice of a nightmare allegory typifies Dunsany's enduring fascination with creating "people, planets, and lands removed from ours in time and temperament" (Hogan 1979, 219). But nothing in his darkest imagination could have prepared him for what he saw on the Western Front.

The second poem Dunsany published during the war was "A Dirge of Victory" (Gardner 1964, 145–46) which first appeared in *The Times* on Armistice Day—11 November 1918. It apparently became a favorite piece for commemorative services as Dunsany read the poem on a couple of occasions for BBC radio on Remembrance Day during the early 1930s (Joshi and Schweitzer 1993, 144–45). The two-stanza poem anticipates Dunsany's subsequent efforts to preserve the memory of the war dead. Victory is hailed not for the edification of the living but for those who will never enjoy the peace:

> Lift not thy trumpet, Victory, to the sky,
>   Nor through battalions nor by batteries blow,
>   But over hollows full of old wire go,

> Where, among dregs of war, the long-dead lie
>   With wasted iron that the guns passed by
>   When they went eastward like a tide at flow;
> . . . .
>   It is not that we have deserved thy wreath.
> They waited there among the towering weeds . . .
> Hundreds of nights flamed by: the seasons passed.
> And thou hast come at last, at last!

Also interesting is how the description of these long dead soldiers trapped among the "towering weeds" serves as an appropriate metaphor for those Irish soldiers whom Dunsany felt were victims not only of the war but of the political expediency of postwar Irish nationalism.

Most of the poems that Dunsany wrote after the war were collected and published in *Fifty Poems*. Even though one critic dismissed the collection as "'pleasantly platitudinous,'" the critical consensus was that the poems were "pleasant" for a "minor poet" (Amory 1972, 214). The one issue that Dunsany takes up again and again in these poems is the gradual distortion of Ireland's war record. It was in response to this historical cleansing that he wrote "To the Fallen Soldiers" (1929, 16). While Armistice Day was still observed throughout the late 1920s and 1930s, especially at Trinity College, where there was "a universal wearing of poppies" (McDowell 1997, 204), wearing a poppy outside the confines of the college could be dangerous. Trinity College historian R. B. McDowell, who was an undergraduate at Trinity in the early 1930s, recalls one incident when he was accosted by a mob at College Green because he was "wearing a poppy" and, but for "the intervention of half a dozen burly Dublin women, wearing their husbands' war medals," he barely escaped being "badly battered" (204).

Unlike Gwynn, who adopts a more conciliatory tone toward those who tried to eradicate all public recognition of the war dead, in "To the Fallen Soldiers," Dunsany is much more accusatory:

> Since they have grudged you space in Merrion
>   Square,
> And any monument of stone or brass,
> And you yourselves are powerless, alas,
> And your countrymen seem not to care;
> Let then these words of mine drift down the air,
> Lest the world think that it has come to pass

> That all in Ireland treat as common grass
> The soil that wraps her heroes slumbering there.

Dunsany distances himself from the prevailing climate of political hostility toward Ireland's war dead, and in the second and last stanza, he expresses Gwynn's faith in a distant future when Irish war heroes will be given their due:

> The ages, that I prophesy, shall see
> Due honours paid to you by juster men,
> You standing foremost in our history.

With the face-lift given to the National War Memorial in Island-bridge and the dedication of the Peace Tower in Messines, the Irish war dead had to wait until the eve of a new millennium before significant steps were taken to remember them.

Elsewhere, Dunsany's fanciful imagination takes an unorthodox view of how the war continues to linger on in the contemporary memory. In "In the Silence" (1929, 49), he imagines what some of the other residents of a bustling city must make of the two minutes of silence on Remembrance Day:

> "Is it dead," said the pigeons, "the city that roared
>   about us?
>   For the silence puzzles and numbs.
> Will the fens come back, and the fields, and the wood-
>   land places?
>   Will there be no crumbs?"
> Two minutes passed, and the bowed heads stirred, and
>   the bugles
> Spoke and the drums.

Irony intrudes again as we remember the cause of this brief, tranquil interlude. Dunsany also suggests that if war is the price of progress, the memory of these silent "wood- / land places" recalls a simpler time—an innocent by-gone era made all the more attractive by pastoral retrospect.

The Great War was to continue to serve as a reference point for Dunsany's understanding of contemporary historical events. In 1941, during the most critical period of the Second World War when Britain stood virtually alone against the Axis powers, he published a volume simply called *War Poems*. What is especially interesting about this collection is how some of the poems draw on places and characters from the First World War to interpret the present conflict. Consequently, memory of the Great War functions as an evaluative filter through which all future experience must be processed. In one poem, "The Lesson" (1941, 46), military pride rallies contemporary resolve:

> In 1914 England opened school
>   To teach the Kaiser. Now it's Hitler's turn
> For the hard learning of the simple rule,
>   Which he must study while the nations mourn
> That this aggression only leads to Doorn.

Names synonymous with the Great War battlefields (then under Nazi control in occupied France and Belgium) also figure prominently in Dunsany's anti-German propaganda. In "A Dream of Cities" (1941, 100–102), he imagines the French army driving back the enemy "Over Marne and over Aisne / And back to again to Germany" and in "Between the Armies," "god-like shapes" stride by the "three sacred streams, / Somme, Bresle, and Aisne." This fixation with the geography of the Great War demonstrates the extent to which that earlier conflict continued to grip the imaginations of those who survived it. The war became part of a public mythography, its battlefields secular shrines invoked to cope with present adversity.

For those whose spiritual faith never survived the trenches, Dunsany's war poetry substitutes a Great War British elán to bolster waning racial confidences, but his belated war poems also elegize the passing ascendancy of his class, the Anglo-Irish, whose political clout significantly diminished in the advent of the new Free State.[2] Political change and a shift in demographics no doubt explain why interest and enthusiasm for commemorating Ireland's war dead dwindled, and Dunsany's postwar verse reflections record one observer's realization that Irish history was in the process of being rewritten and re-recorded.

For most Irish poets who were still writing about the war in the immediate years after the conflict, it was an experience that had to be romanticized or mythologized. Only one Irish poet seems to have largely avoided the temptation to politically subjectify the war according to the way he would like it to be remembered, and his name is Thomas MacGreevy. MacGreevy (1893–1967) was another ex-serviceman whose war poems were not published until well after the Armistice. In March 1916, he was "commissioned as second lieutenant in the Royal Field Artillery" (Knowlson 1996, 98) and later wounded twice during tours of duty on the Somme and in the Ypres Salient (Schreibman 1995b, 15–18). The few poems that address his war experiences were included in the only volume of poetry he ever published, a collection simply entitled *Poems* which appeared in 1934. It could be argued that all of MacGreevy's poems are essentially war poems for their fragmentary style typifies the prevailing sense of rootlessness and displacement that many returning soldiers experienced. But, as we shall see, what distinguishes his work from his Irish contemporaries is its modernist technique and implicit detachment from partisan ideologies.

MacGreevy was among a small group of Irish writers during the 1920s and 1930s who "turned against the romantic sentiment of the convention and the narrow puritanism of popular morality" (Loftus 1964, 18). Before we take a closer look at some of his war poetry, it would be useful to review his place in Irish poetry during the early years of the Free State. In the 1920s and early 1930s, he wrote criticism ("book, ballet and opera") for several English periodicals, taught at the École Normale Superièure, and established a lifelong friendship with Samuel Beckett whom MacGreevy met during his stint as lecteur d'Anglais in Paris (Schreibman 1991, xvi–xvii). He also wrote a couple of critical studies on T. S. Eliot and Richard Aldington, which were published in 1931. Even Yeats thought highly enough of MacGreevy's work to include two of his poems in his *Oxford Book of Modern Verse*. In 1950, MacGreevy assumed the directorship of the National Gallery of Ireland in Dublin where he spent the rest of his years before his death from heart failure in 1967 (Knowlson 1996, 99, 487).

Like Seán O'Faoláin, Frank O'Connor and other notable post-Treaty Irish writers, MacGreevy "reacted against the Romantic idealism of the Literary Revival, which seemed too intimate with the political wave which had broken on the rocks of civil war and republican failure" (T. Brown 1995, 37). If MacGreevy rejected the puerile idealism of the revivalists, as an Irish modernist looking to Europe for his artistic models he must have felt particularly isolated, for literary activity in the early years of the Free State was "increasingly stifled by the narrowly defined nationalism, social conservatism, and blinkered Catholicism that formed its ideological bedrock" (Fogarty 1995, 213). What distinguishes MacGreevy's war poetry, then, from most of his contemporaries is that he appeared to be one of the few Irish writers "around whom a largely ignored tradition of international modernism in Ireland had happened and had been waiting to be rediscovered" (Mays 1995, 107). Even a quick glance at his war poems reveals significant differences in content and form from the work of the other poets surveyed in this chapter. While they continued to work with the more native forms of ballad and lyric and depended heavily on myth, dialect, and landscape synonymous with the aesthetic standards of the revival, MacGreevy embraced modernism: a movement that involved "literary and artistic exile," valued a "cosmopolitan and metropolitan rather than national foci," and practiced "a highly self-conscious eclecticism and near-universality of cultural forms" (T. Brown 1995, 25). What distinguished writers like MacGreevy, Brian Coffey, Denis Devlin, and most notably Samuel Beckett was their eagerness "to develop Joycean techniques in their poetry" (Garratt 1986, 94). Similarities exist between MacGreevy's prose style and some of the techniques he incorporates in his poetry. For our purposes, the most relevant comparison is his penchant for "bold analogies and imaginative parallels," especially his intermedium comparisons between writing and painting (Knowlson 1996, 138). His critical essay on Richard Aldington links the English writer with the French painter Jean Lurçat "as adepts of *natures vivantes*" (138), and this sensitivity to both mediums surfaces especially in his war poem "De Civitate Hominum."

Apart from his lifelong passion for art, MacGreevy's poetry is also influenced by his war experiences. In the essay "Unpublished Poems of MacGreevy," Susan Schreibman sums up the role the Great War played in his development as a writer:

> It should also be borne in mind that MacGreevy's first impulse to write (and I would venture to add many subsequent ones) was a direct result of the First World War: that many of his poems mirrored the essential irrationality of war, and that no matter how heartfelt any attempts to recapture that idyllic past which preceded the war . . . [they] must, by necessity, end in failure. (1995a, 140)

This overwhelming despair dominates a short commemorative piece entitled "Nocturne" (1991, 1), written for a fellow soldier whom MacGreevy met at a training academy in London prior to embarkation for France in 1917 (Schreibman 1991, 97). Geoffrey England Taylor was killed in action in September 1918, and MacGreevy learned of his friend's death only after spotting Taylor's name in the casualty list in one of the daily papers while he himself was recovering from a shoulder wound (97–98). "Nocturne" was first published in *The Irish Statesman* in September 1929 under the title "Nocturne, Saint Eloi, 1929"; the reference to

Saint Eloi was apparently taken from the name of monastic ruins near the village of Mont St. Eloi and a British military cemetery is situated not far from there (98). For Susan Schreibman, the poem "captures the sense of hopelessness and Godlessness that must have plagued, however fleetingly, so many men who fought with an unprecedented spirit of self-sacrifice in the Great War" (1995b, 18):

> I labour in a barren place,
> Alone, self-conscious, frightened, blundering;
> Far away, stars wheeling in space,
> About my feet, earth voices whispering.

As some critics note, the use of the lyric "I" together with the end rhymes indicate that MacGreevy had not turned his back completely on traditional rhetorical and stylistic modes. Also, the presence of a despoiled landscape and the second line's catalogue of war-induced isolation, fear, and ineptitude typify our most common pictorial perceptions about the hazards of life at the front. However, like the more popular features of early modern poetry, the poem's language is stripped to its semantic essentials: "There is little ornament" (Mays 1995, 119). In terms of time and space, the poem breaks free from linear or chronological time; only the present exists. The narrative locale established at the beginning of the poem gives way to a consciousness of infinitesimal time and space in the third line; it is as though the war makes all temporal and spatial notations irrelevant. The speaker's self-deprecatory tone suggests an awareness not only of his own mortality but of the incomprehensible dimensions of "space." At the end, he hears "earth voices whispering" and is sobered by this reminder of mankind's fleeting existence in contrast to the eternity of those cosmic constellations that shine overhead. It has also been noted that the poem's exclamatory despair ("I labour in a barren place") describes MacGreevy's sense of artistic isolation in an Irish culture stifled by the "official anathematizing of everything from jazz to modern fiction, and the symbolic institution of the much-reviled Censorship Board in 1929" (R. Foster 1988, 535). Yet like Eliot in "The Waste Land," MacGreevy makes use of the most powerful images of the Great War to describe the psychological disintegration and decay of a dying civilization.

The poem's title widens the thematic scope of the poem beyond personal loss. A number of MacGreevy's poems are nocturnes, "recreating [in a sense] the world in darkened stillness" (Mays 1995, 121), but in terms of the war, such stillnesses are deceptive, signifying as they often do the end of consciousness. The poem's conclusion with its description of barely audible "earth voices" also indicates a heightened sensitivity as though the trauma of the war refines perception and crystallizes for a moment the individual's sense of place and identity within the vast reaches of a timeless cosmos. This moment of clarity suggests MacGreevy's "devotion to an epiphanic moment in the midst of a fallen universe," a notion that "had, of course, another sponsor in Joyce, whose rejection of all narrowing national traditions inspired MacGreevy" (Kiberd 1995, 462).

In terms of its more obvious genuflections to the modernist mode, MacGreevy's most enduring war poem "De Civitate Hominum" (1991, 2–3) reveals a work "which runs well beyond an outraged Georgianism and whose fragmentary method was far more adequate to the dislocations it reported" (Kiberd 1995, 461). Written between May and July 1927, the poem recounts the death of a British airman who MacGreevy saw shot down a few days after his own arrival in the Ypres Salient in December 1917 (Schreibman 1991, 98–99). Altogether, the poem is the first major experimental war poem written by a modern Irish writer as MacGreevy employs free verse, jolting transitions, connotative intensities, multiple-meaning word play, intermedium reference, montage, and strategic pause. Thematically, the sense of futility that accompanies the passive description, the uncertainty of what is recorded, and the poet's honesty in accepting that some things cannot be understood make the poem a significant departure from the more traditional, prescriptive responses to the war that we have seen so far.

In "MacGreevy as Modernist?" J. C. C. Mays plots the general movements of the poem: "A situation is there, is described as given; an event takes place, which is horrible; but the real action in the mind of the speaker is an interior drama [which] . . . reaches an unresolved stasis" (1995, 115–16). What is initially described is the untainted silence and daybreak dazzle of early light:

> The morning sky glitters
> Winter blue.
> The earth is snow-white,
> With the gleam snow-white answers to sunlight, . . .

But as the sun slowly illuminates the landscape, the scene becomes more ominous:

> Save where shell-holes are new,
> Black spots in the whiteness
>
> A Matisse ensemble.

These lines reveal one of the poem's organizational patterns: "Throughout the early stanzas of the poem he [MacGreevy] alternates between describing the scene and then stepping back to analyse it in painterly terms" (Schreibman 1991, xxiii). These descriptions also focus on the natural beauty and color of the landscape, but when we are taken in for a closer look, the scene's beauty is quickly spoiled by a more sinister reality:

> The shadows of whitened tree stumps
> Are another white.
>
> And there are white bones.

Just as the speaker sees the natural wonder of the scene tarnished by the inescapable presence of the war, any attempt to locate the visually agreeable is quickly sobered by fatalistic resignation:

> Zillebeke Lake and Hooge,
> Ice gray, gleam differently,
>
> Like the silver shoes of the model
>
> The model is our world,
> Our bitch of a world.
> Those who live between wars may not know
> But we who die between peaces
> Whether we die or not.

Again a brief pleasing image is transformed into a moment of despair. This "model"—"Our bitch of a world"—recalls Pound's "old bitch gone in the teeth, / For a botched civilization" in *Hugh Selwyn Mauberley*. Yet while these images confirm the total breakdown of European civilization, they also capture the soldier's sense of futility and anticipation of oblivion.

MacGreevy's penchant for jolting transitions is also much in evidence when the narrative voice suddenly shifts to the first person singular, and the distance of objective description is briefly elided:

It is very cold
And, what with my sensations
And my spick and span subaltern's uniform,
I might be the famous brass monkey,
The *nature morte* accessory.

Again, MacGreevy reveals an eye for the discordant. The speaker's earlier notations of the war's sickening despoliation of the natural scene are complimented by his innate sense of incongruity. A resident of the front lines, he is preened and pomaded like a fastidious martinet, all "spick and span." He concludes this self-portrait with a reference to another artistic medium. We have already seen his painterly eye for detail and color in his descriptions; now the artist becomes part of his own painting. In her annotated notes to the poem, Susan Schreibman points out that a "nature morte accessory" refers to "still life (nature morte) painting" where "an accessory is any object or figure not belonging to the principal subject of the picture, but added solely to furnish background" (1991, 100). This deprecatory self-profile is typical of the modernist's view of contemporary man as a spiritless adjunct, Prufrock's attendant lord, Auden's "Unknown Citizen." MacGreevy's subsequent pun diagnoses modern man's disjointed existence as a symptom of the war:

Morte . . . !
'Tis still life that lives,
Not quick life—

Then the objectifying, descriptive voice returns to the narrative. When the speaker realizes that he "is as useful to the scene dead as alive, he retreats into descriptions which simulate the soft edges of an impressionist painting" (Schreibman 1991, xxiii):

There are fleece-white flowers of death
That unfold themselves prettily
About an airman
Who, high over Gheluvelt,
Is taking a morning look around,
All silk and silver
Up in the blue.

The occasion that inspired the poem—the death of the British airman—is now brought into focus. While the description of the aerial barrage that follows the careening airplane "defamiliarizes the horror" (xxiii), the scene resembles a grotesque sexual

courtship as these "flowers of death . . . unfold themselves prettily." Even the airman's actions are described innocuously as
though he were out for a Sunday joy ride, "taking a morning look
around." But the high-flying romance is quickly shattered by the
sickening quiver of a struck target:

> I hear the drone of an engine
> And soft pounding puffs in the air
> As the fleece-white flowers unfold.
>
> I cannot tell which flower he has accepted
> But suddenly there is a tremor,
> A zigzag of lines against the blue
> And he streams down
> Into the white,
> A delicate flame,
> A stroke of orange in the morning's dress.

The consummation of this aerial courtship and the catalogue of
color create a collage of pigments that form the pattern of "the
morning's dress." The violence of the spectacle is portrayed in bitterly ironic shades. MacGreevy's dissonant metaphor ("flower"/
shell bursts) and the reiterated terms of landscape brushwork
("zigzag of lines," "delicate," "stroke") intensify the surreal quality of the scene and heighten the irony of a human life taken in
a beautiful fireball.

In the final lines, the poem's latent theme emerges:

> My sergeant says, very low, "Holy God!
> 'Tis a fearful death."
>
> Holy God makes no reply
> Yet.

J. C. C. Mays notes that the sergeant's glib response illustrates
man's "inability to respond to it [death] adequately" (1995, 116).
He goes on to argue that the speaker's counter-response is "too-
pat" with the "witty line break giving away his callowness" (116).
If, as Mays argues, the entire description of the scene demonstrates the "inability of art to transcend nature" (116), the poem's
conclusion also presents a range of human responses. The sergeant can only mumble an oath (an ironic one at that given
his own proximity to "fearful death") after what he sees. The
speaker, meanwhile, adopts a self-arrogating posture. His remark, while critical of God's silence, remains uncommitted in

its agnosticism ("no reply / Yet") but points toward man's egotistical expectation that everything can ultimately be explained. If art cannot transcend nature, rational thought or spiritual belief appear equally inadequate in explaining our atavistic instincts. Perhaps MacGreevy's poem reveals the inadequacies of simplifying structures like reason and faith, and as such, echoes the general "assault of war on religious belief" (Jenkins 1994, 151).

As a war poem, "De Civitate Hominum" responds to the "sense of fragmentation" that the war produced, and it is "written with a full consciousness of the pressures of history" (Armstrong 1995, 55). The poem's multiplicity of reference, compressed images, and sequential gaps certainly stamp it as a modernist text. Even the title, meaning "of the City of Men," is richly suggestive: it is taken from St. Augustine's *The City Of God* where he contrasts man's ungodliness in the "City of Men" with the virtue of the "City of God" (Schreibman 1991, 99). Obviously, the horrors of the Western Front mark another depraved episode in man's corrupt self-government.

Clearly the Great War had a major impact on MacGreevy's poetry, and it was to continue to provide him with images and ideas that would intensify his critique of Ireland's cultural and political insularity. One example of how Great War iconography recurs in his work is in his long poem "Crón Tráth na nDéithe" (1991, 14–20) begun in 1925 (Schreibman 1991, xxvi). In the course of a meandering odyssey through the Dublin streets (à la Bloomsday), the speaker passes the wreckage of buildings destroyed during Easter Week 1916. The sight of these hulking ruins recalls memories of the Great War:

> Wrecks wetly mouldering under rain,
> Everywhere.
> Remember Belgium!

Historical ironies collide as MacGreevy alludes to the destruction of two conflicts. Irishmen had been urged to enlist in the British army to protect the interests of small nations, yet the Easter insurgents who rose to protect the rights of their own small nation were punished in draconian fashion. Seeing the destroyed Dublin landscape with its resemblance to the front may have spurred MacGreevy to recall his own "naivety in believing that the Great War would guarantee the sovereignty of small nations" (Schreibman 1991, 112).

The critical consensus is that "Crón Tráth na nDéithe" or "Twilight of the Gods" (Schreibman 1991, 109) is ultimately a critique of life in the post-Treaty Free State. While MacGreevy's unflattering portrait of Dublin seethes with reminders of the historical conflicts that dominated Irish history between 1916 and 1923, especially interesting is his fascination with Ireland's ambiguous social and cultural identity. MacGreevy is one of the first Irish poets to make use of distinct images and icons from the Great War to illustrate the ongoing tensions in an Irish state searching for self-definition yet uncomfortable with certain strands of its narrative past. Everywhere the speaker goes, he sees reminders that "Britannia indeed is not gone." Ireland's colonial past (and role in the Great War) frustrates any attempt to construct a self-sustaining post-Treaty Irish hegemony. Dublin's darkness evokes images of a "green great-coat / And wet lamplit shade" (memories of prepartition Dublin) that complicate the speaker's attempt to remember that he, too, served Ireland as one of those "soldiers of the queen" (Ireland's queen, Kathleen ni Houlihan, that is). The poem's first section concludes with the enigmatic question: "But how long till your swagger-stick blossoms?" Irish self-definition, it seems, can only grow out of the preexisting hierarchies of the past. The "swagger-stick"—synonymous with British military authority—serves as a convenient symbol for Ireland's colonial past. Like Yeats, for MacGreevy, memory of the Great War becomes highly politicized and apparently representative of an adversarial British mindset. As this thinly veiled sniping at British colonial rule in Ireland implies, MacGreevy, despite his past service in the British army, became increasingly hostile toward Ireland's former colonizer, so much so that by the late 1920s, "he had become vehemently anti-British" (Knowlson 1996, 99).

MacGreevy's work confirms the general critical consensus that the Great War was to provide a ready-to-hand iconography with which to describe the contemporary decline of western civilization. Of all the poets still writing about the war during the 1920s and early 1930s, his work reveals a consciousness of styles and themes that began to emerge on the international scene. Yet while some regard him as "a seminal influence in Modern Irish poetry" (Smith 1975, 159), reception to his work has not always been favorable as his poetry has been criticized for its "pale impressions of Eliot and Pound" and dismissed as both "bloodless and stolen" (Ramsay 1996, 33). Furthermore, the recent attention given to MacGreevy's work has been described pejoratively as some kind of political quest for the "spiritual forebears of much southern Irish poetry" (33). These criticisms seem more concerned with present-day disputes about the shaping and re-shaping of the Irish canon, the settling of old scores and the defending of ideological turf in the ongoing anthology wars. At times, MacGreevy's work is excessively self-conscious in its al-lusiveness as some poems do come across as earnest imitations in the modernist mode. But his slim output reveals an aware-ness and interest in European poetry that later more accom-plished poets like Seamus Heaney were to also embrace (Osip Mandelstam, Czeslaw Milosz and Marin Sorescu are particu-lar favorites) as they sidestepped the limitations of native in-sularity. If traditional techniques were traded in for continental ones, if modernism was to replace "antiquarianism" (Beckett's term for revival poetry), as Declan Kiberd points out, the work of Irish modernists like MacGreevy demonstrates that they "never stopped being consciously Irish" (Catterson 1996, 32). Like other poets who wrote about Ireland's Great War legacy, MacGreevy found himself inextricably caught up in the political fallout of a failed colonial experiment, and Ireland's role in the Great War was a reminder of his cultural and political interdependence.

War poetry published by Irish poets during the years between both world wars is marked by the absence of a coherent and unified statement about the First World War. Instead, despite this "complex web of interacting and conflictive tendencies which failed to present possibilities for a homogeneous narrative" (Wes-tendorp 1991, 140), some Irish poets still appropriated war mem-ory for political expediency. Complete detachment appears to have been impossible: even a modernist like MacGreevy was drawn to interpreting the war in terms of Irish history despite international modernism's "view that politics are a threat to the artistic integrity of the artist" (140). As Irish memory of the war became more politically charged, its imagery and vocabulary pro-vided modern Irish writers with a range of archetypes, symbols, and metaphors that continue to function as interpretative signs in Ireland's ongoing political and cultural wars.

6

Modern Memory

Perched on a hill just off the A21 between the Northern Irish towns of Bangor and Newtownards sits the Somme Heritage Centre. It is a rather imperious-looking pale brown block structure, military-like in design, sturdy, resilient, implacable. Resembling a large pillbox, it occupies the high ground like a strategically situated enclosure, and, from a distance, even its long, narrow windows look like ready-made embrasures for gun emplacements. The Gradgrindian exterior seems appropriate, though, given that the Somme Heritage Centre is a curatorial fortress guarding artifacts from a war that wavers on the frontier of time and memory.

Visitors to the center can walk around the exhibition hall or listen to presentations in the lecture theater. For those who prefer their history three-dimensional, there is even a guided tour of a mock-up display of the front lines, complete with the sights and sounds of the battlefront, though the purist will take umbrage at the neatly reconstructed trenches whose antiseptic theatricality inevitably filter out the history and the horror.

But the Somme Heritage Centre is more than just a museum or a repository for war memorabilia. There is more going on than historical preservation, commemoration, or re-creation. In its attractive brochure, the center's mission statement resolves to remember the "sacrifices and achievements" of "Protestant and Catholic, Unionist and Nationalist [who] fought alongside each other in a common cause" (1996). The brochure also makes it clear that the center aims to provide "a basis for the two traditions in Northern Ireland to come together to learn of their common heritage." This attempt to avoid sectarian or political partisanship is certainly a welcome departure from the imperialist ceremonies that still dominate public expressions of Northern Irish war memory. With its trendy interactive audiovisual displays, the Somme Heritage Centre is still part tourist attraction,

224

part historical reclamation. And even though, like the myths it hopes to replace, the center offers up an ideologically processed version of Irish history, it still aims to transcend the totemic memories of tribalism and deliver what Edna Longley has described as an "agreed version of the past" (1994, 150).

Of course such potted histories, with their genuflections toward the secular creed of the politically correct, run the risk of producing an inoffensive yet inaccurate narrative of the past where uncomfortable truths lie buried behind an agreeable pastiche of period color and contemporary political altruism. Heritage centers like the Somme Heritage Centre can be of great service as long they chart the past rather than simply deliver palatable platitudes that offend no one. Value-free readings of Irish history, while they encourage a spirit of tolerance and mutual understanding, can also divert us from grappling with issues of contention so that the root causes of dissension are never tackled in the open glare of debate and dissent. The heritage center industry, while it seeks to inform and not offend, sometimes produces a version of Ireland's past that filters out the less agreeable aspects of the tribal conflict, as though the chief aim of Irish historical recovery is to altruistically locate for both traditions a "mystic point where parallel lines might meet" (E. Longley 1994, 150). Reconstructing an Irish history we can all agree on is all very well, but what we do not need is a Nóh-like drama where all sides don masks of studied acquiescence and artificially induced posturings become de rigeur. Producing an inclusive narrative of the Great War that can negotiate its way around the entrapping cataracts of unionist triumphalism and nationalist amnesia may be a tall order on a partitioned island. Yet the Somme Heritage Centre reminds us of a time in Irish history when the two traditions did share, for the most part, a common purpose. Again, the ongoing peace process has renewed efforts to find common ground between warring nationalist and unionist ideologies, and recent Irish literature is awash with conciliatory dialogues designed to promote new ways of seeing the past.

Yet with the notable exception of Michael Longley (who by my last count has written somewhere in the region of twenty-five poems about the Great War), contemporary Irish poets have written very little about the Great War. This neglect is especially puzzling when we consider the pervasiveness of Ireland's past in Irish poetry over the last quarter century or so. Reading through collections like John Montague's *The Rough Field* (1972), Seamus Heaney's *Field Work* (1979), Eavan Boland's *Outside History* (1990), and Medbh McGuckian's *Shelmalier* (1998), to name a few, is like watching the poet blur the distinctions between poetry and historical forensics work. Yet for all this fascination with the political and personal tragedies of the Irish question, the most catastrophic event in terms of lives lost in twentieth-century Irish history remains largely ignored. Why? In the essay "The Great War in Irish Memory," Tjebbe Westendorp asserts that Irish poets' failure "to do justice to all the complexities of the Great War" is because they have failed to locate "the right metaphors to express the wider dimensions of either the Great War or the present Troubles" (1991, 141–42). One wonders what Westendorp considers are the "right metaphors" as contemporary Irish poets are often chided for being too circumspect in their treatment of the Troubles. Seamus Heaney has spoken about his "search for images and symbols adequate to our predicament" (1980b, 56), and certainly his bog poems draw historical parallels between the sacrificial victims of Iron Age fertility rites and the murdered innocents of Northern Ireland's sectarian conflict. Others like Paul Muldoon, with his dizzyingly allusive exercises in multireferentiality, and Medb McGuckian, with her transhistorical links between the past and contemporary Irish politics (see her treatment of the 1798 rebellion in her volume *Shelmalier*), address the ongoing local dispute via indirect cultural reference and historical deflection. For Westendorp, though, perhaps these soundings of the Troubles are too oblique. In their defense, what metaphors could be "appropriate" for Irish poets as they respond to the tribal brawl in their backyard? No, perhaps Clair Wills is closer to the mark when she writes that while some Irish poets still "fall back on a mythic or symbolic model of representation as the means to speak for the community," others find such "poetic strategies" simply "inadequate to contemporary circumstances in Ireland" (1993, 239). As we have seen already, the Great War and the Easter Rising have become tribal totems for warring unionists and nationalists, so much so that when Irish poets try to negotiate the tribal minefield that is Irish politics, they run the risk of tribal complicity. Grand metaphors offer tidy parallels and little else. Those Irish poets who have responded to the Troubles and the Great War with the most sensitivity recognize that if the past is to be understood at all, it must be tackled at ground zero, in the emotional corridors of family and place.

By focusing their personalized lenses on Irish war memory, modern Irish poets for the most part successfully sidestep the kind of sectarian cant and populist myths featured in some of the earlier war verse. This does not mean that more subtle forms of postpartition political propaganda do not lurk beneath the surface of their work, though. While some poets challenge received wisdom about the war and Ireland's role in it, others provide politicized readings that prop up their respective ideological sermonics. The primary motive, though, for writing about the First World War still remains a private one, in spite of the fact that any statement about the war, however personal, never completely transcends the public event (the war) that necessitates its utterance. For Tjebbe Westendorp, personal memories of the war often trigger debates about "complex, comprehensive, or universal issues" while the example of the Great War poets' dedication to their art in times of violence provides inspiration for many Irish poets who feel caught up in a similar predicament (1991, 130–31). It would appear then that the intimate exercise of retrieving family memories of the Great War cannot be separated from the backdrop of regional and international disputes. The infiltration of submerged political ideologies even in the most highly personalized accounts of Irish war memory demonstrates the unnerving contiguity of private and public identity in a culture where most social habits are tribally translatable.

No doubt the most raw and deeply anguished memories of the war are those of its soldier survivors. For Welsh poet David Jones, the war was a parenthetical experience, a savage and unforgettable episode demarcated from pre- and postwar history. Yet this description seems too commodious, as if the war was only a horrible interpolation or aberration in the lives of those who survived it. On the contrary, for many veterans, the war never ended, and their subsequent attempts to scrabble for a life among its emotional debris is a recurring theme in contemporary Irish war verse.

Quite a number of Irish poets have explored the war's long reach into the lives of its survivors. In Derry-born Robert Greacen's war poetry, we see old soldiers' attempts at social repatriation meet with varying degrees of failure. In two poems in particular, "Oranges" and "Hun," taken from Greacen's *Collected Poems 1944–1994*, the voice of a schoolboy narrator—presumably Greacen himself—highlights the gulf between those who fought and those who did not. In both poems, the naïve narrator reports details and half-truths with little or no note of empathy.

In "Oranges" (1995, 133), we see the war continue to haunt "old sweat Dan McArthur" who could not measure up to the Horatian ideal:

> His mind spewed out dollops of the Great War—
> Dawn raids, mud, rats, heroics.
> In a bayonet charge he had gutted a Hun,
> Was angry still that Boche blood soiled
> His smart uniform, ruined his puttees.

Predictably, McArthur's claims are too good to be true. Appearances deceive. The schoolboy speaker reveals that one day this "lovely man" attacked his wife

> With a butcher's knife, that the police
> Had handcuffed him and what's more
> He had sobbed, told them he had deserted,
> Lived for years with a false discharge.

Burdened by the need to construct a heroic narrative to compensate for his war guilt, McArthur's life is a litany of falsehoods. His guilt is compounded by postwar society's obsession with hero worship where simply to have survived is not enough. We see this emphasis on the myth of individual honor especially in the "military effigies of Ulster war memorials [that] are notably ferocious embodiments of exultant aggression" (Waterman 1992, 24). Those who find themselves unable to measure up to this Sergeant York heroic code end up trapped between myth and truth. For men like McArthur, the war's psychical repercussions never end.

The postwar experiences of another one of Greacen's veterans also demonstrate how the war continues to shape personal and communal perceptions. In "Hun" (1995, 164–65), the schoolboy narrator provides the interpretative commentary once again, but this time, in contrast to McArthur who tried to conceal his inglorious past, a feared school teacher—the "Head of Maths"—is actually rumored to have been one of the enemy:

> The grapevine reckoned him a Hun.
> Kipling and others glossed the word:
> Our lads crucified, babies spiked
> On bayonets by vampire Aryans
> Drunk on the wine of innocents.

Suspected of the worst war crimes, the teacher's culpability is made all the more likely for he had "Beckerman as suspect name." The concluding revelatory formula of "Oranges" is repeated as we discover

> . . . that Beckerman
> Had fought for Country and for King,
> Been wounded twice in World War I.

Perhaps Beckerman was one of Greacen's "masters" at Methody, the Belfast high school where he was educated (Greacen 1995, 14), but the poem demonstrates the power of racial stereotype and the unreliability of equating public signs with historical accuracy. In both poems Greacen explores how old soldiers rarely shake off the residue of their past as their personal identities are appropriated by the war and its defining images. Even if the war ceases to rage in their heads, they are perceived as figures on an urn, trapped in the past and constantly processed by their own and others' self-sustaining historical myths about the war.

As Greacen's war poetry illustrates, observing the effects of the war on its survivors often reveals more about the observer than the survivor. In Seamus Heaney's poem "Veteran's Dream" (1980a, 130), the speaker describes an old neighbor, "Mr Dickson," as a living reliquary

> Who saw the last cavalry charge
> Of the war and got the first gas
> Walks with a limp.

The old soldier's painful daily reminders of the war contrast with the speaker's emotiveless commentary, as though he were thumbing through a lost uncle's old scrap book. Then in the following lines, the war's lingering physical immediacy in the lives of those who survived it is underlined by gaps in memory that make the war's living wounds all the more incomprehensible. Inevitably, recollection of the experience slowly recedes into the mists of senility:

> Into his helmet and khaki.
> He notices indifferently
> The gas has yellowed his buttons
> And near his head
>
> Horses plant their shods.
> His real fear is gangrene.

As the poem ends, the speaker notes the "cankered ground" where Mr. Dickson lies and the "scatter of maggots, busy / In the trench of his wound." With his memory gone, the war survives in this literal and metaphorical cicatrix. What the speaker only vaguely comprehends is that the war is not some distant historical event, for it still possesses the lives of those who fought, rendering them prisoners of its psychic geography.

Yet coping with the ongoing psychic trauma of the war is made all the more personal and debilitating for those poets who lost family members during the war or who witnessed the effect of postwar trauma on their loved ones. One of the unassailable truths about any war is that those who do the actual fighting are not the only casualties. War trauma observes no cease-fire or respects any boundaries of pain. While for some poets, family memories of the war often reveal the extent of the war's impact on future generations, childhood recollection of the war intensifies other feelings of insecurity and political and cultural disorientation. Perhaps the most recurring concern of contemporary Irish poetry about the war is the struggle of the soldiers' families to cope with their loved ones' psychological trauma. In the course of coping say with a father or an uncle's emotional and physical disabilities, poets often are forced to confront war memories that contradict the more acceptable narratives of public glory, honor, and sacrifice.

In Ulster poet Frank Ormsby's work, we encounter characters whose lives continue to be defined by the distant past. In "McConnell's Birthday" (1986, 5), taken from Ormsby's second collection *A Northern Spring*, the middle-aged speaker's petty servility as the caretaker at the "the manor farm" is mitigated only by his sense of family and place. One of the reasons why McConnell's buried life consists of compromised dreams and troubled relationships is presumably his sense of emotional disinheritance. Losing his father when he himself was entering manhood, McConnell appears to be living a twilight existence, stumbling through life devoid of emotion and direction:

> My father died among the Guinchy brickstacks
> in the First World War, before I was seventeen.
> Daily I stopped to read his weathered name
> on the dull statue in the village square
> until I forgot him.
>
> I worked the manor farm, my children grew
> in a green place at the foot of the Major's trees.

The year that Bridie left they filled my days,
riding the tractor to the stable yard.
We were closer when she returned.

Convinced that the war is the source of his present problems, McConnell lives a posthumous existence, still unconsciously trying to cope with the legacy of a missing father. As a belated casualty of the war, his life consists of meaningless routines:

I've no urge to watch how the world goes,
or cry for the century and its latest war.
At forty-four I'm fed up with the first light
to feed the Major's pheasants.
I close his gates at night.

Haunted by the loss of his father in the Great War, the irony that that war was the war to "end all wars," and the paralysis of middle-age introspection, McConnell discovers a small, private consolation: a way to make something of a "diminished thing":

Today there are shouts on the road, McCusker's boy
going home from the creamery, Donnelly taking his
   time
on a creaky bike. Slyly he stops to roar:
"We're not getting any younger."
In this part of the world they know it's my birthday.

In this rural backwater, McConnell clings to a sense of a shared place and the daily reminders that quiet lives have their own vitality. If the war heightened a global sense of vulnerability and increased the need for a defense mechanism against obsolescence and confusion, Ormsby's brief character study celebrates the local as opposed to the crowding anonymity and overwhelming complexity of the outside world. McConnell recognizes one of life's paradoxes—that happiness can be found even in deprivation.

Coping with the psychological trauma of the war is made all the more personal and debilitating for those poets whose relatives died in the war or who survived the carnage yet continued to suffer the effect of postcombat anxiety. In a 1995 interview, Michael Longley explained why the war continues to feature prominently in his work:

My father's own experiences, which he recounted vividly on only
a couple of occasions, have allowed me to participate in the com-

munity's glum pride. My mother's mentally retarded brother disappeared in the trenches—and from family conversation. His vanishing
act haunted my childhood much more than the vast catastrophe ever
did. (M. Longley 1995b, 558)

Indeed, in a number of his war poems (many of which appear in
Poems 1963–1983 and *Selected Poems*) Longley's exploration of
family war casualties is as much an exercise in self-exploration
as it is an attempt to understand the war. Part of this self-
exploration involves locating one's place in the family history—
a difficult task when, as in Longley's case, certain parts of the
family narrative get excised or, in time, confused and distorted.

In "Master of Ceremonies" (1987, 133), Longley recalls the
fate of the aforementioned uncle who, because he had "molested"
Longley's mother, "was thrown out of the house" and, according
to family memory, "was last heard of following the stretcher
parties across No Man's Land with a sack into which he was
putting bits and pieces of soldiers" (1994, 20):

> My grandfather . . .
> Had thrown out his only son, my sad retarded uncle
> Who, good for nothing except sleepwalking to the Great War,
> Was not once entrusted with a rifle, bayonet but instead
> Went over the top slowly behind the stretcher parties
> And, as park attendant where all hell had broken loose,
> Collected littered limbs until his sack was heavy.

According to Brian McIlroy, the grisly details of this last line,
especially the fascination with body parts, form a "kind of imagery that is predominant in Longley's work," namely a fetish
for parts that McIlroy argues reflect the poet's "partial loyalties"
with regard to his ethnic and political identity (1990, 60–61). But
perhaps the "retarded" uncle's insane attempt to clean up the
battlefield can also be read as an unconscious act of exculpatory
penance for past sins; his subsequent omission from the family history, however, indicates how the war becomes not only a
repository for unsavory family memories but how it also provides
opportunities to revisit the ghosts of one's past. In the final four
lines, Longley acknowledges that despite the attempt to remove
all memory of his uncle, the memories still persist:

> In old age my grandfather demoted his flesh and blood
> And over the cribbage board ("Fifteen two, fifteen four,
> One for his nob") would call me Lionel. "Sorry. My mistake.
> That was my nephew. His head got blown off in No Man's Land."

Like the forgotten uncle banished to the "No Man's Land" of the family history, Longley's identity appears momentarily ambiguous given his grandfather's unreliable memory, and his confusion over his relationship with his son ("nephew") also illustrates how the more unpleasant parts of our heritage can be altered to meet the needs of an agreeable narrative. The flippant tone of the last line signifies how sometimes emotional pain can only be handled from an extremely detached perspective. For Longley, these memories of shame and annulled identity demonstrate the necessity of confronting the truths of one's past, however unpalatable.

In a number of other poems, Longley reads his "father's 'personal history' as a means of comprehending the death and nightmare of the Great War" (E. Longley 1994, 156). In "In Memoriam" (1987, 48–49), the poet resolves to "read" his father "like a book" in order to "Let yours / And other heartbreaks play into my hands." In the subsequent stanzas, Longley relives his father's war experiences: his mistaken enlistment with the London-Scottish and his charging into battle "wearing an unwarranted kilt" (M. Longley 1994, 18). But the obsession with identity forms the poem's chief thematic concern. Once, after a German attack, his father returned to his dugout to discover "that he had been shot through his scrotum, [and] that the top of his penis had been severed" (19). After his father's mutilation, the poet imagines his own prenatal death:

> That instant I, your most unlikely son,
> In No Man's Land was surely left for dead,
> Blotted out from your far horizon.
> As your voice now is locked inside my head,
> I yet was secure, waiting my turn.

And as Longley notes, he and his sibling "owe their existence to skilled medical orderlies" (19). In this case, war memory actually strengthens the son's sense of identity as he is reminded of the fragility of life and the links between father and son as creators and curators of memory.

Later in the poem, the poet recalls how his father's "old wounds woke / As cancer." And

> Death was a visitor who hung about,
> Strewing the house with pills and bandages,
> Till he chose to put your spirit out.

Cognizant of his father's recurring bouts of pain and depression, the poet chooses to end his elegy "on a healing and amatory note as the women Longley's father went with in France are conjured up by the poet to occlude some of the harshness of death" (Peacock 1988, 63). The final indignities of death with the waiting ambulance and the "lingering in the hall" are set aside, as the poet celebrates his father's affirmations of love and peace:

> I summon girls who packed at last and went
> Underground with you. Their souls again on hire,
> Now those lost wives as recreated brides
> Take shape before me, materialise.
> On the verge of light and happy legend
> They lift their skirts like blinds across your eyes.

By calling from the grave his father's "experimental lovers," Longley celebrates his own life, one that was given the chance to be conceived. The point of these historical analyses is ultimately to repossess the past and its tragic consequences in order to extract familial significance from the Great War's overpowering and incomprehensible scale of suffering. By focusing on his father's memory, Longley intensifies our capacity for empathy so that the sheer scale of the tragedy does not numb us into apathy.

Despite the attempt to reinhabit the past in order to comprehend one's own relationship to it, sometimes the incommunicable horror of the war preserves an unbridgeable gap between the old soldier and his family. In "Last Requests" (1987, 150), for example, Longley crosscuts between scenes from the front and the present (a favored technique) in order to establish emotional ties between father and son. The image of his father coming up for a "long remembered drag" of a cigarette after surviving an explosion shifts to a present-day hospital ward as the dying old soldier motions for a

> . . . Woodbine, the last request
> Of many soldiers in your company,
> The brand you chose to smoke for forty years
> Thoughtfully, each one like a sacrament.

The final effect is one of distance and disengagement. The poet confuses his father's waving of his "bony fingers . . . to and fro" for a "kiss" and cannot share in the old soldier's battlefield ritual. The last two lines confirm this generational and experiential gap as the son realizes the distance between them: "I who brought peppermints and grapes only / Couldn't reach you through the oxygen tent." Instead of providing opportunities to establish a link to the past, the war preserves the psychological gap between those who fought and those who did not. Ultimately the poem fails to locate a salve for the heartbroken "but instead point[s] up the inadequacy of traditional elegiac resources" (Brearton 2000, 260). The war's memory defines the pain of present agony in terms of noncommunication and the inevitable loneliness of the survivors.

Memories of his father's war service constantly surface and resurface in Longley's work. In some cases, the stress of the present rouses memories of the past where emotional links between different modes of experience actually preserve memory. In "The Kilt" (1995, 35), the son recalls one of his father's dreams where he chased "a tubby little German who couldn't run fast enough" and who "turned around to face . . . [him] and burst into tears" (1994, 18). Such memories are grist for the poet's imagination as the pain of the past is evoked to describe present nightmares:

> I waken you out of your nightmare as I wakened
> My father when he was stabbing a tubby German
> Who pleaded and wriggled in the back bedroom.
>
> He had killed him in real life and in real life had killed
> Lice by sliding along the pleats a sizzling bayonet
> So that his kilt unravelled when he was advancing.

In other poems from Longley's collection *The Ghost Orchid*, even the annual memorial services and pilgrimages to the battlefields resurrect old family ghosts. In "A Pat of Butter" (1995a, 36), Longley still sees his long dead father keep step with all the other "doddery English veterans": "My dad's ghost rummages for his medals / And joins them for tea after the march-past." Sometimes the burden of memory also conditions the imagination to view everything in antithesis. In "Behind a Cloud" (1995a, 36), Longley's father's stewardship over a living reliquary at the front is ironically contrasted to the poet's veneration of a scene of natural beauty:

> I
> When my father stumbled over gassy corpses
> And challenged the shadow of himself on duck boards,
> A field of turnips had filled with German helmets
> And under his feet eyes were looking at the moon.

II
When I heard the storm petrel that walks on tiptoe
Over the waves, pattering the surface, purring
And hiccupping, the moon had gone behind a cloud
And changed the sea into a field full of haycocks.

But it is ultimately Longley's desire to piece together his family's past that lies behind his frequent treatment of the war, and again it is his "father [who] focuses questions of belonging rather than longing" (E. Longley 1994, 156).

In the poem "The Third Light" (1987, 200), Longley again exhumes his father's memory, only this time he reunites the old soldier with his bride as the poet-son rekindles a romantic passion smothered by familiarity and private withdrawal:

> The sexton is opening up the grave,
> Lining with mossy cushions and couch grass
> This shaft of light, entrance to the earth
> Where I kneel to remarry you again. . . .

In this case, the war provides a common ground to cross connect the young lovers' separate fields of experiences; consequently, the front serves as a metaphorical landscape for the emotional offensives and counteroffensives between the poet's parents. In *Tuppenny Stung*, Longley's short collection of "Autobiographical Chapters," he describes his parents' sometimes strained relationship, contrasting his father's "passivity" with his mother's moodiness (1994, 20). Near the end of the poem, the poet imagines his mother "Waiting to scramble hand in hand with him [his father] / Out of the shell hole," and the war becomes an unlikely place for emotional mediation as the poet imaginatively assembles the disparate fragments of his own past in order to set things right once again.

This desire to relive the past in order to reconnect tenuous relationships and secure a direct line of contact with one's familial origins also figures prominently in "Second Sight" (1987, 151). The poet "imagines a disorienting visit to London during which the speaker asks: 'Where is my father's house, where my father?'" (E. Longley 1994, 156). But besides this search for his father, the poet reveals a desire to establish contact with relatives whom he never knew, namely his paternal grandmother whose gift of "second sight" elides time and geography:

> My father's mother had the second sight.
> Flanders began at the kitchen window—

> The mangle rusting in No Man's Land, gas
> Turning the antimacassars yellow
> When it blew the wrong way from the salient.

It is his grandmother's miraculous vision that serves as a spiritual gateway through which the poet reunites his family. He and his father connect like still shots in his grandmother's visions. She sees her son "going over the top" "carrying flowers out of the smoke" like a Lawrentian penitent bearing "Bavarian Gentians" to light up the underworld, and, in turn, her grandson imagines her seeing "through" him "and the hallway / And the miles of cloud and sky to Ireland." Her special gift serves as a conduit through which the poet relives a real and imagined past where identities might cohere and the exiles of different generations once again return "home."

For Longley the past opens up new vistas of understanding. He recognizes how the immediate and distant victims of the war cannot shake off their physical and psychological scars with the result that the war serves as a kind of heritage center of the mind where past identities, narrative gaps, and repressed memories are explored and reevaluated. Longley has said as much about his own family:

> I missed out on the usual familial hinterland of aunts and uncles and cousins. Perhaps I am now trying to compensate. Outside of the immediate family circle, my relatives are a crowd of ghosts. I'm interested in ghosts. Genetically each one of us is a ghost story. (M. Longley 1995b, 561)

But it is the ghost of his father who continues to haunt the poet's imagination. In "January 12, 1996," one of several elegies first collected in the chapbook *Broken Dishes* (1998) and later included in *The Weather in Japan* (2000), Longley reveals just how immediate the past is in his life as he commemorates the centenary of his father's birth by reaching out across the No Man's Land of time and space (2000, 25):

> He would have been a hundred today, my father,
> So I write to him in the trenches and describe
> How he lifts with tongs from the brazier an ember
> And in its glow reads my words and sets them aside.

The poem suggests "a hollowness somewhere inside the man sustained forever after the war, and a loss shared by the poet" (Tinley 1999, 18). But again it is the war that is the imaginative meeting place where fathers and sons reunite and where fathers can be fathers and sons can be sons again and be loved.

Longley's concerns are shared by other Irish poets who recognize how the past has shaped their identity. Memories of dead relatives provide a field of vision where one's place in the family and community can be charted by analyzing past actions through contrast. We see how the past serves as a recognition scene In "Uncle Jack" (Simmons 1986, 107–8), a poem taken from *Poems, 1956–1986* by Derry-born James Simmons, where the poet recounts the memory of a shell-shocked veteran who on returning "To Derry, to the old homestead . . . brought war with him in his head."[1] Traumatized by his war experiences, his farm becomes an extension of the front where "every turning of the lane / hid snipers. Any sudden sound flicked him face-down on the ground." When death comes, it is a release:

> My mother's glad the Asian Flu
> killed him. "He was so much like you,"
> she often tells me. Jack and I,
> bookish, intelligent and shy.

For the poet, the remote bond of kinship with a long "dead uncle" is superseded by a sense of debt. What he owes is what his uncle never had:

> I have this feeling that I owe
> something that you will never know
> to you, Jack—*my* life lived with care.
> I'm older than you ever were.

(Often by being reminded of what others have lost we learn to cherish what we have.)

A different message is drawn from John Hewitt's memory of his uncle in "The Volunteer" (1991, 267) where his reminiscence features a customary antithetical framework juxtaposing prewar domesticity and innocence with the inevitable oblivion of the trenches.[2] The poet recalls "an artist, [who] by compulsion made / his living at the lithographic trade." With his "tilted boater and his swagger cane," the uncle fits the classic Edwardian/Georgian profile of all those idealistic and chivalrous young men whose obituaries filled the daily newspapers during the war. In the end, his compulsive nature proves his undoing:

> Months after war broke out he wrote to say
> he had enlisted by deliberate choice,

> not waiting for conscription, lest his boys
> might think of that with shame some future day.
> I still recall my father's countenance
> that day we learned he had been killed in France.

Why does Hewitt still recall the memory of someone he hardly knew? Is it reckless vanity that led his uncle to enlist? Or the romantic gesture and dash for glory? Memory of the pained look on his father's face reveals the extent of the tragedy. It is only later that the poet grasps the gravity of the news from France and the unfulfilled years of absence that that early death entailed.

While some of these family war poems tackle contemporary dilemmas within the extended historical framework of the war, and thus search for the particular within the universal, their chief value appears to be one of instruction. Debts are acknowledged, personal ghosts exorcised, the past sorted through for direction. For Irish poets, family memories of the war resemble runic tablets that require deciphering. It is as if the war continues to demand our attention, telling us, like Heaney's Chorus in *The Cure at Troy* that

> I have opened the closed road
> Between the living and the dead
> To make the right road clear to you.
> (1990, 78)

We have seen how memory of the Great War transmits messages from the past to the present, but its soldier poets also fascinate Irish poets to the extent that a common purpose and experience is engendered. Perhaps the most important strand of kinship that links these writers from different generations is shared grievances in times of violence, a connection made all the more palpable by the sense of a lost innocence. Apart from living in violent times, perhaps the major concern for both groups of writers is the role of the poet during political upheaval. How should one proceed? What is the purpose of poetry in a time when all other civilized values are threatened? Another point of intersection is how echoes of the earlier war verse also crop up in recent Irish war poetry as biographical parallels and favored figurative devices create a familial as well as artistic bond. In fact, it is the soldier poets themselves who are quite often the subject of modern Irish war poetry.

Tjebbe Westendorp notes that "contemporary poets, living in the age of the Troubles and faced with the same predicament of

being an artist in the midst of violence, have a very special relationship to these predecessors" (1991, 131). James Simmons's
"Death of a Poet in Battle-dress" (1969, 47) imagines a dying
soldier poet who communicates his (and all poets') fear of death
and literary oblivion. The poem's epigraph—"I shall forget in
Nineteen-twenty, / *You* ever hurt a bit!"—is taken from a poem
Rupert Brooke wrote in early 1910 called "The One Before the
Last" in which a young man's nostalgic reflections about a past
lover give way to a new-found cynicism about the transitory nature of youthful emotional attachment (Brooke 1916, 65). The
flippant reference to 1920 comes across as particularly ironic considering Brooke's subsequent death in 1915. Simmons's poem,
though, features a brief dialogue between the speaker and the
dying poet whose death bears striking similarities to Brooke's
own premature death from blood poisoning just prior to the disastrous Gallipoli campaign:

> His body was broken. Blood still pushing round,
> Fulfilled no function, spilled out on the ground.
> He prayed, "Oh Jesus, please let me fulfil
> My early promise, if it be Thy will."
> And I embarrassed, said, "What can he do?
> Christ may be understood not spoken to."

Poetry and faith offer little protection from the shells, and the
soldier poet's faith in the divine is countered by a more sardonic
voice that appears less deceived about the exclusivity of artistic
expectation and equally aware that in the tragedy of war, all men
are culpable:

> He said, "To me war's crazy, it was the others
> Brought me here."
>   I said, "All men are brothers."

Simmons reminds us that poets and poetry are just as com-
bustible as everything else. The poem concludes on an even more
despairing note as the soldier poet recognizes the naked truth of
his death:

> " . . . Now I'm dying,
> My good mind never used, and all you see
> Is a soldier in a uniform, not me.
> Help me unbutton this. . . ." and then he tried
> To strip himself. Half dressed for war he died.

Dying before he can reclaim his individuality, the soldier poet's death recalls the names of other poets whose voices were silenced by the Great War: names like Thomas, Sorley, Owen, Rosenberg, and Ledwidge. In some ways this poem challenges the notion that good war poetry equals good politics. The soldier poet's self concern only raises false hopes and intensifies despair. And Simmons suggests that even when poetry has a vatic role to play, that role is usually prescribed.

But honesty has its price, too. In another of Simmons's poems, "Remembrance Day" (1968, 5), a poet who was once "the conscience of this nation" laments years later how his poems' topicality has doomed them as period pieces:

> Now I'm dream-marching at some cenotaph
> Which is my poems; some wounded veterans start
> To break ranks, piss on it and me and laugh,
> While others walk away and break my heart.

The writer's abortive attempt to rework his "old poems" suggests that responding to immediate tragedy has its risks, too. Even more sobering is that time defuses the importance and urgency of topical poetry. Dismissed as an ideologue and played-out versifier, the poet discovers that his work is as static as a monument.

With Michael Longley, his memory of the soldier poets seems more preoccupied with their status as historical victims and Arcadian innocents. In "The War Poets" (1987, 168), the "purpose is not so much pointed historical analysis and comparison as a broadly compassionate view of the tragic consequences of conflict" (Peacock 1988, 62):

> Unmarked were the bodies of the soldier-poets
> For shrapnel opened up again the fontanel
> Like a hailstone melting towards deep water
> At the bottom of a well, or a mosquito
> Balancing its tiny shadow above the lip.

The second stanza portrays the soldier poets forever fixed in our memory, frozen between expectation and fulfillment:

> It was rushes of air that took the breath away
> As though curtains were drawn suddenly aside
> And darkness streamed into the dormitory
> Where everybody talked about the war ending
> And always it would be the last week of the war.

Symbolizing an optimism that did not survive the war, what we cherish most about the soldier poets is their innocence before horror; for them, the end of the war is always imminent.

Another Longley poem that explores the poet's sense of kinship with the war poets is "The War Graves" (2000, 22–23), a powerful elegy where Longley vaults spatial and temporal gaps to explore psychological interiors.[3] In the poem, the speaker tours places that saw some of the worst fighting on the Western Front and stops every so often at some of the war cemeteries where soldiers and soldier poets lie buried side by side. Instead of the customary inventory of dates and battles, Longley portrays the scarred landscape as a living tapestry of personal commemoration where individual outpourings of grief are registered amid the loftier platitudes and rhetoric of the official markers and monuments. The poet intermingles a naturalist's notes about the local wildflowers and ornamentals that beautify the landscape with the untold stories of the war dead as he intuitively reconstructs imagined pieces of their narrative that never make the official histories:

> The headstones wipe out the horizon like a blizzard
> And we can see no farther than the day they died,
> As though all of them died together on the same day
> And the war was that single momentous explosion.
>
> Mothers and widows pruned these roses yesterday,
> It seems, planted sweet william and mowed the lawn
> After consultations with the dead, heads meeting
> Over this year's seed catalogues and packets of seeds.

Anyone who has visited the military cemeteries on the Western Front will recognize the poignancy of Longley's descriptions here. In an attempt to transcend the awfulness of the place's history, the war graves are lovingly maintained as a floral tribute. Only the border plantings on each grave, with their small herbaceous perennials and floribunda roses, provide relief from the row on row of imperious masonry.

Stopping periodically at various sites along the front, the speaker elegizes the war dead, rescuing them from the grand sweep of history:

> At the Canadian front line permanent sandbags
> And duckboards admit us to the underworld, and then
> With the beavers we surface for long enough to hear

The huge lamentations of the wounded caribou.
Old pals in the visitors' book at Railway Hollow
Have scribbled "The severest spot. The lads did well"
"We came to remember", and the woodpigeons too
Call from the wood and all the way from Accrington.

While the boundaries of some of these war cemeteries are often
marked out by low flint walls, those maintained by the Commonwealth War Graves Commission usually feature a visitor's book
stored in a small bronze register in an alcove in an arched en-
tryway. The speaker's guided tour of such commemorative simulacra borders on a religious experience as though he were a
penitent touring the stations of the cross. As in some of his other
poems, Longley's by-now trademark list accomplishes more by
indirect inference:

I don't know how Rifleman Parfitt, Corporal Vance,
Private Costello of the Duke of Wellingtons,
Driver Chapman, Topping, Atkinson, Duckworth,
Dorrell, Wood come to be written in my diary.

In an essay on Longley's affinity for lists, John Lyon points out
how they function as an "act of reclamation and consecration,"
imposing as they do an elegiac "order" (1996 236, 239). Lyon also
notes that Longley's passion for lists honors "a debt to Edward
Thomas, a fellow keeper of country diaries and notebooks" (243).
Similarities in technique between contemporary Irish poets and
the soldier poets of the First World War are especially evident
in Longley and Thomas's poetry. Thomas's poem "If I were to
Own" provides a good example of the sort of cataloguing of rural
place names and flora found frequently in Longley's recent work.
Yet the poet-venerator cannot recall why he has written these
names in his "diary." This is no heroic catalogue. Confronted by
the sheer numbers of the dead, perhaps the only way the poet
can retrieve some sense of each dead soldier's individuality is to
record his name, to affirm his humanity amid the overwhelming
magnitude of the war's slaughter.

It is only in the poem's last three stanzas, with their references to Charles Sorley, Edward Thomas, and Wilfred Owen,
that we see the poet renew his dialogue with the war poets. In
a way, these stanzas not only serve as memorial headstones for
the dead soldier poets, but also as mnemonic devices as Longley
links surrounding images and impressions of the war memorials
with the war poets. The result is that these images, which accu-

mulate throughout the poem's inner architecture, gather round like symbolic wreaths, ironically juxtaposed alongside familiar pastoral standbys, natural wonders and oblique references to the war poets' own poems:

> For as high as we can reach we touch-read the names
> Of the disappeared, and shut our eyes and listen to
> Finches' chitters and a blackbird's apprehensive cry
> Accompanying Charles Sorley's monumental sonnet.
>
> We describe the comet at Edward Thomas's grave
> And, because he was a fisherman, that headlong
> Motionless deflection looks like a fisherman's fly,
> Two or three white after-feathers overlapping.
>
> Geese on sentry duty, lambs, a clattering freight train
> And a village graveyard encompass Wilfred Owen's
> Allotment, and there we pick from a nettle bed
> One celandine each, the flower that outwits winter.

Each stanza draws connections between the speaker's field of vision and the war poets. For Sorley, the youngest of the major soldier poets to lose his life in the Great War, Longley emotionally cross connects their shared grief at the scale of the war's carnage. A "blackbird's apprehensive cry" echoes Sorley's poem "Rooks," with their "cawing all the day," while the allusion to the "monumental sonnet" recalls that haunting first line to Sorley's best-known poem, "When you see millions of the mouthless dead." Like Sorley before him, Longley's poems not only speak for the dead, but they also remind us of the personal stories behind the soldiers' uniforms (a sensibility found throughout Longley's poetry where the innocent victims of Northern Ireland's Troubles, like the greengrocer and the ice-cream man, are also movingly elegized).

At the grave of another soldier poet, Longley describes one of his fondest images of Edward Thomas, the fisherman poet casting a fly rod, by detecting similarities between a glowing comet's trajectory and the "fisherman's fly" with its "overlapping" feathers. (A subtle irony here is the reference to white feathers that women handed out during the war to men not in uniform to symbolize their supposed cowardice.) Then we arrive at a "village graveyard" where Wilfred Owen lies buried.[4] Not far off, the noise of a passing "freight train" faintly recalls another train, one which Owen himself wondered to which front it was bound in his bluntly ironic poem, "The Send Off." Then, as with many of Longley's poems, we are left with a final image that is both symbolic and curatorial. Celandines growing among a "nettle bed" testify to beauty's tentative yet persistent grip among the crowding weeds of historical neglect. The celandine is also a poppy. With its bright yellow flowers, it is not the easily recognizable scarlet poppy that has become the defining commemorative icon of the Great War. Instead of the traditional poppy with its evocations of sacrifice and loss, Longley's celandine poppy signifies survival. The celandine has long been associated with the swallow, so much so that the plant only flowers when swallows return in the spring, its colors fading when the birds begin their winter migration: hence "the flower that outwits winter."[5]

Longley's richly imaginative elegy for the war dead and the soldier poets concludes with this memorable image of life where to survive is victory enough. Faced with the appalling scale of the war, the elegy celebrates life in a way the Great War poets would have appreciated: through a faith in the cathartic powers of the pastoral.

Longley also seems drawn to the war poets' determination to maintain private fidelity to their art in spite of their surroundings. As we have seen, Edward Thomas remains a personal favorite (Longley edited Thomas' *Selected Poems*), and in "Edward Thomas's War Diary" (Longley 1987, 134), the war poet is pictured ensconced in the trenches dreaming of home:

> One night in the trenches
> You dreamed you were at home
> And couldn't stay to tea,
> Then woke where shell holes
> Filled with bloodstained water,
>
> Where empty beer bottles
> Littered the barbed wire—still
> Wondering why there sang
> No thrushes in all that
> Hazel, ash and dogwood,
>
> Your eye in what remained—
> Light spangling through a hole
> In the cathedral wall
> And the little conical
> Summer house among trees.

Pastoral retrospective enables Thomas to "interpret his world in the trenches in his own way" (Westendorp 1991, 137). With the "sods" of his dugout decorated with "Green feathers of Yarrow," his poetic sensibility remains connected to nature. Not even the war can annul his aesthetic instincts. And yet Longley's ironic counterpoint between a natural English Eden and a foreign wasteland ("barbed wire") reminds us of the fate of those restorative pastoral continuities of fellowship, faith and solitude (the tea, the cathedral wall, the summer house) as Thomas's war diary records an antedeluvial and disappearing England.

Besides being symbols of a bygone innocence, the war poets' spiritual disembodiment and personal tragedies provide Longley with an interpretative key with which to read his own family's past. In "No Man's Land" (1987, 199), he resuscitates the ghost of Isaac Rosenberg in an attempt to reimagine lost memories of his own ancestry. Ethnic and biographical parallels collide as he compares his "Jewish granny" (Jessica Braham disappeared from family history after her premature death at twenty) to Rosenberg whose body was "not recovered either" (Westendorp 1991, 137):

> I tilt her head towards you, Isaac Rosenberg,
> But can you pick out that echo of splintering glass
> From under the bombardment, and in No Man's Land
> What is there to talk about but difficult poems?
>
> Because your body was not recovered either
> I try to read the constellations of brass buttons,
> Identity discs that catch the light a little.
> A shell-shocked carrier pigeon flaps behind the lines.

In trying to retrieve the lost narrative of his own past as well as Rosenberg's, Longley's abortive attempt to read the dead soldier's personal effects for clues suggests the "difficulty of carrying messages from the past to the present, and the impossibility of reading the signs of history both in time of war and peace" (137). The image of the "shell-shocked carrier pigeon" seems a fitting image for the confusing messages and gaps in all our pasts.

Looking back to the soldier poets of the Great War as literary precursors has also provided some contemporary Irish poets with a field of reference with which to respond to the ongoing "war" in their own backyard. Indeed, excavating contemporary Irish war poems for their overt and oblique commentaries on contemporary Irish politics provides a wealth of interpretative possibilities. The most overt form of appropriation of the Great War has been its adoption as a framework drama through which to explore the ongoing complexities of the Irish situation. The final objective of this chapter, then, will be to take a look at how two Irish poets' treatment of the war reveals submerged unionist and nationalist ideologies.

In their sometimes overt and sometimes oblique interrogation of Irish history, Seamus Heaney and Michael Longley "search for adequate words and symbols to express the human cost of [the Irish] conflict" (Peacock 1988, 62). In reference to how his poetry has tried to respond to the violence in Northern Ireland, Longley has admitted that he continues to be "dumbfounded by the awfulness of our situation" (M. Longley 1995b, 560). He has also been forthright about the consequence of any poems he has written about the victims of the Troubles: "I have written a few inadequate elegies out of my bewilderment and despair. I offer them as wreaths. That is all" (560). But Longley's typical modesty here should not conceal the fact that when he does write poems that tackle the recent violence in Northern Ireland, he does so with a gravity and sensitivity that go beyond registering the platitudes of ritual grief. In fact, despite his dismissive attitude about his efforts to confront his community's terrible tragedies, his poems reveal a range of sympathies and understandings that cut across the customary political geographies. It is Longley's father's experiences during the First World War that provide him with the resource from where he can explore some of the historical sources of Northern Ireland's recent sectarian disturbances.

With all the talk nowadays about cultural and political identities, much has been written about the Ulster Protestant's so-called identity crisis. Rejecting the either/or fallacy (Irish or British), quite a number of Protestants instead settle for the regional/archipelagic construct of Ulster-British. Of course, assigning a label to a place where rival groups remain in political and cultural contention quickly becomes an exercise in semantics, and in Northern Ireland, political, ethnic, or sectarian labels are rarely homogeneous. Longley is one poet whose work reveals how "shaky the concept" of "identity" in poetry really is (McDonald 1992, 81). His elegies for his father not only reveal disturbing parallels between past and present violence but also how the past can be "processed by state ideologies" (E. Longley 1994, 69).

In reference to perhaps Longley's most memorable war poem, "Wounds" (1987, 86), Peter McDonald claims that when Longley addresses the Troubles in his poetry, "the only perspectives he will allow himself are domestic ones" (1992, 77). To support this observation, McDonald cites a passage from the poem where a bus-conductor is murdered in his own house by a young boy. McDonald's reading of the poem distinguishes between the "domestic" violence of the Troubles and the grand carnage of a foreign war—the Great War. However, as we shall see, Longley's poem draws ironic parallels between both theaters of conflict in order to explore how the Great War and the current hostilities in Northern Ireland share many of the same tensions despite the gaps in time and geography. As Longley disinters the psychological scar tissue of ethnic and family wounds, he not only explores the conflicting loyalties of Ulster Protestants who fought during the Great War but how these self-divisions still impact Northern Ireland today.

Given Longley's ongoing interrogation of the myths of Ulster Protestant war memory and the war's calamitous effect on that community, it is difficult to accept James Liddy's argument that the work of practically all of the so-called poets of "the Ulster majority" (read Protestant) lacks "a sense of calamity through race" or a "[c]loseness to catastrophe" (1978, 127). By claiming that these qualities only animate the poetry of "most Northern Irish of the minority" (read Catholic) (127), Liddy fails to grasp the importance of the Great War in Ulster Protestant folk memory. Reading through Longley's (a so-called poet of the "majority") poem "Wounds" quickly dispels the notion that it is only Catholic poets whose work is edged with a sense of the catastrophic. The poem itself consists of two stanzas: the first one describes memories of the poet's father—a survivor of the Ulster Division's suicidal charge on 1 July 1916:

> Here are two pictures from my father's head—
> I have kept them like secrets until now:
> First, the Ulster Division at the Somme
> Going over the top with "Fuck the Pope!"
> "No Surrender": a boy about to die,
> Screaming "Give 'em one for the Shankill!"
> "Wilder than Gurkhas" were my father's words
> Of admiration and bewilderment.

By now, the price paid for such heroics (the Ulster Division incurred 5,500 casualties on the first day of the Somme) has become engraved in Ulster memory (Bardon 1992, 455). But Longley's recollection of his father's war memory reveals other tensions. We are given "two pictures" from his "father's head" that Longley has kept "like secrets until now." A couple of questions go begging here: why has the poet repressed these memories and why the need to reveal them now? Perhaps the "secrets" themselves provide clues. The battle cries screamed during the terror of the attack reveal an interesting gallimaufry of antipapist ("Fuck the Pope!"), proloyalist ("No Surrender!"), and autarkic ("Give 'em one for the Shankill!") sentiments, but they also imply a hierarchical sense of values that appear absurdly misplaced amid the larger Armageddon of the Somme.

The sectarian nature of the first slogan, a basic feature of loyalist ideology, can be traced to a Protestant fear that the Irish Catholic church is "in such a position of entrenched power" that it is "able to dictate policy to the State on matters which the church considers essential to the maintenance of its position" (Whyte 1990, 151). Of course the Catholic conservatism of the early successive Free State governments did little to allay this fear. But unionist ideology also thrives on tribal triumphalism, which the annual marching season seems to encourage, by glorifying past military victories. The cry of "No Surrender" aptly describes the nature of unionist siege mentality with its commemorative genuflections to the defiance of the Apprentice Boys of Londonderry who boldly closed the gates of their city rather than capitulate to the besieging forces of James II during the Williamite war of 1690. Naturally, for Ulster loyalists, "No Surrender" has become synonymous with "The basic themes of the siege myth—defiance, solidarity, sacrifice, deliverance" (McBride 1997, 12). The third epithet hurled at the German enemy—"Give 'em one for the Shankill"—signifies a parochial and sectarian identity as the Shankill is the predominantly Protestant enclave in largely Catholic West Belfast.

What Longley's recollection of his father's war memories illustrates is how Ulster Protestant identity is often defined by its response to a nationalist culture that appears exclusively Catholic and antipartitionist. Another tension emerges when we compare Longley's father's memories of the war with his last words as he lies dying, still haunted by the "lead traces":

> At last, a belated casualty,
> He said—lead traces flaring till they hurt—
> "I am dying for King and Country, slowly."
> I touched his hand, his thin head I touched.

Longley's father was originally from London and did not settle permanently in Belfast until 1927 (M. Longley 1994, 16), but tensions emerge between his recollection of the Ulster Division's sectarian slogans on the Somme and his own deathbed attempts to make sense of the terrible sacrifices by describing them as purely patriotic acts rendered gladly for "King and Country." The sectarian nature of his first recollection of the battle and the imperial allegiances the old soldier utters on his deathbed dramatize Ulster Protestantism's shifting loyalties. In the past, Ulster Protestant loyalty to the British monarchy has been implicitly conditional: as long as the monarch is Protestant, Ulster will be loyal. In fact, there always has been the notion that Ulster is not "bound by the 'will of the British parliament'" (Miller 1978, 2–3). As we have seen, many Ulster Protestants enlisted to fight in the Great War because of the implicit understanding that after the war their efforts would be rewarded by the shelving of the Home Rule Bill. Longley's father's deathbed effusions arguably represent the old soldier's attempt to convince himself that Ulster's war effort was motivated by a larger sense of British patriotism. It would appear, though, that there were other more regional imperatives that sent over 2,500 Ulstermen to kingdom come in a matter of hours on the first day of the Somme offensive.

Perhaps the possibility that the Ulster Volunteer Force, which made up the nucleus of the Thirty-sixth division, might have taken up arms against its own government had Home Rule become a reality is one of the two "secrets" with which men like Longley's father have had to grapple; the Great War removed the ironic likelihood that Ulster unionists would have to wage war against their own government in order to remain part of a union that Home Rule threatened to dissolve. Consequently, the old soldier's acknowledgement of his comrades' ambiguous allegiances suggests that many Ulster "Protestants [continue to remain] more uncertain about their national identity than Catholics" (Whyte 1990, 245). While most Ulster Catholics describe themselves as "Irish," Protestants have been more inclined to "tack between the labels 'British,' 'Ulster,' and even 'Irish'" (245).

Clearly the sacrifice on the Somme has become part of Protestant/unionist mythology. However, another of the poem's subsurface narrative tensions calls into question how this attempt to mold an ethnic identity has evolved. Longley's objective description of the past and present violence exposes ironies that remind us how violence, telescoped through historical perspective and subjectivity, can be mythicized as part of the oral narrative of the tribe. The dates 1690 ("No Surrender") and 1916 serve as cultural referents to consolidate tribal solidarity, and Longley's blunt description of the war dead and the three recent victims of the Troubles raises questions about the whole fabric of an identity whose defining moments are characterized by tribal tub-thumping and bloodshed.

Memories of the battlefield then give way in the second stanza to an imaginative conceit where the poet buries his father along-side recent victims of the Troubles:

> Next comes the London-Scottish padre
> Resettling kilts with his swagger-stick,
> With a stylish backhand and a prayer.
> Over a landscape of dead buttocks
> My father followed him for fifty years.
> . . . .
> Three teenage soldiers, bellies full of
> Bullets and Irish beer, their flies undone.
> A packet of Woodbines I throw in,
> A lucifer, the Sacred Heart of Jesus
> Paralysed as heavy guns put out
> The night/light in a nursery for ever;
> Also a bus-conductor's uniform—
> He collapsed beside carpet-slippers
> Without a murmur, shot through the head
> By a shivering boy who wandered in
> Before they could turn the television down
> Or tidy away the supper dishes.

The poem's comparisons between the past and present violence challenge the sanctification of blood sacrifice. First of all, the soldiers' deaths are deromanticized: a "London-Scottish padre," with an absurd sense of propriety given the carnage of the bat-tlefield, steps through the "landscape of dead buttocks," reset-tling kilts with his "swagger-stick," while the recent victims of the Troubles—the "three teenage soldiers"—are discovered with their "bellies full of / Bullets and Irish beer" and "their flies un-done." These lines imply that while the past can be cosmetically altered (the padre's settling of the kilts), present atrocities have to be confronted. Longley reminds us of our moral obligation to recognize the truth about violence and how past horrors can be sanitized to support tribal ideology.

Eventually even the cultural icons the poet mourner casts into the figurative grave reflect the sectarian tensions that color Ulster's Great War experience and how it is commemorated. The "Woodbines" and "lucifer,"[6] basic staples of the British Tommy's few creature comforts at the front, are conflated with a distinctly Catholic icon, a picture of the "Sacred Heart of Jesus." These incongruous items suggest that those being interred share one unenviable common denominator: they are all "victims of Irish history" (Roulston 1983, 110).

By examining his father's memory of the war, Longley reveals how the violence in Northern Ireland "originates in a conflict [over] national identities" (T. Brown 1975, 206). He also implies that his father's shell shock may function as a paradigm for an entire community's cultural disorientation, a likelihood that Longley forecasts could have serious political implications:

> Terrified of Irishness—the cultural ideology of the Free State and then of the Republic—Unionists have clung to what after 1968 has increasingly become known as "the Mainland," and to cultural importation. Those who depend on imports run the risk of themselves being exports. (1995a, 74)

There is also the issue of how the past can be mythologized to serve a collective will: like the Easter Rebellion, the Great War's commemoration has been shaped by "sectarian idioms" (E. Longley 1994, 69). A good example of this mythologizing would be the legend that grew up around the Ulster Division's fateful attack on that July morning in 1916. The story goes that many of the troops marched into battle remembering that the date—July 1— was the same date as the Battle of the Boyne in 1690. Years later, one Ulster veteran recalled, "I don't know why they plaster such incidents on our battle. Nothing was further from my mind than the Boyne on the Somme" (Orr 1987, 218).

Just as Longley's antiwar statements conceal other political discourses that locate the particular (the Irish situation) in the universal (the Great War), Seamus Heaney's treatment of the war also indicates that quite often the best way to approach the potentially incendiary nature of local cultural and political tensions is to locate them within a larger drama. In Heaney's most impressive war poem "In Memoriam Francis Ledwidge" (1979, 59–60), the war provides a framework drama through which to examine political and cultural conflicts, in particular, the antagonism between a nationalist/"Celtic /Catholic *mythos*" and an intrusive Anglo presence (Parker 1993, 175). While Steven Matthews argues that Heaney undermines "Ledwidge's pious, nostalgic conflation of religion with nationalism" (1997, 8), Heaney's response to the war is also clouded by the pull of tribal constraints.

Heaney's elegy for Ledwidge—the Irish soldier-bard—laments the loss of a promising poet, but the poem's first five stanzas contain no reference to Ledwidge himself. Instead, Heaney begins by describing, from childhood memory, the war memorial in the small seaside town of Portstewart. In the poem's next six stanzas, he imaginatively crosscuts between pastoral scenes from his Aunt Mary's childhood and Ledwidge's Boyne Valley youth to the trenches in the Dardenelles and Flanders:

> It's summer, nineteen-fifteen. I see the girl
> My aunt was then, herding on the long acre.
> Behind a low bush in the Dardenelles
> You suck stones to make your dry mouth water.

Then the elegy's final two stanzas address the purported irony of Ledwidge (an Irish Catholic) serving in a British uniform while his fellow Irishmen fought for their country's independence during Easter Week, 1916:

> In you, our dead enigma, all the strains
> Criss-cross in useless equilibrium
> And as the wind tunes through this vigilant bronze
> I hear again the sure confusing drum
> You followed from Boyne water to the Balkans
> But miss the twilit note your flute should sound.
> You were not keyed or pitched like these true-blue ones
> Though all of you consort now underground.

As stated earlier, there has been a long tradition of Irish Catholics serving in the British army, so Heaney's assumption that Ledwidge remains an "enigma" shows either a lack of historical consciousness on his part, or it implies another political bias: that Irish Catholic service in the British army was and is ideologically unsound. As a consequence, Heaney's language reveals historical and cultural references endemic to Irish nationalist ideology. Submerged narrative tensions emerge when Ledwidge's pastoral Gaelic "ethos" is threatened by the intrusion of the Great War (Parker 1993, 176). Heaney's elegy, then, subscribes to a fairly narrow definition of Irish ethnicity, for we see Ledwidge's "Celtic/Catholic" pastoralism favorably contrasted to a non-Celtic presence which threatens the "native" order. Judging by the way Heaney's poem associates Irishness with landscape and Catholicity, we see further evidence of his love affair with romantic nationalism. The poem's construction of a counter-narrative featuring Ledwidge as tribal representative of an indigenous bardic tribe is sustained as binary images accumulate.

Stanza seven contains several of these "Celtic/Catholic" cultural referents: the "hill-top raths" associated with Ledwidge's prewar experiences recall Ireland's megalithic past, before the arrival of the Norman and Saxon invaders, and the connection between these ancient enclosures and Ledwidge, the bard, reinforces the idea of his membership in a Celtic tribal hegemony. Other images associated with Ledwidge's youth, like the "May altar," the "Easter water," and the "Mass-rocks" denote his Catholicism; the "Mass-rocks," in particular, arouse memories of seventeenth-century Irish recusancy when the Penal Code condemned Catholics to worship at remote sites in order to avoid religious persecution.

Certainly these selective historical referents add "great depth to the heritage Ledwidge embodies" (Di Nicola 1986, 50), but this "heritage" is a narrow construct in which Irishness is associated almost exclusively with a gaelic/Catholic ethos. In direct conflict with Ledwidge's "Celtic/Catholic" heritage is the intrusion of the Great War, which infects the bard's "countrified" innocence like a foreign antibody. In contrast to the prewar "literary, sweet-talking poet," we now see the "haunted Catholic face" enduring the blistering heat of the Dardenelles before being "rent / By shrapnel" in Flanders two years later. If the war is perceived as a British cause, Ledwidge's death implies that it is also the destroyer of the Irish bardic tradition and its Celtic "twilit note": for Heaney, the war is the enemy of Irish culture and refinement. Also important is that Heaney's insinuations conveniently ignore the thousands of Catholic nationalists who fought in the war with the result that selective allusions breed selective histories. As James Simmons has noted about Heaney's poetry in general, this elegy for Ledwidge "is dominated by his tribal pieties without [his] being able to [fully] dramatise or examine them" (Simmons 1992, 63).

Far from illustrating his more "sceptical [view] of nationalist pieties" (Matthews 1997, 8), then, Heaney's portrayal of Ledwidge actually embraces the notion that Irish cultural identity can be largely defined by the poet's bond to the Irish landscape and that age-old trope in Irish literature—Mother Ireland. Despite the fact that the Great War represents a force which obstructs self-discovery, both Ledwidge and Heaney discover their emerging sense of selfhood and nationality through female personifications of Ireland.

That Irish cultural identity is inextricably linked to Irish landscape is borne out by Heaney's ironic intercutting between Ledwidge's suffering on foreign battlefields and the pastoral continuities associated with Heaney's Aunt Mary. While Ledwidge endures the heat of the Dardenelles (and the implied cultural aridities), Aunt Mary, the mother earth figure, is pictured "herding on the long acre," and when Ledwidge is killed in Flanders, "She still herds cows." In the essay, "A More Social Voice: *Fieldwork*," Tony Curtis doubts whether there is any "direct association" between Heaney's Aunt Mary and Ledwidge (1985, 122). But both figures are "brought together" by more than Heaney's "memory of the statue" (122). Instead, the intercutting references to Aunt Mary and the dead soldier poet reveal Heaney's reading of the war as a cross-cultural conflict. Ledwidge's death on foreign soil signifies the demise of bardic Ireland, while at home, the Irish pastoral ideal, embodied by Heaney's aunt, endures as a timeless rural ceremony. Furthermore, Aunt Mary represents in Irish poetry what Patricia Coughlan calls the now familiar "female icons of ideal domesticity" which are usually "associated with unmediated naturalness" (1991, 90).

If Heaney's aunt functions as an unshakable pastoral continuum, for Ledwidge, the hardships of the war are mitigated by romantic fancy; he imagines his "soul is by the Boyne, cutting new meadows" and perceives Ireland as a Catholic female ego awaiting her reception into nationhood garbed in her "confirmation dress." Heaney also appears betrothed to this standard nationalist ideal, for he readily admits that for him the "feminine element . . . involves the matter of Ireland" (1980b, 34). Not surprisingly, for "Heaney the feminine is associated with the Irish and the Celtic, the masculine with the English and the Anglo-Saxon" (Green 1983, 3). His Aunt Mary's stewardship of the land reveals how the "feminine principle" sustains man's "participation in the domestic and religious rituals which give life continuity" (4). Ledwidge's death in Flanders illustrates the potency of Heaney's image of the dying bard severed from the very earth that gives him life while his Aunt Mary represents an act of cultural as well as political affiliation, too, thus demonstrating Heaney's more easily stereotyped fascination with romantic nationalism. Fran Brearton believes that the poem struggles "with reductive histories" (2000, 193). But it could be argued that the poem itself is a reductive history as Heaney's memory of the soldier poet is flawed by his misreading of Irish history (Ledwidge's British citizenship in prepartition Ireland is largely ignored) with the result that the poem is not so much an elegy for the dead poet but a wreath for an anachronous Irish nationalism. Heaney's selective narrative of the dead poet's life focuses on how Ledwidge misguidedly followed a "confusing drum" to the Great War only to end up in a British army grave, consorting now with those "true-blue ones underground." This reductionist portrait of Ledwidge as some sort of naïve nationalist conveniently glosses over his complex motives for fighting in the war. Yet by serving as the soldier poet's elegist, Heaney also rescues him from literary oblivion as Ledwidge is no longer the "Irish poetic ruralist forgotten in the trenches of British war poetry" (Tamplin 1989, 87). In this respect, the poem serves as an act of cultural as well as ideological reclamation.

Ultimately, Heaney and Longley's retrospective treatment of the war reveals how nationalist and unionist ideologies permeate Irish cultural utterance. Perhaps here lies the value in examining how the Great War is perceived in modern Irish memory. If the war continues to be appropriated by rival political groups in order to consolidate their tribal myths, then Irish "cultural apartheid" will continue to flourish to the "mutual impoverishment of both communities" (M. Longley 1994, 75). One can only hope that the war will become a recognition scene in Irish history: one that reminds us that the various strands of Irish identity cut across convenient cultural, religious, and political divides. If Heaney's final image of Ledwidge interred with all the other "true-blue ones" suggests that a common thread of suffering unites these former adversaries, it also reveals that any hope of political reconciliation has to transcend both sides' martyr culture. The inability of Longley's father and Ledwidge to peg out a homogeneous ethnic identity demonstrates the extent to which our notions of Irishness and Britishness are sustained by selective histories. In reference to the Northern Irish situation, Longley has stated that "Reconciliation does not mean all the colours of the spectrum running so wetly together that they blur into muddy uniformity" (75). As Irishmen's various motives for fighting in the Great War demonstrate, defining Irishness and Britishness was and still is a confusing and perhaps futile exercise.

7

Conclusion

In IRISH WRITER CARLO GÉBLER'S NOVEL *HOW TO MURDER A MAN*, THE NAR-
rator begins the story by laying bare the inadequacy of simply
viewing historical struggles as generalized ideological conflicts:

> All histories are really murder stories. Sometimes they are epic and
> there are generals, and battlefields, and regiments of cavalry and
> foot, and sometimes there are pairs of men and alleyways and pistols
> in the back pocket. (1998, 1)

This is one of the most basic ironies about human violence, this
shared notion that killing on a grand scale in the name of some
lofty ideology is somehow more acceptable than a backstreet
tribal execution. With war, we get the pious platitudes and encomiums thrown like yesterday's wreaths around the memory of
the glorious dead. With the individual homicide, we get revulsion
at the unspeakable act of naked brutality. In the previous chapter, I examined how modern Irish poets return again and again to
the Great War to excavate family histories and address the current political situation in Northern Ireland, and what they recognize is this fundamental fallacy in human nature that translates yesterday's atrocities into today's cherished myths: ritual
murder becomes sacrifice, duty and honor. By acknowledging
that all histories are "murder stories," most Irish poets recognize that, on some level, present-day conflicts in Ireland are a
continuation on a much smaller scale of the global hostilities of
the First World War as centuries-old ethnic animosities continue
to separate communities who have never enjoyed an unconditional peace with their neighbors. In the work of contemporary
Irish poets, the Great War's storehouse of images provides an instantly translatable set of symbols through which to address the
ongoing political disturbances on both sides of the Irish border.
As a result of the Great War's omnipresence in modern sensi-

bility, even in poetry not ostensibly about the war itself, we see its iconography, enduring myths and traditions continue to be contentiously negotiated in contemporary Irish poetry.

For Irish poets interested in restoring a sense of responsibility toward the past, selecting enduring images from the Great War to "dramatize man's existential condition in our age" has become a favorite pastime (Westendorp 1991, 130). As contemporary Irish poets grapple with the disposable nature of modern culture, we see in their poetry how the Great War serves as a historical Rubicon whose crossing continues to reshape contemporary thought and the global landscape. Even when the Great War is not directly addressed in their work, a number of Irish poets call upon powerful images from the Great War to serve as catechistic texts on modern man's alleged sociocultural decline. The idea that the war made the past seem even more remote to present experiences is borne out in Tom Matthews's poem "Chaine of Chaine Park" (1968, 27), where the emotiveless description of a local war hero's despoiled memorial in the town of Larne epitomizes the cultural and historical estrangement between the present and the past:

> Dressed in full
> Dressed for a ceremony
> Captain Chaine stands
> Stiff as a sentry
>
> He stands on a hill
> Overlooking the North Channel
> He stands there all day
> And all night as well.

With his outmoded ceremonial dress and frozen gait, Chaine is reduced to an historical icon cut off from the present by unrelenting time and the prospect of oblivion. He is also a prisoner of his own history and Irish history:

> It is a park
> He stands in
> Chaine Park
> Named after him.
>
> He sees not the lighthouse
> On the horizon dim
> Knows not the park
> Named after him.

In the final stanza, the poem completes its accretion of layers of irony:

> His uniform
> Is rotted
> As are his eyes
> In their sockets.

The statue's state of decay robs the war hero even of posthumous recognition. Like a latter-day Ozymandias, Chaine's eyeless image faces eastward toward the Scottish coast. Ironically, the statue's physical deterioration presents a more truthful monument to the war dead than the tidy, marmoreal orderliness we see at most war memorials, and Chaine's vapid seaward gaze contrasts man's brittle existence with the ceaseless energy of nature. As a comment on the contemporary world, the staccato lines (appropriately devoid of emotion or critical discernment) present a bitter vision of a time when heroism and tradition seem outmoded. Bounded by a "dim" horizon, we live with the relics of a past that we ignore or cannot comprehend. As Matthews's poem suggests, the war has also led us to romanticize the prewar era even more so than those who lived through it. Like John Crowe Ransom's "Captain Carpenter," Chaine resembles a fallen idol whose gradual spoliation serves as a mute testimony to our proclivity for falsely sentimentalizing the past.

In a similar vein, Derek Mahon's allusive poem "The Kensington Notebook" (1991, 90–95) makes use of Great War iconography to expose the modern age's intellectual conceit and processed representations of the past. Mahon's chronicle of urban and imperial decline also acknowledges the demise of prewar traditions and ceremonies. Divided into four sections, the poem reads like the selected highlights of London's political, artistic, and literary culture between the years 1912 and 1920. Each of the first three sections chronicles the lives of Ford Madox Ford, then Ezra Pound, and finally Wyndham Lewis as Mahon's extremely compressed style weaves together reported snatches of conversation, literary reference, political allusion, and biographical minutiae about each writer in a form that reads at times like a "telegrammatic resumé" (Haughton 1992, 114). As the title suggests, Kensington is the center for this literary-historical tour de force due to its associations with three writers whose values and experiences reveal the tensions that characterized Britain's transformation from an elitist, tradition-bound society

to a modern welfare state. The Great War's role in all this is
to provide ironic counterpoints to the prevailing intellectual and
artistic pieties of the time period.

Toward the end of the first section, which focuses on significant
moments in Ford's life, the arrogating optimism of prewar intel-
lectualism and innocence is bitterly contrasted to the sobering
realities of the Somme:

> What price the dewy-eyed
> Pelagianism of home
> To a lost generation
> Dumbfounded on the Somme?

Mahon's questioning of Pelagian faith in free will is particularly
ironic considering how that free will was abrogated by a generation's willing participation in its own slaughter.

In addition to exposing the inadequacies of early modernist
optimism, Mahon's account of Lewis focuses on his attempt to
reflect the war's horror through his art while other war artists
simply rehash the same old stylized glorifications of the war and
its warrior-leaders:

> A moonscape, trees like gibbets,
> Shrapnel, wire, the thud
> Of howitzers, spike-helmeted
> Skeletons in the mud.
>
> War artist, he depicts
> The death-throes of an era
> While Orpen glorifies
> Haig, Gough etc.;

This unfavorable comparison between Irish painter Sir William
Orpen's stately portraitures of the British army top brass with
Lewis's frightening landscapes is unfair, though. While Lewis's
artwork challenged the sanitized version of the war that the
military wished to perpetuate, Orpen's war paintings were not
all simple glorifications. Certainly, along with Sir John Lav-
ery, Orpen was one of Ireland's most accomplished "society por-
traitist[s]" (Cork 1994, 195) when war erupted in 1914, but while
both men did not graphically reproduce the carnage of the front
in their war paintings, Orpen's work did eventually take on a
harder edge after his subsequent experiences on the Western
Front while working as an official war artist "from his base at

Amiens" (195). But it was not until after the war that his work became controversial.

In 1922, Orpen's painting, *To the Unknown British Soldier in France*, created quite a stir when it was rejected for inclusion in the Imperial War Museum. The canvas featuring a lone coffin covered with a Union Jack with partially clad British soldiers standing guard on either side served as an ironic commentary on the price of peace. The painting also seemed to mock the classical piety and pretentiousness of the British war-monument industry. This flair for the satirical, though, does not fit in with Mahon's image of Orpen as the official war artist. Orpen did go on to produce a second version of the painting without the offending imagery in order to appease the trustees of the Imperial War Museum. Perhaps, as noted war art critic Richard Cork suggests, "official disapproval affected the artist's attitude to his picture" (1994, 267), but Mahon's image of Orpen as a war propagandist still seems far too narrow. As we have already seen in other Irish poets' war poems, ambiguity is usually the first casualty of war memory.[1]

Finally, in the poem's fourth and final section, Mahon's elliptical style concludes the portraits of these literary mavericks by noting how all three died in exile. In reference to Ford, the old soldier, Mahon cleverly mingles Great War iconography with references to and from Ford's novels, *Parade's End* and *The Last Post*:

> No more parades . . .
> Ghostly bugles sound
> The "Last Post"; the last fox
> Has gone to ground . . . .

These images write the obituary to an era as Mahon's depiction of these isolated romantic outsiders and their disillusionment with the war reminds us of the war's legacy of political, cultural, and psychological fragmentation.

Modernist angst and attendant nostalgias aside, echoes of the Great War, as already noted, inform contemporary responses to other wars, most notably the Northern Irish Troubles. As we shall see later, there may be more overarching reasons to explain why contemporary Irish women poets have been generally silent about the Great War, but they can hardly be accused of avoiding the subject of war within an Irish context. In some cases, their work is particularly preoccupied with the "devaluing of the warrior culture in Ireland, past and present" as they continue to "challenge the glorification of war and other themes and imagery found in male poetry" (East 1996, 12). Two of the most vociferous critics of Ireland's love affair with war and its corresponding mythologies are Eavan Boland and Eiléan Ní Chuilleanáin. Unfortunately, their condemnation of these war myths has received scant recognition due to the popular conception that women rarely make "any kind of comment on Irish history and politics" (Haberstroh 1996, 24). Commenting on her own work, Boland has acknowledged a sense of isolation from the mainstream historical narratives, noting that she has "never felt" like she has "owned history" or ever "felt entitled to the Irish experience" (1995, 489). In addressing her self-perception that history as a subject for poetry was off limits to her, Boland reveals how she has shied away from writing overt political poetry. This feeling of not having what she describes as the right "credentials" (489) has not stopped her, though, from engaging in a critique of Ireland's obsession with violence. A number of her poems illustrate that "the failure to see the tragic consequences of the mythic celebration of war [still] persists in contemporary Ireland" (Haberstroh 1996, 63). The extent to which the First World War is the source of many of these myths can be gauged by how Boland's poems about the Troubles explore similar themes and borrow the very iconography of Great War poetry.

In her second collection of poems, *The War Horse* (1975), she explores various fields of conflict ranging from the familial, to the sexual, to the political, and what unifies these excursions into personal and public war zones is her desire to "suggest the need for peaceful alternatives" (Haberstroh 1996, 62). The focus of Boland's "war" poems is the Irish conflict. Nowhere do we find direct reference to the Great War; however, several of the themes of that greater struggle inform Boland's treatment of this more local fight. As we have already seen, the Great War undoubtedly exacerbated the political and sectarian divisions in Ireland, but Boland's war poems also share the outrage of earlier antiwar poetry.

In "A Soldier's Son" (1975, 12), Boland's reading of the cult of violence pinpoints the same hollow myths of war that AE also examined in his pacifistic verse. In the poem's first stanza, she acknowledges war's hypnotic hold on youth with its false promises of victory, adventure, and honor:

> A young man's war it is, a young man's war,
> Or so they say and so they go to wage
> This struggle where, armoured only in nightmare,
> Every warrior is under age—. . . .

Boland demonstrates here that the myth of war as a glorious struggle did not die on the Western Front. If anything, history teaches us nothing. The blind allegiances and the eternal instinct for bloodlust seem endless as martial traditions defy time and memory. Later, in the second stanza, her critique of the timeless pull of violence reveals the ironic distance between myth and reality. The archaic notion that war is a valorous carnival of high-mindedness and noble sacrifice is contrasted to the dirty realities of street violence:

> In a backstreet stabbing, at a ghetto corner
> Of future wars and further fratricide.
> Son of a soldier who saw war on the ground,
> Now cross the peace lines I have made for you
> To find on this side if not peace then honour,
> Your heritage. . . .

Boland's vision is epochal. The war in Ulster, like the Great War, and all the other wars fought in the field of foggy ideals, is cast as further confirmation of our inability to learn from our mistakes. Boland's use of the high-flown language of chivalric, martial poetry ("armoured," "warrior") again underlines the inadequacy of such terms, especially in a modern context, to describe the horror of war. And like all subsequent conflicts, the parlance of the front is accessed once again to articulate the empty spaces of ignorance and misunderstanding. The poet's assembly of metaphoric "peace lines" resembles Michael Longley's authorial excursions into the landscape of his father's war memory where the poet searches for consolatory emblems to come to terms with what has been lost. In Boland's war poetry, the aftershocks of the Great War color her reaction to the "glorification" of war "in the Western heroic tradition" (Haberstroh 1996, 24).

In another poem, "Suburban Woman" (1975, 42–44), a different sort of conflict is described in terms that again employ unforgettable images from the front as powerful metaphors. Consisting of five sections, the poem explores one woman's (presumably Boland's) domestic isolation. Boland herself recalls how shortly after getting married (in the early 1970s), she "went to live at the foothills of the Dublin mountains" in a sparsely furnished and poorly heated suburban house during a "time of violence in Northern Ireland" (1995, 487). It was here on the edges of the city that she wrote the twenty-five poems that make up *The War Horse*. Seemingly trapped by stultifying daily housekeeping routines, the measuring of time by the quotidian and her uneventful, spiritual exile on the fringes of a world where things supposedly happen, Boland's interior world is described as a battlefield, where combative platoons of conflicting emotions attack and counterattack. In an ongoing struggle to contend with the afterglow of suffocated aspirations and the ever-present aridities of empty domestic ritual, Boland portrays a female persona who recognizes that her strength is her ability to remake her own self-conception through daily compromise. Boland accomplishes this by making liberal use of the Great War's vocabulary.

In section one of the poem, she depicts the sense of rootlessness brought on by the geographical dislocation of a city-bred woman now exiled to the country. The homesickness and displacement wrought by these warring places in her psyche advance and recede like offensive and counteroffensive:

> She woke
> one morning to the usual story: withdrawing,
> neither side had gained, but there, dying,
>
> caught in a cross-fire, her past lay, bleeding. . . .

As the poem moves chronologically through the slow hours of the day, in section four, late sunlight in the garden exposes a landscape of weeds and flowers whose appearance symbolizes her own wasting vitality and sexuality:

> she perceives
> veteran dead-nettles, knapweed
> crutched on walls, a summer's seed
> of roses trenched in ramsons, and stares
> at her life falling with her flowers,
> like military tribute or the tears
> of shell-shocked men, into arrears.

The cumulative effect of these war images creates a powerful metaphoric train of associations cross connecting the remote historic images of war and suffering with the personal hormonal battlefield of loss and self-perceived obsolescence. Once again, the Great War's iconography transcends time and space to communicate the disintegrative ego of a woman floundering on the margins of existence.

In the final section, section five, Great War emblemata continue to provide a language to articulate the psychic war within as the day draws to an end:

> Her kitchen blind down—a white flag—
> the day's assault over, now she will shrug
>
> a hundred small surrenders off as images
> still unborn, unwritten metaphors, blank pages
>
> and on this territory, blindfold, we meet
> at last, veterans of a defeat. . . .

In these lines, we see that the conflict is not only one of displacement and coping with alien surroundings. It is also the struggle for words as the poet battles with the endless demands of house and family and her poetic persona and its creative struggle to find a voice amid the debris of domestic obligation, emotional anxiety, and the certitude of the daily grind.

Boland's use of military metaphors may seem inappropriate in describing her personal traumas and yet her very use of these terms underlines just how dependent women are on metaphors forced on them by a culture that can only interpret conflict in the argot of a militaristic patriarchy. Boland's achievement here is to take the Great War's vernacular and make it relevant in other arenas of conflict. The result is that the war becomes a repository of images and memories that provide the Irish imagination with an inexhaustible trove of associations with which to address political, sectarian, and interpersonal discord.

Like Boland, Eiléan Ní Chuilleanáin has periodically challenged the myths of Irish militarism, too. Unlike Boland, though, her work does not reveal a direct link to the iconography of the Great War. Instead, she examines war's attendant mythologies through the use of metaphorical landscapes. In her collection *Site of Ambush,* published in the same year as Boland's *The War Horse* (1975), the title poem intermingles meditative sequences with a narrative scene featuring a lorry full of soldiers that overturns into a stream during an ambush. The soldiers and a local boy, who was presumably caught in the crossfire, are all killed.

Patricia Haberstroh believes that the political backdrop in "Site of Ambush" (Ní Chuilleanáin 1975, 22–28) is "the Irish civil wars of the 1920s" (1996, 105), but the poem is actually about the

"Black and Tan War in Co. Cork" and the dead soldiers are Black and Tans or Auxiliaries.[2] Despite the lack of a direct connection to the Great War, the poem tackles themes common to some of the antiwar verse discussed earlier. Again, Haberstroh notes the poem's critique of the usual platitudes of warmongering. In the poem's second section, the soldiers' "military calculations and the attempts to control life and death are [later ironically] contrasted to the timeless flow of the stream, which eventually passes indifferently over their dead bodies" (1996, 105):

> The enemy commanders synchronised their heartbeats:
> Seven forty-five by the sun.
> At ten the soldiers were climbing into lorries
> Asthmatic engines drawing breath in even shifts.
> The others were fretting over guns
> Counting up ammunition and money.
> At eleven they lay in wait at the cross
> With over an hour to go.

Another theme here is the vilification of war as a noble and chivalric pursuit. The fact that the troops themselves plan an ambush is hardly in keeping with the pre-Great War sense of fair play on the battlefield. Also, the "fretting over guns," "ammunition and money" is not the sort of behavior one would expect to be extolled in martial verse. Instead, the selfish interests in self-preservation and the squalid squabbling over money (looted spoils?) portray war in far more realistic terms. (The concern over dividing the spoils could strongly suggest that this is a scene from somewhere in West Cork where local republican flying columns and Black and Tans engaged in a series of tit-for-tat atrocities.)

Other myths of war (and especially the Great War and the Anglo-Irish War) that Ní Chuilleanáin explodes are the usual pieties associated with good death on the battlefield as the innocent die alongside the uniformed:

> Deafly rusting in the stream
> The lorry now is soft as a last night's dream.
> The soldiers and the deaf child
> Landed gently in the water
> They were light between long weeds
> Settled and lay quiet, nobody
> To listen to them now.
> They all looked the same face down there:

Water too thick and deep to see.
They were separated for good.
It was cold, their teeth shrilling.
They slept like falling hay in waves.

Haberstroh notes that the flowing waters of the stream, with their naturally eternal, restorative associations, contrast with the fragile mortality of the war dead who lie face down in the current (1996, 105). Unlike Yeats's stone in the living stream, the war dead here are not impervious to flux; their deaths signify their estrangement from the natural order. Just as with some of the earlier pacifistic poems written in response to the Great War, Ní Chuilleanáin "warns against the celebration of traditional heroism" (106). In this regard, her work shares the same measured outrage as other antiwar commentators. What lends a further irony to her description of the dead, though, is its dependence on pastoral images and trite elegiac euphemisms that heighten the ironic effect. In essence, she deromanticizes war by using romantic clichés: death is described as lying "quiet"; as the eternal parting ("separated for good"); and as the endless sleep ("They slept like"). Even in contemporary poetry, the power of pastoral still dominates the Irish elegiac tradition—a tradition of commemoration that Great War poetry undoubtedly also shares.

Making use of the enduring imagery of the Great War and responding to its elaborate mythology has obviously served Irish poets well as they continue to reexamine inherited assumptions about ethnic identities and gender roles. But besides the thematic similarities, the iconic echoes and the ironic cross-connections between contemporary Irish poetry and Great War verse, other Irish poets view Irish war memory as a portal through which to explore the sacred narratives that purportedly chronicle the making and shaping of a new nation—the Irish Republic.

Perhaps no other contemporary Irish poet has taken such a dispassionate look at modern Ireland and all her contradictions than Paul Durcan. Yet his iconoclasm is not merely a proleptical reading of past sins. Durcan rarely assumes the vatic pose; his poetry is rarely prescriptive. For him, all sides share a collective guilt in prolonging Ireland's nightmare, and he sees recent Irish history littered with ignominious acts perpetrated by those convinced that Ireland's future depends on their self-proclaimed acts of selflessness. Durcan is particularly interested in how the misdeeds of the past continue to condition and nourish the duplicities of the present.

In "Lament for Major-General Emmet Dalton" (1982, 99–100),
Durcan pays tribute to another Irishman whose posterity has
been marginalized in favor of a more homogeneous Irish narrative. Dalton served with the Sixteenth Irish Division, fought on
the Western Front, and was with Tom Kettle when he was killed
in action in September 1916. In Durcan's poem, the "Lament"
for the old soldier becomes a lament for Ireland as the poet sees
Dalton as the representative of a more pragmatic nationalism
whose willingness to compromise with other political groups offered greater potential for securing peace than the adversarial
homilectics practiced by republican extremists. Throughout the
poem, the Great War and the Irish Civil War provide the historical backdrop for Durcan's critique of Irish politics. Like those
before him, Dalton in death joins the other forgotten dead: those
whose ideals and actions are no longer serviceable to the republican myth of a unified nationalist front against British rule:

> The gun-carriage bearing your coffin
> Trundled unnoticed through Dublin streets:
> The mob, in tune with the mobsters,
> Disowned you, Emmet Dalton;
> Disremembering Michael Collins also
> Whom you held in your trembling arms
> As he lay dying at the Mouth of Flowers.

As a former British soldier and major figure in the Free State's
armed forces, Dalton is a discomforting reminder of another
branch of Irish nationalism, one that saw the value of political
compromise rather than unyielding and unrealistic devotion to
a nationalist ideal. Buried without fanfare, Dalton's historical
vanishing act illustrates how memory of the Great War continues to undermine nationalist identity in Ireland.

The old soldier's role in Irish history recalls other tensions
in the national psyche. His subsequent withdrawal from Irish
politics after the Civil War reveals gaps between republicanism's
lofty idealism and historical actuality:

> When civil war arrived at the pit of degradation
> With fiats of summary executions,
> And revenge and counter-revenge assumed their sway,
> You resigned from the army; in the post-war scramble
> For dividing-up the lolly, you kept well out of it,
> Preferring the art of film-making (a new art in Ireland)
> To that old Celtic game—Tammany Hall politics.

For Durcan, Dalton's refusal to be dragged into the mire of gang-land reprisals, parochial politics and pocket-lining obsequies represents a refreshing alternative to the insular and proscriptive government policies of the 1920s. Durcan's critique of institutionalized repression also includes larger historical events. He deromanticizes the war by remembering Dalton as one of the crowd whose hunger for heroism was complicitous in staging the bloodbath of the Western Front:

> You were twenty, then, a moustachio'd young captain
> Dreaming of deeds of derring-do; instead, you had the privilege
> Of seeing Tom Kettle having his head blown off on the road to
>   Guinchy.

The shift in tone and image in these lines from romantic retrospect to blunt reportage also communicates Durcan's aim to demonstrate the gulf between expectation and reality.

Years later the old soldier returns to places forever associated with bitter memories, and it is there that Durcan singles out the historical burdens of Dalton's past:

> Sixty years later you revisited those pastoral scenes
> Of that most dreadful carnage; they were as unrecognisable
> As the nearby dales of white crosses to the anonymous dead:
> You leaned back on your stick, gazed out through your spectacles;
> Sadly and gracefully, bewildered and bemused:
> At the Mouth of Flowers you re-enacted the Ambush—
> Yet the deed remained as sinister as the location itself.

Geographical ironies intersect as neither the Western Front's pastoral makeover nor the arcadian beauty of a name (the "Mouth of Flowers" or Beál na Bláth) can cover up the sins of the past. Kettle and Collins form part of recent Irish history's enigmatic narrative, and yet while it is pointless to conjecture what role they would have played in the new Ireland had they lived, like Dalton, their historical roles have been either forgotten (Kettle) or distorted (Collins). Neither man can be easily reconciled with the republican version of history as one was a British officer and the other was instrumental in creating the terms for Irish partition. Another irony is that their truest venerator, the one whose fate it was to be present when they both were killed, shows symptoms of historical amnesia, too. Unlike the Ancient Mariner condemned to suffer until his "ghastly tale is told," Dalton's memory sleepwalks through the present, his past "unrecognisable." His loss of memory also has larger historical sig-nificance in that the horror of the past has been altered. The on-going political appropriation of Irish history ignores the human cost of past victories and defeats as the dead remain "anony-mous." Dalton's participation in a staged reenactment also calls to mind how commemorative ceremony can be exploited for po-litical purposes, yet these acts which perpetuate popular myth can never thoroughly erase their "sinister" origins. Their bloody realities haunt us still.

Ultimately for Durcan, Emmet Dalton is a victim of the polar-izing forces of Irish history. As Durcan's symbol of a pragmatic and progressive force in Irish politics, he has no place in an Ire-land where all rivers must become one. Dalton's fate, like many of Ireland's best hopes, is historical exile:

> What are we left with? At dusk, on the River Lee, a steamer
> Steams out to sea with a dead King's coffin on board,
> And, beside it, keeping guard, the dead King's young friend;
> Whose habit was truth, and whose style was courage.

Perhaps Ireland could do with a few less Hamlets and a few more Horatios. As a dissentient voice raised against Irish national-ism's sacred narratives, Durcan recognizes how certain episodes in Irish history like the Great War present problems for those determined to interpret Irish affairs from an intertribal perspec-tive.

Other Irish poets share Durcan's eagerness to challenge the sacred doxologies of opposing Irish political ideologies as the use of war iconography features prominently in recent Irish verse about the Troubles. It would seem that the enduring images and vernacular of the First World War were especially tailored for the Northern Irish situation where booby traps, land mines, check-points, peace lines, observation posts, foot patrols, "No Go Ar-eas," sandbags, and barbed wire have become integral parts of the province's landscape and vocabulary. Battle lines exist not only on maps but cut across social consciousnesses, too, and bi-nary oppositions are intuited rather than contrived. Even con-temporary culturespeak borrows freely from the Great War's lex-icography as one of the first accounts of the paramilitary cease-fire brokered in 1994 to be published carried the title: *Behind the Lines: The Story of the IRA and Loyalist Cease-Fire*. In an anthol-ogy devoted exclusively to poetry about the Troubles (*A Rage for Order*) the sheer multiplicity of reference to Great War imagery is also astonishing. Ciaran Carson's Belfast landscapes in particular echo the grisly theater of the front with their references to "duck patrol[s] ("Army"), the "broken rhythm / Of machine gun fire" ("Night Out"), and "crossfire" ("Hairline Crack"). The paraphernalia of war pervades Padraic Fiacc's war-torn Belfast streets, too, with its "barbed-wire Irish / Twilight" (from "Tears") and crouching soldiers "hiding" in trench-like culverts ("Enemy Encounter"). The result is that the combat zones of the Western Front and Northern Ireland become almost indistinguishable. We see these striking parallels between both fields of conflict in Norman Dugdale's description of Ulster's geopolitical topography in his poem, "Some Notes for Impartial Observers" (1997, 42):[3]

> Lived in, it is a minefield triggered
> By invisible trip-wires. Wayleaves by day
> Give access to some common zones, where the inhabitants
> Frat cautiously, ears cocked for trouble.
>
> By night, it drops all civic pretension
> To assume a true plurality. Each warring village
> Stands to, mobilised against the stranger,
> Its strong points pubs, back alleyways its fields of fire. . . .

Minefields, trip-wires, mobilizations, strategic "strong points," lines of fire: in Ulster, the Great War's vernacular has a long shelf life as the sectarian fault lines of the Ulster landscape resemble the adversarial trench network of the front.

While the war provides convenient metaphors to describe not only the hunkered-down siege mentalities of the opposing sides, in John Montague's poem "Red Branch (A Blessing)" (1995, 157), images from the Great War are conjured up as emblems of hope:

> Sing our forlorn hope then—
> the great Cross of Verdun,
> Belfast Tower on the Somme—
> Signs raised over bloody ground
> that the two crazed peoples make an end.

For Montague, these war monuments symbolize a common ground between Ulster's warring traditions, but as we have seen, the shared grievances of the Great War did little to initiate communal reconciliation.

Sometimes the Great War and the Troubles cross-collide literally rather than figuratively. In Conor Carson's poem "Marie

Wilson" (1992, 159–60), the poet elegizes one of the victims of
the IRA bombing of the Remembrance Day Sunday service in
Enniskillen in November 1987:[4]

> Under the Statue
> of the Unknown Soldier
> a man prepares
> a bomb. He is
> an unknown soldier.

Historical ironies link the unknown war dead with this new
breed of unknown "soldier." Victims and victimizer share the
impersonality of war as we remember the deed rather than the
dead. The destruction of the cenotaph as a symbol of British Ulster reminds us that terrorists are rarely blessed with a cogent
historical consciousness: some of those whose names were inscribed on the memorial had also been nationalists. Ironically,
Ireland's war dead continue to be victims of political expediency
as innocent people lose their lives honoring another generation's
sacrifice:

> Today there was no Last Post.
> Her last words
> were "Daddy, I love you."
> He said he would trust
> God. But her poppy
> lay in the dust.

Even Rosenberg's poppy was "safe behind his ear," albeit ironically as Paul Fussell points out (1975, 253). Carson's arrange-
ment of these ironic images from two different theaters of conflict
not only provides an interpretative vocabulary for the present political violence in Northern Ireland but also demonstrates how, in
some circles, Irish memory of the Great War is still perceived as
a political act. Commemoration is encoded as another partisan
ritual in a society dominated by sectarian signs, symbols, and
gestures.

Certainly some contemporary Irish poets recognize how Ireland's role in the Great War continues to provide interpretative
paradigms with which to analyze the numerous contradictions
in Irish political culture, but when we take a more generalized
view of the range of poetry written by Irish poets about the
war, several conclusions begin to emerge. The year 1996 marked
the 80th anniversary of the Somme, but in Northern Ireland,

memorial ceremonies (organized under the auspices of the Orange Order) were marred by violent exchanges between Orangemen, who were determined to parade along traditional routes through largely nationalist areas, and local residents' groups who regarded these commemorative marches as nothing more than loyalist processions. Nationalist opposition rallied behind another divisive slogan of "No Consent No Parade." This latest reminder of the deep divisions that still exist between the two traditions demonstrates perhaps the most prevalent theme in Irish war poetry—how Irish memory of the First World War continues to be manipulated for political and sectarian expediency. The fact that the war can still stir up controversy on both sides of the Irish border should confirm the value of listening "carefully to the beat of that 'sure, confusing drum' of August 1914, for its echo reverberates down the history of Ireland, and is still heard today" (Boyce 1993, 33).

In our survey of the soldier poets, we saw the earliest rumblings of how future memory of the war would be processed for political gain. While soldier poets like Willoughby Weaving and Patrick MacGill were apparently untroubled by the political implications of their service in the British army, others like Francis Ledwidge and Tom Kettle were clearly disturbed by the likelihood that their decision to fight in the war would later be construed as an act of political betrayal. Saddled with the remnants of their colonial identity and suddenly rendered irrelevant by the emergence of a more militant Irish nationalism, they were caught in the front lines of a struggle between rival political, aesthetic, and cultural ideologies that is still being fought today.

Another general conclusion that can be drawn from Irish soldier poetry is that it was largely unconcerned with making pacifist statements about the war. On the contrary, a prowar spirit can be traced from Weaving's romanticizing of modern combat through to the pan-British front championed by Patrick MacGill's *Soldier Songs*. In contrast to "mainland" soldier poets, Irish soldier poets were also generally more concerned with tackling national issues that had been temporarily set aside by the war. These political tensions in Irish soldier poetry also reveal how the fairly modest political ambitions of constitutional nationalism were overwhelmed by the emergence of a more militant republicanism. Perhaps the deaths of prominent Home Rulers like Tom Kettle meant that the war effectively removed from the scene the very voices of moderation who may have been able to defuse the bellicose passions of more extreme nationalists.

As for the home front, poets like Katharine Tynan were less concerned about war aims and Irish politics than they were with their roles as poetic paracletes providing comfort and hope to the bereaved, while AE's war poetry was more preoccupied with philosophical issues raised by the war's threat to civilized society. For AE, the war sparked off a debate that would result in an introspective reassessment of personal political theory. Yeats's political ideals also came under self scrutiny as a result of the war and its violent offspring—the Rising. His fascination with men of action and Ireland's participation in the grand conflict coalesced his semiaffiliated nationalist sympathies that may have continued to list vaguely between what could be best described as a form of cultural nationalism and a quietistic tolerance of the political status quo. The result of this shift in political outlook led to Yeats's partisan reading of the war and, like the propagandist poetry of pro-imperialists like F. S. Boas, contributed in its own small way to the postwar divisions in Irish war memory.

Apart from engendering political realignment in individual attitudes about Ireland's domestic affairs, the war also raised questions about what constitutes Irishness. In the war poetry written during the decade or so after the war ended, the various motives for fighting and the postwar determination to either preserve or dispel war memory reveal a diversity of views about Irish identity. Lord Dunsany's Anglo-Irish lineage, Stephen Gwynn's constitutional nationalism, and Samuel McCurry's Ulster-British loyalism all share a basic love of the land and what distinguishes it from the rest of the United Kingdom. Yet in retrospect, all three strands of Irishness were to be further alienated from each other as a result of the Great War and Irish partition. The irreplaceable loss of many leading Anglo-Irishmen in the war was to hasten not only their class's demise but also widen the political gulf between unionists and nationalists. Hubert Butler certainly thought so. As a member of the Ascendancy and one of Ireland's most insightful and articulate voices, Butler understood better than most the consequences of the Great War, the War of Independence, and the Civil War in Irish history. His class, he observes, could have provided a counter balance against the more narrow interpretations of who was Irish and who was not. He argued that

A new and more suffocating ascendancy, that of international commerce, was on the way; many of those ruined houses [of the Anglo-Irish] would have been strongholds of resistance to it, and the Anglo-

Irish with their easy-going pragmatic Christianity would certainly have tempered the religious and political passions of our northern countrymen. (1985, 103)

Given the raw hatred and sectarian passion of Ulster unionist and nationalist extremists that we see paraded on the streets of Northern Ireland each marching season, Butler's belief that southern pragmatism could have moderated northern bellicosity seems highly unlikely. For other former soldiers like Thomas MacGreevy, the Free State's general amnesia about the war and its insular attitude toward foreign (chiefly British) cultural intrusion actually served as reminders of Ireland's political and cultural contiguity to Britain and Europe.

Apart from reminding us of the diverse ways that Irish men and women define their ethnicity, Irish war poetry demonstrates how the war continues to provide materials for those in search of origin myths. The most obvious way in which the war has been laundered for its mythical possibilities has been the unionist appropriation of the Somme as a rallying point for tribal solidarity. Like 1690, 1916 has now become another tribal totem for Ulster loyalism. But the war also functions as a source of personal discovery. Michael Longley's exhumations of his family's war memories not only enable him to imaginatively fill in the narrative gaps of his family history but also to come to a closer understanding of the various identities that have helped to define his own. In this sense, the Great War serves as a reference point for personal as well as ethnic, political, and cultural definition.

Consequently, the range of political and cultural rereadings of the war indicate the extent to which many Irish men and women define their Irishness. World-renowned culture critic Ernest Gellner has argued for years that a "national state" is not simply a "political and cultural unit" (Kirk-Smith 1995, 28), and this survey of Irish war poetry seems to confirm the validity of his claim as the range of dissonant voices in Irish war poetry represents various strands of Irish identity that overlap the customary political, religious, and cultural binarisms. Ultimately, Irish poets' treatment of the Great War illustrates how the past continues to be contested in Irish memory. In looking for more oblique ways to confront the complexities of the political situation in Northern Ireland, Irish poets have heeded Robert Graves's advice that "In poetry the implication is more important than the manifest statement" (1922, 14). Not everyone agrees, though. Shortly after it was announced that Seamus

Heaney had won the 1995 Nobel prize for literature, Irish novelist Robert McLiam Wilson begged to disagree with "Those who
would maintain that in writing about hedges and blackberries,
Heaney has actually treated the manifestations of political violence in a different manner" (1995, 24). Wilson claims that such
notions are "entirely fraudulent and must be termed so" (24).
However, his criticism of Heaney's circumspection and avoidance
of real political dialogue overlooks Heaney's active engagement
with Irish history as the poet explores what Wilson describes
as "definitions of nationhood" (24). Perhaps it is Heaney's nationalist perspective that Wilson has a problem with. Certainly
Heaney has imported exotic metaphors and excavated images
from pre-Christian cultures in order to approach the Irish situation from an oblique frame of reference. But like the other
poets featured in this study, his treatment of the Great War in
Irish memory shows that he has not shied away from active
engagement with historical antecedents (the Great War) that
still provoke divisive political, cultural, and sectarian interpretations. Indeed, writing about Ireland's Great War legacy does
"really pass muster as an investigation of modern Northern Ireland" (24).

And yet, the reluctance of many contemporary poets to address
the war (and the Troubles) in their work may be due in part to
the general shift in attitudes toward poetry in the last fifty years
or so. On the one hand, the retreat into a more highly personalized, confessional poetry can be partly ascribed to the belief that
"local possibilities of subject matter and attitude were exhausted
by Yeats and Joyce": hence the desire for some poets to elide "geographical and historical particulars" in their work (Crotty 1994,
2). Looked at as a remote event coated with historical ambiguity
and smothered by stereotypical posturing, the Great War in Irish
memory, ironically, may seem too parochial to those Irish poets
who look to Europe, especially, for their models and influences.

An equally convincing reason why the war has been neglected
as a topic for exploration in contemporary poetry is due to its
incarceration within a "neo-romantic aesthetic enclosure" (Wills
1993, 238). For most poets born after the Second World War,
memory of the Great War and its poetry has been largely shaped
by the impression created by secondary school anthologies. War
poetry was written in a neopastoral, self-consciously aesthetic,
and excessively rhetorical style: all sermon and sentiment and
seemingly irrelevant to contemporary realities. And yet, as Clair
Wills points out, contemporary Irish poets prefer to explore pri-

vate experiences (rather than myth and symbol) in order to give utterance to "communal concerns" (1993, 239, 238). We have seen this idea that "personal and public experience are already imbricated with one another" (239) clearly illustrated in Michael Longley's soundings of his father's war memory with its familial and political implications.

Regarding the war as not a fit subject for poetry can also be traced to the gender demarcations in Irish poetry. As Eavan Boland suggests, some Irish women poets generally felt estranged from the masculine genuflections to Irish history, and the relative silence about the war among recent Irish women poets is no doubt due to the traditional attitude (which women subscribed to themselves) that the world of public events (like the war) was generally off limits. Instead, women were more apt to identify with the "internal spaces" of personal and domestic experience rather than the externalities of the "'public' world of their male colleagues" (Haberstroh 1996, 21).[5] Katharine Tynan's war poetry certainly affirms the sentimental stereotypes of women as her war poems focus on the customary roles of mother, deserted lover, and helpless widow, and even though women continue to battle with disempowerment and marginalization in Boland's poetry, there is no longer a rote passive acceptance of the status quo. If Irish war poetry contributed to the portrayal of women as domestic icons, the recent responses to war by poets like Boland and Ní Chuilleanáin not only demonstrate that women are certainly as accomplished as their male counterparts in responding to the local political crises, but that they are also, through the very act of writing war poetry, able to demolish the perceptions of Irish women and Irish women poets as obeisant, sentimentalized nurturers.

Yet the act of confronting the past seems to carry its own tribal freight and the general neglect of the war in modern Irish poetry must be chiefly ascribed to years of state neglect in the Irish Republic, sectarian appropriation in the north, and the omission of the Irish experience in the war in the secondary school history curricula. Perhaps with the most recent public manifestations of reexamining Ireland's role in the war, such attitudes will change but like everything else in Ireland, such change will come slowly.

Self-serving interpretations of Irish memory of the Great War remain as part of a wider practice in Ireland where the past continues to be manipulated in order to validate tribal narratives (Kiberd 1988, 30–33). Looking for consensus about the role Ireland played in the First World War may be a futile pursuit. A willingness to confront the past rather than rely on inherited mythologies may be the most valuable directive we can extract from studying how Irish poets write the Great War. The presence of propaganda, platitude, illusion, evasion, excision, ambivalence, and ambiguity in Irish war poetry makes us aware of just how many other voices there are that deserve to be heard in the rewriting of Irish history. In other ways, literature can remind us of the true direction that political debate should take, and Irish war poetry, in its own small way, demonstrates where the focus of real dialogue about Ireland's future should be, not in circuitous rhetoric about traditions but in tackling Louis MacNeice's question, "what is a nation?"[6]

And yet Irish poets' treatment of the First World War is much more than a dialogic narrative on the issue of Irish/British identity. Their work serves as a remembrance wreath for the thousands of Irish soldiers whose remains lie scattered across the numerous British and Allied cemeteries on the Western Front, the Balkans and the Dardenelles. The act of poetry may seem a flimsy device with which to record the loss of friends and family in a conflict that was until recently largely forgotten in the Irish Republic, but the written tribute is a more sacred act of commemoration than the cold veneer of ornamental masonry. It is more sacred because, with all its imperfections, poetry, unlike the agreeable tidiness of monuments, reminds us of our and its incompletion.

The dedication of the Irish Tower at Messines in 1998 is a belated yet commendable attempt to ensure that the thousands of Irishmen who perished in the Great War will not be forgotten. Yet all the memorials, auspicious speeches, and wreath-laying ceremonies will never expiate the price of our history—a price only a visitor to the battlefields of the Great War can begin to comprehend. Only in the individual act of remembrance can we understand the importance of not forgetting. Today, near the Ieper (Ypres) Salient, a place that saw some of the most horrific fighting of the war, lies the Tyne Cot Memorial, located roughly nine kilometers northeast of the town of Ieper. In the northeastern corner of the cemetery is the Tyne Cot Memorial to the Missing. Panels 140 and 141 record the name and rank of an ordinary Irish soldier, one Private David McGrann MM, Ninth battalion Royal Irish Fusiliers, who died on Thursday, 16 August 1917, aged thirty-six. The names of thousands of other Irish soldiers like him are engraved on cross, stone, and obelisk across the French and Belgian countryside, and now, with the advent of a new millennium, one would think that the politics of their deaths would have faded into retrospect. But not far from the memorial, which is the only resemblance to a grave marker that Private McGrann and many others like him have, lies the Tynecotstraat and beyond that the Zonnebeekseweg where traffic rolls unceasingly to other arterial routes leading to Brussells, home of the European Parliament and headquarters of N.A.T.O. and a Europe radically altered from the one these dead fought for over eight decades ago. With the enduring agonies of an Ireland still not at peace and ethnic hatreds still fanning afresh in the Balkans, if the Irish dead could rise miraculously unscathed from their graves, they would wonder why so little has changed. Yet in the face of such chilling ironies, Irish poets continue to provide us with voices that testify to the emotional absences that still linger with us long after the First World War officially ended. Their war poems register our eternal need to transcend all that is obscene in the human experience and remind us of our duty not to forget our war dead, a duty Francis Ledwidge acknowledged with such ironic prescience in his last poem "To One Who Comes Now and Then" (1992, 72–73), written at the front just days before his death:

> Come often, friend; with welcome and surprise
> We'll greet you from the sea or from the town;
> Come when you like and from whatever skies
> Above you smile or frown.

Notes

CHAPTER 1: INTRODUCTION

1. Ormsby 1992.
2. Binchy 1998, 64.
3. The Commonwealth War Graves Commission estimates that "38,000 Irish people" were killed during the war "out of a total of nearly 250,000 who fought." See Attempts to identify Irish dead of First World War. *Irish Times* (Dublin), 29 May 2000 (http://www.irish-times.ie/). See also Casey 1997.
4. Other noteworthy fictional works that examine the Irish war experience are Liam O'Flaherty's novel *The Return of the Brute* (1929) and *Somme Day Mourning* (1994), a play written by Brian Irvine and produced for the stage by the Shankill (West Belfast) Community Theatre and later performed as part of a series of activities marking the eightieth anniversary of the Thirty-sixth Ulster Division's heroic yet ultimately doomed attack at Thiepval during the first day of the Somme offensive. Hugh Cecil describes O'Flaherty's book as a "tale of superstitious emotional Irish Guardsmen grumbling and hating in the mud of Arras," and despite the general consensus that it is O'Flaherty's "worst book," Cecil notes that it possesses a "monstrous vigour" (Liddle 1985, 220).
5. See Sheridan 1998.
6. See Kevin Myers's An Irishman's Diary. *Irish Times* (Dublin), 20 March 1998 (http://www.irish-times.ie/).

CHAPTER 2: MYTH AND MEMORY

1. From Daire McMahon's The Day a Generation Died. *Lurgan Mail*, 27 June 1996.
2. Another reason for the war memorial's location is that this area of Lurgan used to be a tree-lined mall, and parades were traditionally held there throughout the eighteenth and nineteenth centuries (Clendinning 1999).
3. Catholic involvement in Armistice Day services in Lurgan (and most likely throughout the rest of Northern Ireland) largely ended after World War Two and especially after nationalist celebrations of the Easter Rising's twenty-fifth anniversary (Clendinning 1999).
4. Among the memorabilia found in the Royal Irish Fusiliers Regimental Museum in Armagh are embroidered "postcards" made from pieces of silk that

French women routinely sold to British soldiers who sent them home to their loved ones. Flags were also embroidered, but one of the most popular "post-cards" purchased by Ulster troops consisted of a circle of shamrock enclosing a red hand topped by a green flag with harp and crown and a Union Jack with the logo: "Ulster Forever." Postwar memory obviously could not accommodate such a collection of supposedly incongruous political and cultural insignia.

5. Distaste for the trappings of a British military burial were also shared by Major Willie Redmond's family who, rather than have him buried in a British military cemetery, had his body interred in its own plot beside the Belgian village of Loker's military graveyard. See Patrick Smyth's Flanders Irish War Memorial Completed. *Irish Times* (Dublin), 5 October 1998 (http//:www.irish-times.ie/).

6. *Irish News* columnist Andy Wood's anecdote about a trip he made to Drogheda with the then Northern Ireland Secretary, Sir Patrick Mayhew, provides another example of the extent to which the Great War and World War Two were erased from living memory in the Irish Republic. After Mayhew placed a wreath at the town's war memorial, which honors Irish dead from both world wars, Wood spoke with a small group of "ex-servicemen and service widows [who] said it had been years since they felt able to wear their poppy openly." Wood also noted that "the tablets on the memorial bore the names of disbanded Irish regiments, long since ignored or airbrushed out of popular memory." See Coffee and Buns and Not a Sword in Sight. *Irish News* (Belfast), 25 May 2000 (http://www.irishnews.com/).

7. Somme and Easter Rising mythographies also generate rival martyrologies. When comparing the Ulster Division's offensive at the Somme to the Easter Rising, David Harkness, Professor of Irish history at Queen's University Belfast, notes: "Here was a blood sacrifice far greater and in a mightier cause than that offered up in Dublin." See *Ireland in the Twentieth Century: Divided Island* (1996, 30).

8. This connection between the contemporary UVF and their predecessors who fought at the Somme was further consecrated during the 1980s when UVF prisoners in Long Kesh "called their huts after battlefields where the Ulster Division had fought over 71 years before" (Rolston 1991, 33). More recently, the UVF has taken to appropriating the literature of the Great War to honor its dead. A wall mural and plaque were dedicated on the Shankill Road to several UVF men who were shot dead by the INLA in June 1994. Under the names of the UVF dead appear several lines from Laurence Binyon's Cenotaph favorite, "For the Fallen" (McKittrick et al. 1999, 1364).

9. Another example of the appropriation of Irish iconography associated with the Great War is the adoption of the Irish Guards' motto "Quis Separabit" ("Who Will Separate Us") by various loyalist paramilitary factions. See Rolston 1991, 21.

10. Servia, or Serbia as it came to be known, is, as any student of the Great War knows, where arguably the first shots of the war were fired with the assassination of the Archduke Francis Ferdinand in June 1914. See Fussell, 1975, 175, for further details about how Servia was subsequently renamed Serbia by the British press.

11. In postindependence India, memory of that former colony's Great War veterans also proved to be a point of embarrassment for the new state, which was determined to downplay its imperial past in order to procure an agreeable nationalist narrative. See Omissi 1999.

12. See Sheridan 1998.

13. See Michael O'Toole's Wearing a Poppy is Not a Problem, Says McAleese. *Irish News* (Belfast), 9 November 1999 (http://wwww.irishnews.com/).

14. Getting one's photograph taken in full uniform was apparently a ritual for many soldiers as most army depots had a photography studio where they would go to get their image made for family posterity (Clendinning 1999).

15. The poem was later published in *The Nation* and is reproduced in her autobiography (Gregory 1974).

16. In Lurgan, tenters (those men who were responsible for repairing the looms in the linen factories) were especially good army recruiters as they often sent any weavers who could not produce the requisite beams of cloth directly to the local recruiting sergeant (Clendinning 1999).

17. See Anita Gallagher's Nationalism in East Down (90–108) in Fitzpatrick 1988.

18. *The Fureys and Davey Arthur in Concert*. 1984. Ritz Productions. LC 0025.

19. Even Irish literature about the Great War gets adapted into Irish popular culture (in this case Frank McGuinness's play *Observe the Sons of Ulster Marching Towards the Somme*). In 1994, during the All-Ireland Gaelic football final between Down (the eventual winners) and Dublin, a banner spotted among the Ulster county's faithful following read "Observe the Sons of Ulster Marching Towards the Sam." The "Sam" in question is the Sam Maguire trophy awarded to the winning team.

CHAPTER 3: THE SOLDIER POETS

1. Personal diaries were "forbidden" at the front (Powell 1993, xiv), and as the war dragged on, there was "less mention . . . of the overall purpose of the war" in the "letters and diaries of front soldiers" (Eksteins 1989, 180).

2. Submitted for publication in the *Armagh Guardian* by Rev. Gabriel Ryan, Catholic Chaplain of the First Royal Irish Fusiliers.

3. A second edition of the *Complete Poems of Francis Ledwidge* with an introduction by Lord Dunsany was published in 1955. Subsequent editions were edited by Alice Curtayne (1974) and Liam O'Meara (1997).

4. See also Tom Farrell's column in An Irishman's Diary. *Irish Times* (Dublin), 4 August 1997 (http://www.irish-times.ie/).

5. Boland discusses Ledwidge's subscription to the "orthodoxies" of the Irish Literary Revival and criticizes his conventional depiction of women as symbols for Mother Ireland (1990, 32–38).

6. Records of where Ledwidge was killed have not always been accurate. According to Piet Chielens, the In Flanders Fields Museum coordinator, the inscription on Ledwidge's bronze memorial plaque in Slane is erroneous as it states that he was killed in France rather than in Belgium. The inscription on his grave at Boezinge also gets his age wrong; he was twenty-nine when he was killed, not twenty-six.

7. Treitschke or Treitsche, Heinrich Gotthard von (1834–1896). German historian.

8. *Soldier Songs* was published in 1917 and not 1919 as some sources report.

9. There appears to be some confusion about when MacGill died. Volume

116 of *Contemporary Authors, The Dictionary of Irish Literature* (1996 ed.) and *The Oxford Companion to Irish Literature* (1996) all report that he died in November 1963 after a lengthy bout with multiple scerlosis. However, Dungan (1997, 134) claims that MacGill died in 1940, also from multiple sclerosis. There is consensus about where he is buried. The Notre Dame Cemetery in Fall River, Massachusetts is MacGill's final resting place, an ocean apart from his native Glenties (May 1986, 294; Aspinwall 1991, 321).

10. Brandon Books published *The Navvy Poet: The Collected Poetry of Patrick MacGill* in 1984; the collection includes poems from *Songs of the Dead End* (1912), *Soldier Songs (1917), and Songs of Donegal* (1921).

CHAPTER 4: THE HOME FRONT

1. Most of these war poems were later included in Russell 1935.

2. First published in *The London Times* in September of 1914 and later included as the first poem in Russell 1915.

3. This poem was not included in Russell 1935.

4. This poem does not appear in Russell 1935.

5. See letter of 13 October 1915 to Lady Gregory in Gregory 1974, 523.

6. First published in the *Dublin Evening Telegraph* on 22 May 1918.

7. Besides her son, Lady Gregory lost four nephews (Rudolph, Dudley, Henry, and Aubrey Persse) while a fifth ("another Dudley Persse") later died of his wounds after being invalided home (Gregory 1974, 550). Other relatives who were killed in the war were Geoffrey Persse, who died at Gallipoli, a great-nephew, Percy Trench, who was killed near the Tigris, and Hugh Lane, who went down with the *Lusitania* (550).

8. This version of the poem appears in Allt and Alspach's *The Variorum Edition of the Poems of W. B. Yeats* (Yeats 1957, 791). Despite Allt and Alspach's claim that no variants exist, another version of the poem can be found in volume 1 of Richard J. Finneran's 1989 edition of *The Collected Works of W. B. Yeats: W. B. Yeats: The Poems* (Yeats 1989, 561–62). While both versions consist of twenty-four lines, half of the lines in the Finneran edition differ slightly in content, word selection, and tone. For example, lines three and four in Allt and Alspach sound more recriminatory: "We called it a good death. Today / Can ghost or man be satisfied?" In Finneran, the underlying bitterness of these lines is replaced by a more hesitant, mollifying voice: "I think that you were satisfied, / And life at last seemed worth the pains."

CHAPTER 5: POSTWAR REFLECTIONS

1. Ulster historian George Fleming disputes the Orange Order's claim that many of its members died at the Somme, arguing, among other things, that there is no documented evidence to support the Order's contention that many of those who served with the Thirty-sixth Ulster Division during the July 1916 offensive were members of Orange lodges. To support his claim that there were no Orangemen on the Somme, Fleming cites "King's Regulations 1912

paragraph 451" which forbade members of the British military from joining politically partisan organizations like the Orange Order or the Ancient Order of Hibernians. See letter to the editor, *Irish News* (Belfast), 8 October 1998 (http://www.irishnews.com/).

2. Population figures for Anglo-Irish Protestants in the south of Ireland were in decline since the onset of the Home Rule crisis. The number of southern Irish Protestants dropped by "32.5 percent" between 1911 and 1926 (McDowell 1997, 164).

CHAPTER 6: MODERN MEMORY

1. Simmons (1933–2001) and his wife and fellow poet Janice Fitzpatrick ran The Poets' School near Falcarragh in Co. Donegal.

2. In honor of the poet's memory, the John Hewitt Summer School is held each July on the campus of St. Mac Nissi's College, Garron Tower, Carnlough.

3. The poem was first published in *The Observer* (Sunday edition), 9 November 1997.

4. According to the Commonwealth War Graves Commission, Owen's grave is not in a military cemetery. Instead, he is buried in the Ors Communal Cemetery, a small village graveyard where sixty Great War dead are interred. The village of Ors is in the North of France, not far from the villages of Le Cateau and Landrecies. See the Debt of Honour Register at the Commonwealth War Graves Commission website: (http://www.cwgc.org/).

5. The red poppy (or "de klaproos" as it is known in the local Flemish vernacular) has a reputation for being a hardy annual. It generally flourishes in uprooted soil, so it is not surprising that it would have prospered among the shell holes and craters of the Western Front.

6. Longley must be accorded his poetic license, but his reference to the "lucifer" is apparently anachronistic. Brophy and Partridge (1965, 216) note that "lucifer" matches were "long out of date" by the outbreak of the Great War.

CHAPTER 7: CONCLUSION

1. For further discussion of Orpen as a war artist, see Jeffery 1993.

2. Quote taken from Ní Chuilleanáin's note in a letter to the author, 10 July 2000.

3. Born in Burnley, Lancashire, Dugdale (1931–95) moved to Belfast in 1948 to work for the Northern Ireland Civil Service. The author of four volumes of poetry, his *Collected Poems* was published in 1995.

4. Born in 1976, Carson was the youngest poet to appear in Frank Ormsby's 1992 anthology of poems about the Northern Irish Troubles—*A Rage for Order*.

5. Medbh McGuckian has also acknowledged her initial reluctance to directly address war and politics in her poetry. See When Hope and History did Rhyme (Emmit 1999, 16).

6. Taken from MacNeice's poem "Prologue" (Stallworthy 1995, 489).

Works Cited

Adamson, Ian. 1974. The *Cruthin: A History of the Ulster Land and People*. Belfast: Pretani.

———. 1982. *The Identity of Ulster*. Belfast: Pretani.

Amory, Mark. 1972. *Lord Dunsany: A Biography*. London: Collins.

Archibald, Douglas. 1983. *Yeats*. Syracuse, N.Y.: Syracuse University Press.

Armstrong, Tim. 1995. Muting the Klaxon: Poetry, History, and Irish Modernism. In *Modernism and Ireland: The Poetry of the 1930s*, edited by P. Coughlan and A. Davis. Cork: Cork University Press.

Aspinwall, Bernard. 1991. Patrick MacGill, 1890–1963: The Voice of the Irish, British and Universal Man. *Contemporary Review* 258: 320–25.

Asquith, Cynthia (Lady). 1968. *Lady Cynthia Asquith Diaries, 1915–1918*. London: Hutchinson.

Bardon, Jonathan. 1992. *A History of Ulster*. Belfast: Blackstaff.

Barry, Sebastian. 1995. *Three Plays by Sebastian Barry*. London: Methuen.

———. 1998. *The Whereabouts of Eneas McNulty*. London: Picador.

Bartlett, Thomas. 1993. "A Weapon of War Yet Untried": Irish Catholics and the Armed Forces of the Crown, 1760–1830. In *Men, Women, and War*, edited by T. G. Fraser and K. Jeffery. Dublin: Lilliput.

Binchy, Maeve. Five Sisters Alone Against Their World. *The New York Times*, 13 September 1998, 64.

Birmingham, George A. 1919. *A Padre in France*. New York: Doran.

Boas, Frederick S. 1917. *Songs of Ulster and Balliol*. London: Constable.

Boland Eavan. 1975. *The War Horse*. Dublin: Arlen House.

———. 1990. Eavan Boland: Outside History. *American Poetry Review* (Mar./Apr.): 32–38.

———. 1990. *Outside History: Selected Poems 1980–1990*. New York and London: Norton.

———. 1995. Writing the Political Poem in Ireland. *The Southern Review* 31, no. 3: 485–98.

———. 1996. *An Origin Like Water: Collected Poems 1967–1987*. New York: Norton.

Bowman, John, 1993. Introduction to *The Tenth Irish Division in Gallipoli*, by Bryan Cooper. 1918. Reprint, Dublin: Irish Academic Press.

Bowman, Timothy. 1996. The Irish at the Somme. *History Ireland* 4, no. 4: 48–52.

287

Boyce, D. G. 1991. Northern Ireland: A Place Apart? In *Culture and Politics in Northern Ireland 1960–1990*, edited by E. Hughes. Milton Keynes, England: Open University Press.

———. 1993. *The Sure Confusing Drum: Ireland and the First World War.* Swansea, Wales: University College of Swansea.

Bradley, Anthony. 1988. Literature and Culture in the North of Ireland. In *Cultural Contexts and Literary Idioms in Contemporary Irish Literature*, edited by M. Kenneally. Totowa, N.J.: Barnes and Noble.

———. 1989. The Irishness of Irish Poetry after Yeats. In *New Irish Writing: Essays in Memory of Raymond J. Porter*, edited by J. D. Brophy and E. Grennan. Boston: G. K. Hall.

Brantlinger, Patrick. 1988. *Rule of Darkness: British Literature and Imperialism, 1830–1914.* Ithaca: Cornell University Press.

Brearton, Fran. 2000. *The Great War in Irish Poetry: W. B. Yeats to Michael Longley.* Oxford: Oxford University Press.

Bredin, A. E. C. 1987. *A History of the Irish Soldier.* Belfast: Century Books.

Breen, Jennifer. 1990. Representation of the "Feminine" in First World War Poetry. *Critical Survey* 2: 169–75.

Breen, Muriel. 1993. *Liquorice All-Sorts: A Girl Growing Up.* Dublin: Moytura.

Bridges, Robert. 1916. Introduction to *The Star Fields and Other Poems,* by Willoughby Weaving. Oxford: Basil Blackwell.

Brooke, Rupert. 1916. *The Collected Poems of Rupert Brooke.* New York: John Lane.

Brophy, John, and Eric Partridge. 1965. *The Long Trail: What the British Soldier Sang and Said in the Great War of 1918.* London: André Deutsch.

Brown, Stephen J. 1970. MacGill, Patrick. In *Ireland in Fiction: A Guide to Irish Novels, Tales, Romances and Folklore.* 2d ed. New York: Burt Franklin.

Brown, Terence. 1975. *Northern Voices: Poets from Ulster.* Dublin: Gill and Macmillan.

———. 1985. *Ireland: A Social and Cultural History, 1922 to the Present.* Ithaca and London: Cornell University Press.

———. 1992. British Ireland. In *Culture in Ireland: Division or Diversity*, edited by E. Longley. Belfast: Institute of Irish Studies Q.U.B.

———. 1995. Ireland, Modernism, and the 1930s. In *Modernism and Ireland: The Poetry of the 1930s*, edited by P. Coughlan and A. Davis.

Buckley, Anthony. 1991. Uses of History Among Ulster Protestants. In *The Poet's Place: Ulster Literature and Society*, edited by G. Dawe and J. W. Foster. Belfast: Institute of Irish Studies Q.U.B.

Burnham, Richard. 1979. O'Sullivan, Seumas (1879–1958). In *Dictionary of Irish Literature,* edited by R. Hogan. Westport, Conn.: Greenwood Press.

Bushrui, Suheil Badi. 1982. Images of a Changing Ireland in the Works of W. B. Yeats. In *Literature and the Changing Ireland*, edited by P. Connolly. Totowa, N.J.: Barnes and Noble.

Butler, Hubert. 1985. *Escape from the Anthill.* Mullingar, Ireland: Lilliput.

Byers, John. 1922. Introduction to *The Ballads of Ballytumulty,* by Samuel McCurry. Belfast: Carswell.

Cadogan, Mary, and Patricia Craig. 1978. *Women and Children First: The Fiction of Two World Wars*. London: Gollancz.

Caesar, Adrian. 1993. *Taking It Like a Man: Suffering, Sexuality and the War Poets, Brooke, Sassoon, Owen, Graves*. Manchester: Manchester University Press.

Callan, Patrick. 1987. Recruiting for the British Army in Ireland During the First World War. *Irish Sword: The Journal of the Military History Society of Ireland* 17: 42–56.

Callow, Heather Cook. 1990. James Joyce and Politics. In *Irish Writers and Politics*, edited by O. Komesu and M. Sekine. Savage, Md.: Barnes and Noble.

Cardinal, Agnès. 1993. Women on the Other Side. In *Women and World War One: The Written Response*, edited by D. Goldman. London: Macmillan.

Carnduff, Thomas. 1924. *Songs From the Shipyards and Other Poems*. Belfast: E. H. Thornton.

———. 1932. *Songs of an Out-of-Work*. Belfast: Quota.

———. 1993. *Poverty Street and Other Belfast Poems*. Belfast: Lapwing.

———. 1994. *Thomas Carnduff: His Life and Writings*. Edited by John Gray. Belfast: Lagan Press.

Carter, D. N. G. 1988. W. B. Yeats and the Poetry of the First World War. *Focus on Robert Graves and his Contemporaries* 1: 13–22.

Casement, Roger. 1958. *The Crime Against Europe*. Edited by Herbert O. Mackey. Dublin: C. J. Fallon.

Casey, Patrick J. 1997. Irish Casualties in the First World War. *The Irish Sword* 20: 193–206.

Catterson, Simon. 1996. Re-inventing Revisionism. *Fortnight* (Belfast) 346: 33–34.

Cecil, Hugh. 1996. *The Flower of Battle: How Britain Wrote the Great War*. South Royalton, Vt.: Steerforth Press.

Cheng, Vincent. 1995. *Joyce, Race, and Empire*. Cambridge: Cambridge University Press.

Chielens, Piet. 1997. Letter to author, 17 November.

Clayton, Pamela. 1996. *Enemies and Passing Friends: Settler Ideologies in Twentieth Century Ulster*. London: Pluto Press.

Clendinning, Kieran. 1994. Lurgan Soldiers Who Fought in the Great War. Typescript.

———. 1999. Interview by author. Lurgan, N. Ireland, 11 June.

Clifford, Brendan. 1992. Introduction to *Ireland in the Great War: The Irish Insurrection of 1916 Set in Its Context of the World War,* by Charles James O'Donnell and Brendan Clifford. Belfast: Athol.

Cooper, Bryan. 1993. *The Tenth (Irish) Division in Gallipoli*. 1918. Reprint, Dublin: Irish Academic Press.

Cork, Richard. 1994. *A Bitter Truth: Avant-Garde Art and the Great War*. New Haven and London: Yale University Press.

Coughlan, Patricia. 1991. "Bog Queens": The Representation of Women in the Poetry of John Montague and Seamus Heaney. In *Gender in Irish Writing,* edited by T. O'Brien Johnson and D. Cairns. Milton Keynes, England and Philadelphia: Open University Press.

Coughlan, Patricia, and Alex Davis, eds. 1995. *Modernism and Ireland: The Poetry of the 1930s*. Cork: Cork University Press.

Cross, Tim. 1989. *The Lost Voices of World War One*. London: Bloomsbury.

Crotty, Patrick, ed. 1994. *Modern Irish Poetry*. Chester Springs, Pa.: Dufour.

Cullingford, Elizabeth. 1981. *Yeats, Ireland, and Fascism*. New York: New York University Press.

Curtayne, Alice. 1972. *Francis Ledwidge: A Life of the Poet (1887–1917)*. London: Martin Brian and O'Keeffe.

———. 1980. Appreciation: Francis Ledwidge, Who Fought in Another Man's War. *Éire-Ireland* 15, no. 2: 114–27.

Curtis, Tony. 1985. A More Social Voice: *Field Work*. In *The Art of Seamus Heaney*, edited by T. Curtis. Chester Springs, Pa.: Dufour; Bridgend, Mid Glamorgan: Poetry Wales Press.

Dangerfield, George. 1935. *The Strange Death of Liberal England*. New York: Harrison Smith and Robert Haas.

Davis, Robert Bernard. 1977. *George William Russell ("AE")*. Boston: Twayne.

Dawe, Gerald. 1988. A Question of Imagination—Poetry in Ireland Today. In *Cultural Contexts and Literary Idioms in Contemporary Irish Literature*, edited by M. Kennelly. Totowa, N.J.: Barnes and Noble.

———. 1993. Review of *Heresy: The Battle of Ideas in Modern Ireland*, by Desmond Fennell. *Fortnight* (Belfast) 323: 43–44.

Dawson, Hugh J. 1988. Thomas MacGreevy and Joyce. *James Joyce Quarterly* 25, no. 3: 305–21.

Deane, Seamus. 1989. Yeats: The Creation of an Audience. In *Tradition in Anglo-Irish Poetry*, edited by T. Brown and N. Grene. Totowa, N.J.: Barnes and Noble.

Dearmer, Mabel. 1916. *Letters from a Field Hospital*. London: Macmillan.

Deeny, James. 1989. *To Cure and to Care: Memoirs of a Chief Medical Officer*. Dun Laoghaire, Ireland: Glendale Press.

Denman, Terence. 1991. The Catholic Irish Soldier in the First World War: the "Racial Environment." *Irish Historical Studies* 27: 352–65.

———. 1992. *Ireland's Unknown Soldiers: The Sixteenth (Irish) Division in the Great War, 1914–1918*. Dublin: Irish Academic Press.

———. 1995. *A Lonely Grave: The Life and Death of William Redmond*. Dublin: Irish Academic Press.

Di Nicola, Robert. 1986. Time and History in Seamus Heaney's "In Memoriam Francis Ledwidge." *Éire-Ireland* 21, no. 4: 45–51.

Dole, Carole M. 1983. Francis Ledwidge. In *The Dictionary of Literary Biography*. Vol. 20, edited by D. E. Stanford. Detroit: Gale.

Dooley, Thomas P. 1995. *Irishmen or English Soldiers? The Times and World of a Southern Catholic Irish Man (1876–1916) Enlisting in the British Army During the First World War*. Liverpool: Liverpool University Press.

Drinkwater, John. 1918. The Poetry of Ledwidge. *Edinburgh Review* 228: 180–89.

Dugdale, Norman. 1997. *Collected Poems 1970–1995*. Belfast: Lagan Press.

Dungan, Myles. 1993. *Distant Drums: Irish Soldiers in Foreign Armies*. Belfast: Appletree.

———. 1995. *Irish Voices from the Great War*. Dublin: Irish Academic Press.

———. 1997. *"They Shall Not Grow Old": Irish Soldiers and the Great War*. Dublin: Four Courts Press.

Dunsany, Lord. 1916. Introduction to *Songs of the Fields*, by Francis Ledwidge. London: Jenkins.

———. 1918. *Tales of War*. London: G. P. Putnam's.

———. 1929. *Fifty Poems*. London: G. P. Putnam's.

———. 1938. *Patches of Sunlight*. London: William Heinemann; New York: Reynal and Hitchcock.

———. 1941. *War Poems*. London: Hutchinson.

Durcan, Paul. 1982. *The Selected Paul Durcan*. Edited by Edna Longley. Belfast: Blackstaff.

East, Joyce E. 1996. Exploring Irish Women's Poetry. *Irish Literary Supplement* 15: 12.

Eksteins, Modris. 1989. *Rites of Spring: The Great War and the Birth of the Modern Age*. New York: Houghton Mifflin.

Ellis, John. 1976. *Eye-Deep in Hell: Trench Warfare in World War One*. Baltimore: The Johns Hopkins University Press.

Ellmann, Richard. 1948. *Yeats: The Man and the Masks*. New York: Macmillan.

———. 1954. *The Identity of Yeats*. London: Macmillan.

———. 1959. *James Joyce*. New York: Oxford University Press.

Emmitt, Helen V. 1999. When Hope and History Rhyme. *Irish Literary Supplement* 19: 16.

Espey, John J. 1955. *Ezra Pound's "Mauberley."* Berkeley and Los Angeles: University of California Press.

Eyler, Audrey S., and Robert F. Garratt. 1988. Introduction to *The Uses of the Past: Essays on Irish Culture*. Edited by Audrey Eyler and Robert Garratt. Newark: University of Delaware Press.

Fairhall, James. 1993. *James Joyce and the Question of History*. Cambridge: Cambridge University Press.

Fallon, Ann Connerton. 1979. *Katharine Tynan*. Boston: Twayne.

Falls, Cyril. 1922. *The History of the Thirty-sixth (Ulster) Division*. Belfast: McCaw, Stevenson, and Orr.

———. 1930. *War Books: A Critical Guide*. London: Davies.

Featherstone, Simon. 1995. *War Poetry: An Introductory Reader*. New York: Routledge.

Feeney, William J. 1979. Letts, Winifred M. In *Dictionary of Irish Literature*, edited by R. Hogan.

Fennell, Desmond. 1994. *Heresy: The Battle of Ideas in Modern Ireland*. Chester Springs, Pa.: Dufour.

Fiacc, Padraic. 1994. *Ruined Pages: Selected Poems*. Belfast: Blackstaff.

Finneran, Richard J., George Mills Harper, and William M. Murphy, eds. 1977. *Letters to W. B. Yeats*. Vol. 2. London: Macmillan.

Fitzpatrick, David. 1982–85. Ballads as History. *Irish Folk Music Studies* 4: 58–62.

———. ed. 1988. *Ireland and the First World War*. Mullingar, Ireland: Lilliput.

———. 1998. *The Two Irelands: 1912–1939*. Oxford and New York: Oxford University Press.

Flanagan, Thomas. 1975. Yeats, Joyce, and the Matter of Ireland. *Critical Inquiry* 2: 43–67.

———. 1988. Contrasting Fables in *The Year of the French*. In *The Uses of the Past: Essays on Irish Culture*, edited by A. S. Eyler and R. F. Garratt. Newark: University of Delaware Press.

———. 1996. The Literature of Resistance: An Inquiry into the Relationship between Irish Culture and British Imperialism. *New York Times Book Review*, 17 March.

Fogarty, Anne. 1995. Gender, Irish Modernism and the 1930s. In *Modernism and Ireland: The Poetry of the 1930s*, edited by P. Coughlan and A. Davis.

Foster, John Wilson. 1991. *Colonial Consequences: Essays in Irish Literature and Culture*. Dublin: Lilliput.

Foster, Roy. 1988. *Modern Ireland, 1600–1972*. London: Penguin.

———. 1997. *W. B. Yeats: A Life, The Apprentice Mage, 1865–1914*. Oxford: Oxford University Press.

Foster, Thomas C. 1989. *Seamus Heaney*. Boston: Twayne.

Fox, R. M. 1958. *Louie Bennett: Her Life and Times*. Dublin: Talbot.

Francis Ledwidge. 1987. In *Twentieth-Century Literature Criticism*. Vol. 23, edited by D. Poupard, M. Lazzari, and T. Ligotti. Detroit: Gale.

Friel, Brian. 1990. *Dancing at Lughnasa*. Boston: Faber and Faber.

Fuller, J. G. 1990. *Troop Morale and Popular Culture in the British and Dominion Armies, 1914–1918*. Oxford: Clarendon.

Fussell, Paul. 1975. *The Great War and Modern Memory*. London and New York: Oxford University Press.

Gardner, Brian, ed. 1964. *Up the Line to Death*. London: Methuen.

Garratt, Robert F. 1986. *Modern Irish Poetry: Tradition and Continuity from Yeats to Heaney*. Berkeley: University of California Press.

Gébler, Carlo. 1998. *How to Murder a Man*. London: Little, Brown.

Gerstenberger, Donna. 1990. W. B. Yeats: Politics and History. In *Irish Writers and Politics*, edited by O. Komesu and M. Sekine. Savage, Md.: Barnes and Noble.

Gibbon, Monk. 1968. *Inglorious Soldier*. London: Hutchinson.

Gilbert, Susan, and Susan Gubar. 1988. *No Man's Land: The Place of the Woman Writer in the Twentieth Century*. Vol. 2. New Haven, Conn.: Yale University Press.

Goldring, Maurice. 1995. *Pleasant the Scholar's Life: Irish Intellectuals and the Construction of the Nation State*. London: Serif.

Gore-Booth, Eva. 1929. *Poems of Eva Gore-Booth*. London: Longmans, Green.

Graves, Robert. 1922. *On English Poetry*. London: William Heinemann.

Gray, John. 1994. Introduction to *Thomas Carnduff: His Life and Writings*, by Thomas Carnduff. Belfast: Lagan Press.

Greacen, Robert. 1981. *Patrick MacGill: Champion of the Underdog*. Glenties, Ireland: Glenties Development Association.

———. 1995. *Collected Poems, 1944–1994*. Belfast: Lagan Press.

Green, Carlanda. 1983. The Feminine Principle in Seamus Heaney's Poetry. *Ariel* 14: 3–13.

Gregory, Isabella Augusta (Lady). 1974. *Seventy Years: Being the Autobiography of Lady Gregory*. Gerrards Cross, England: Colin Smythe.

———. 1978. *Lady Gregory's Journals, Volume I: Books One to Twenty-Nine, 10 October 1916–24 February 1925*. Edited by Daniel Murphy. New York: Oxford University Press.

———. 1995. *Selected Writings*. Edited by Lucy McDiarmid and Maureen Waters. London: Penguin.

Gwynn, Stephen. 1924. *Collected Poems*. New York: Appleton. Original Edition, London: Blackwood, 1923.

Haberstroh, Patricia. 1996. *Women Creating Women*. Syracuse, N.Y.: Syracuse University Press.

Hall, Michael. 1993. *Sacrifice on the Somme*. Newtownabbey, N. Ireland: Island Publications.

Hanley, Lynne. 1991. *Writing War: Fiction, Gender, and Memory*. Amherst: University of Massachusetts Press.

Harkness, David. 1996. *Ireland in the Twentieth Century: Divided Island*. London: Macmillan.

Harris, Henry. 1968. *The Irish Regiments in the First World War*. Cork: Mercier.

Haughton, Hugh. 1992. Place and Displacement in the Poetry of Derek Mahon. In *The Chosen Ground: Essays on the Contemporary Poetry of Northern Ireland*, edited by N. Corcoran. Chester Springs, Pa.: Dufour.

Heaney, Seamus. 1979. *Field Work*. New York: Farrar.

———. 1980. *Poems: 1965–1975*. New York: Farrar, Straus, and Giroux.

———. 1980. *Preoccupations: Selected Prose 1968–78*. London: Faber and Faber.

———. 1990. *The Cure at Troy*. London: Faber and Faber.

———. 1992. Introduction to *Francis Ledwidge: Selected Poems*. Edited by Dermot Bolger. Dublin: New Island Books.

———. 1999. *Opened Ground: Selected Poems*. New York: Farrar.

Heaney, Seamus, and Ted Hughes, eds. 1997. *The School Bag*. London: Faber and Faber.

Hennessey, Thomas. 1998. *Dividing Ireland: World War I and Partition*. London and New York: Routledge.

Hewitt, John. 1991. *The Collected Poems of John Hewitt*. Edited by Frank Ormsby. Belfast: Blackstaff.

Higonnet, Margaret, et al., eds. 1987. *Behind the Lines: Gender and the Two World Wars*. New Haven, Conn.: Yale University Press.

Hogan, Robert, ed. 1979. *Dictionary of Irish Literature*. Westport, Conn.: Greenwood Press.

———. 1996. *Dictionary of Irish Literature*. Westport, Conn.: Greenwood Press.

Holmes, Carrie Ellen. 1916. *In the Day of Battle: Poems of the Great War.* Toronto: W. Briggs.

Hughes, Michael. 1994. *Ireland Divided: The Roots of the Modern Irish Problem.* New York: St. Martin's Press.

Hynes, Samuel. 1990. *A War Imagined: The First World War and English Culture.* London: Bodley Head.

Inglis, Brian. 1973. *Roger Casement.* London: Hodder and Stoughton.

Innes. C. L. 1993. *Woman and Nation in Irish Literature and Society, 1880–1935.* Athens: University of Georgia Press.

Irish Writers Protest. 1918. *Dublin Evening Telegraph,* 22 May.

Jackson, Alvin. 1994. Unionist History. In *Interpreting Irish History: The Debate on Historical Revisionism, 1938–1994,* edited by C. Brady. Dublin: Irish Academic Press.

Jeffares, A. Norman. 1968. *A Commentary on the Collected Poems of W. B. Yeats.* Stanford: Stanford University Press.

———, ed. 1982. *Anglo-Irish Literature.* Dublin: Gill and Macmillan.

Jeffery, Keith. 1993. The Great War in Modern Irish Memory. In *Men, Women, and War,* edited by T. G. Fraser and K. Jeffery. Dublin: Lilliput.

———. 2000. *Ireland and the Great War.* Cambridge: Cambridge University Press.

Jenkins, Lee. 1994. Thomas MacGreevy and the Pressure of Reality. *The Wallace Stevens Journal* 18, no. 2: 146–56.

Johnston, Dillon. 1985. *Irish Poetry After Joyce.* South Bend, Ind.: University of Notre Dame Press; Dublin, Dolmen.

Johnston, Jennifer. 1974. *How Many Miles to Babylon?* London: Hamish Hamilton.

Johnston, John. 1964. *English Poetry of the First World War: A Study in the Evolution of Lyric and Narrative Form.* Princeton: Princeton University Press.

Johnstone, Tom. 1992. *Orange, Green, and Khaki: The Story of the Irish Regiments in the Great War, 1914–1918.* London: Macmillan.

Joshi, S. T. 1995. *Lord Dunsany: Master of the Anglo-Irish Imagination.* Westport, Conn.: Greenwood Press.

Joshi, S. T., and Darrell Schweitzer, eds. 1993. *Lord Dunsany: A Bibliography.* Metuchen, N.J.: The Scarecrow Press.

Joyce, James. 1959. *The Critical Writings of James Joyce.* Edited by Ellsworth Mason and Richard Ellmann. New York: Viking.

———. 1991. *James Joyce: Poems and Shorter Writings.* London: Faber and Faber.

Kain, Richard M., and James H. O'Brien. 1976. *George Russell.* Lewisburg, Pa.: Bucknell University Press.

Kelly, James. 1995. *Bonfires on the Hillside: An Eyewitness Account of Political Upheaval in Northern Ireland.* Belfast: Fountain.

Kelly, John S. 1990. The Fifth Bell: Race and Class in Yeats's Political Thought. In *Irish Writers and Politics,* edited by O. Komesu and M. Sekine. Savage, Md.: Barnes and Noble.

Kermode, Frank. 1961. *Romantic Image.* New York: Chilmark Press.

Kerrigan, John. 1997. Birth of a Náision. *London Review of Books* 19, no. 11: 16–17.

Kettle, T. M. 1916. *Poems and Parodies*. London: Duckworth.

———. 1917. *The Ways of War*. New York: Scribner's.

Khan, Nosheen. 1988. *Women's Poetry of the First World War*. Lexington: University Press of Kentucky.

Kiberd, Declan. 1988. The War Against the Past. In *The Uses of the Past: Essays in Irish Culture*, edited by A. S. Eyler and R. F. Garratt. Newark: University of Delaware Press.

———. 1995. *Inventing Ireland*. London: Jonathan Cape.

Kime Scott, Bonnie. 1979. Kettle, Thomas. In *Dictionary of Irish Literature*, edited by R. Hogan.

Kirk-Smith, Ian. 1995. Ruthless Liberalism. *Fortnight* (Belfast) 338: 28–30.

Knowlson, James. 1996. *Damned to Fame: The Life of Samuel Beckett*. New York: Simon and Schuster.

Krimm, Bernard G. 1981. *W. B. Yeats and the Emergence of the Irish Free State, 1918–1939: Living in the Explosion*. Troy, N.Y.: Whitston.

Ledwidge, Francis. 1916. *Songs of the Fields, with an Introduction by Lord Dunsany*. London: Jenkins.

———. 1955. *Complete Poems of Francis Ledwidge*. Edited by Lord Dunsany. London: Jenkins.

———. 1974. *The Complete Poems of Francis Ledwidge*. Edited by Alice Curtayne. London: Brian and O'Keeffe.

———. 1992. *Selected Poems*. Edited by Dermot Bolger. Dublin: New Island Books.

———. 1997. *The Complete Poems of Francis Ledwidge*. Edited by Liam O'Meara. Newbridge, Ireland: Goldsmith.

Leonard, Jane. 1988. Lest We Forget. In *Ireland and the First World War*, edited by D. Fitzpatrick.

———. 1996. The Reaction of Irish Officers in the British Army to the Easter Rising of 1916. In *Facing Armageddon: The First World War Experienced*, edited by Hugh Cecil and Peter H. Liddle. London: Leo Cooper.

Letts, Winifred. 1916. *Hallowe'en and Poems of the War*. London: John Murray.

———. 1917. *The Spires of Oxford and Other Poems*. New York: E. P. Dutton.

Lewis, Gifford. 1988. *Eva Gore-Booth and Esther Roper: A Biography*. London: Pandora.

Liddle, Peter H., ed. 1985. *Home Fires and Foreign Fields: British Social and Military Experience in the First World War*. London: Brassey's.

Liddy, James. 1978. Ulster Poets and the Catholic Muse. *Éire-Ireland* 13, no. 4: 126–37.

Littlefield, Hazel. 1959. *Lord Dunsany: King of Dreams*. New York: Exposition Press.

Loesberg, John, ed. 1979. *Folksongs and Ballads Popular in Ireland*. Vol. 2. Cork: Ossian Publications.

Loftus, Richard J. 1964. *Nationalism in Modern Anglo-Irish Literature*. Madison: University of Wisconsin Press.

Longenbach, James. 1988. *Stone Cottage: Pound, Yeats, and Modernism*. New York and Oxford: Oxford University Press.

Longley, Edna. 1985. Poetry and Politics in Northern Ireland. *The Crane Bag* 9, no. 1: 26–40.

———. 1987. *Poetry in the Wars*. Newark: University of Delaware Press.

———. 1991. "Defending Ireland's Soul": Protestant Writers and Irish Nationalism after Independence. In *Literature and Nationalism*, edited by V. Newey and A. Thompson. Liverpool: Liverpool University Press.

———. 1994. *The Living Stream: Literature and Revisionism in Ireland*. Newcastle: Bloodaxe Books.

Longley, Michael. 1987. *Poems, 1963–1983*. Winston-Salem, N.C.: Wake Forest University Press.

———. 1994. *Tuppenny Stung: Autobiographical Chapters*. Belfast: Lagan Press.

———. 1995a. *The Ghost Orchid*. London: Jonathan Cape.

———. 1995b. An Interview with Michael Longley. By Dermot Healy. *The Southern Review* 31: 557–62.

———. 1998. *Broken Dishes*. Belfast: Abbey Press.

———. 1999. *Selected Poems*. Winston-Salem, N.C.: Wake Forest University Press.

———. 2000. *The Weather in Japan*. Winston-Salem, N.C.: Wake Forest University Press.

Lost Music. 1917. *Times Literary Supplement*, 16 August.

Lyon, John. 1996. Michael Longley's Lists. *English* 45: 228–46.

Lyons, F. S. L. 1979. *Culture and Anarchy in Ireland, 1890–1939*. Oxford: Clarendon.

———. 1994. The Burden of Our History. In *Interpreting Irish History: The Debate on Historical Revisionism, 1938–1994*, edited by C. Brady. Dublin: Irish Academic Press, 1994.

Lyons, J. B. 1983. *The Enigma of Tom Kettle: Irish Patriot, Essayist, Poet, British Soldier, 1880–1916*. Dublin: Glendale Press.

Lysaght, Sean. 1996. The Scourge of Nationalism. *The Irish Literary Supplement* 15: 33.

MacDonagh, Michael. 1916. *The Irish at the Front*. London: Hodder and Stoughton.

MacDonagh, Thomas. 1916. *Literature in Ireland*. London: T. Fisher Unwin.

MacGill, Patrick. 1917. *Soldier Songs*. London: Herbert Jenkins.

———. 1984. *The Navvy Poet: The Collected Poetry of Patrick MacGill*. Dingle, Kerry: Brandon.

MacGreevy, Thomas. 1934. *Poems*. London: William Heinemann.

———. 1991. *Collected Poems of Thomas MacGreevy: An Annotated Edition*. Edited by Susan Schreibman. Washington, D.C.: The Catholic University of America Press.

Mahon, Derek. 1991. *Selected Poems*. London: Viking.

———. 1999. *Collected Poems*. Dublin: Gallery.

Manganiello, Dominic. 1980. *Joyce's Politics*. London: Routledge.

Martin, F. X. 1967. 1916—Myth, Fact, and Mystery. *Studia Hibernica* 7: 7–124.

Marwick, Arthur. 1977. *Women at War, 1914–1918*. London: Fontana.

Matthews, Steven. 1997. *Irish Poetry: Politics, History, Negotiation: The Evolving Debate 1969 to the Present*. New York: St. Martin's Press.

Matthews, Tom. 1968. Chaine of Chaine Park. *The Honest Ulsterman* (October).

May, Hal, ed. 1985. MacGill, Patrick. In *Contemporary Authors*. Vol. 116. Detroit: Gale.

Mays, J. C. C. 1995. How is MacGreevy a Modernist? In *Modernism and Ireland: The Poetry of the 1930s,* edited by P. Coughlan and A. Davis.

McAuley, James W. 1991. Cuchulainn and an RPG-7: The Ideology and Politics of the Ulster Defence Association. In *Culture and Politics in Northern Ireland, 1960–1990*, edited by E. Hughes. Philadelphia: Open University Press

McBride, Ian. 1997. *The Siege of Derry in Ulster Protestant Mythology*. Dublin: Four Courts Press.

McCaffrey, Larry J. 1989. Components of Irish Nationalism. In *Perspectives in Irish Nationalism*, edited by T. E. Hachey and L. J. McCaffrey. Lexington: University Press of Kentucky.

McCartney, Clem, and Lucy Bryson. 1994. *Clashing Symbols? A Report on the Flags, Anthems, and Other National Symbols in Northern Ireland*. Belfast: The Institute of Irish Studies Q.U.B.

McCurry, Samuel S. 1922. *The Ballads of Ballytumulty*. Belfast: Carswell.

McDonald, Peter. 1992. Michael Longley's Homes. In *The Chosen Ground: Essays on the Contemporary Poetry of Northern Ireland*, edited by N. Corcoran. Chester Springs, Pa.: Dufour.

———. 1996. Yeats and Remorse, Chatterton Lecture on Poetry. *Proceedings of the British Academy* 94: 173–206.

McDonnell. 1996. *The Oxford Companion to Irish Literature*. Edited by Robert Welch. Oxford: Clarendon.

McDonnell, Randal. 1932. *Songs of Seaside Places and Other Verses*. Dublin: Talbot.

McDowell, R. B. 1997. *Crisis and Decline: The Fate of the Southern Unionists*. Dublin: Lilliput.

McGuckian, Medbh. 1998. *Shelmalier*. Winston-Salem, N.C.: Wake Forest University Press.

McGuinness, Frank. 1986. *Observe the Sons of Ulster Marching Towards the Somme*. London: Faber and Faber.

McHugh, Roger. 1960. Thomas Kettle and Francis Sheehy-Skeffington. In *The Shaping of Modern Ireland*, edited by C. C. O' Brien. Toronto: University of Toronto Press.

McIlroy, Brian. 1990. Poetry Imagery as Political Fetishism. *The Canadian Journal of Irish Studies* 16: 59–64.

McKittrick, Seamus et al. 1999. *Lost Lives: The Stories of the Men, Women and Children Who Died as a Result of the Northern Ireland Troubles*. Edinburgh and London: Mainstream Publishing.

Middlebrook, Martin. 1972. *The First Day on the Somme*. New York: Norton.

Millar, Frank, and Ian Adamson. 1991. Introduction to *The Great War 1914–1918*. Belfast: Citizens Committee, City Hall, 1919. Reprint, Belfast: Pretani.

Miller, David. 1978. *Queen's Rebels: Ulster Loyalism in Historical Perspective.* Dublin: Gill and Macmillan.

Montague, John. 1972. *The Rough Field.* Winston-Salem, N.C.: Wake Forest University Press.

————. 1995. *Collected Poems.* Winston-Salem, N.C.: Wake Forest University Press.

Montefiore, Janet. 1993. "Shining Pins and Wailing Shells": Women Poets and the Great War. In *Women and World War 1: The Written Response,* edited by M. Goldman. London: Macmillan.

Moorhouse, Geoffrey. 1993. *Hell's Foundations: A Town, Its Myths, and Gallipoli.* London: Sceptre.

Morrison, Danny. 1996. Fantasy Festival. *Fortnight* (Belfast) 353: 30–31.

Murphy, Cliona. 1989. The Tune of the Stars and Stripes: The American Influence on the Irish Suffrage Movement. In *Women Surviving: Studies in Irish Women's History in the 19th and 20th Centuries,* edited by M. Luddy and C. Murphy. Dublin: Poolbeg.

Ní Chuilleanáin, Eiléan. 1975. *Site of Ambush.* Edited by Peter Fallon. Dublin: Gallery Press.

————. 1986. *The Second Voyage.* Dublin: Gallery.

O'Casey, Sean. 1949. *Collected Plays.* Vol. 2. London: Macmillan.

Ó huanacháin, Micheál. 1984. "A Few Notes on German Treatment": The Diary of Sergeant Charles Mills, Royal Munster Fusiliers, 1918. *The Irish Sword: The Journal of the Military History Society of Ireland* 15: 159–75.

Omissi, David, ed. 1999. *Indian Voices of the Great War.* London: Macmillan.

Ormsby, Frank. 1986. *A Northern Spring.* London: Secker and Warburg.

————, ed. 1992. *A Rage for Order: Poetry of the Northern Ireland Troubles.* Belfast: Blackstaff.

Orr, Philip. 1987. *The Road to the Somme.* Belfast: Blackstaff.

O'Sullivan, Seumas. 1918. *The Rosses and Other Poems.* Dublin: Maunsel.

————. 1940. *Collected Poems.* Dublin: Orwell Press.

O'Sullivan, Thaddeus. 1996. *Nothing Personal.* London: Channel Four Films.

Owens, Rosemary Cullen. 1984. *A History of the Irish Women's Suffrage Movement, 1887–1922.* Dublin: Attic Press.

The Oxford Companion to Irish Literature. 1996. Edited by Robert Welch. Oxford: Clarendon Press.

Palmer, Roy. 1988. *The Sound of History: Songs and Social Comment.* Oxford: Oxford University Press.

Parfitt, George. 1990. *English Poetry of the First World War: Contexts and Themes.* New York: Harvester Wheatsheaf.

Parker, Michael. 1993. *Seamus Heaney: The Making of the Poet.* Dublin: Gill and Macmillan.

Peacock, Alan J. 1988. Prologomena to Michael Longley's Peace Poem. *Éire-Ireland* 23, no. 1: 60–74.

Pierce, David. 1995. *Yeats's Worlds: Ireland, England and The Poetic Imagination.* New Haven, Conn.: Yale University Press.

Platt, Len. 1995. Review of *James Joyce and the Question of History*, by James Fairhall. *New Odyssey: A Journal of Joycean Studies* 1, no. 2 (Summer): 2–3.

Pound, Ezra. 1920. *Hugh Selwyn Mauberley*. N.p.: Ovid Press.

Powell, Anne, ed. 1993. *A Deep Cry: A Literary Pilgrimage to the Battlefields and Cemeteries of First World War British Soldier-Poets Killed in Northern France and Flanders*. Aberporth, Wales: Palladour Books.

Quinn, Patrick. 1994. *The Great War and the Missing Muse*. Selinsgrove, Pa.: Susquehanna University Press.

Ramsay, Patrick. 1996. Pathologically Unsound. *Fortnight* (Belfast) 346: 33–34.

Rhyme from the Trenches. 1915. *Armagh Guardian*, 22 January.

Richards, Shaun. 1991. Field Day's Fifth Province: Avenue or Impasse? In *Culture and Politics in Northern Ireland, 1960–1990*, edited by E. Hughes. Philadelphia: Open University Press.

Rolston, Bill. 1991. *Politics and Painting: Murals and Conflict in Northern Ireland*. Rutherford, N.J.: Fairleigh Dickinson University Press.

———. 1994. *Drawing Support: Murals in the North of Ireland*. Belfast: Beyond the Pale.

———. 1999. Music and Politics in Ireland: The Case of Loyalism. In *Politics and Performance in Contemporary Northern Ireland*, edited by J. P. Harrington and E. J. Mitchell. Amherst: University of Massachusetts Press.

Roper, Esther. 1929. Introduction. *Poems of Eva Gore-Booth*. London: Longmans.

Ross, Robert H. 1965. *1910–1922: Rise and Fall of a Poetic Ideal*. Carbondale: Southern Illinois University Press.

Roulston, Stewart. 1983. Past Tense, Present Tension: Protestant Poetry and Ulster History. *Éire-Ireland* 18, no. 3: 100–123.

Rowland, Thomas J. 1996. Irish-American Catholics and the Quest for Respectability in the Coming of the Great War, 1900–1917. *Journal of American Ethnic History* 15: 2. Academic Abstracts, EBSCO, item number 9602203659.

Ruane, Joseph, and Jennifer Todd. 1991. "Why Can't You Get Along With Each Other?": Culture, Structure and the Northern Ireland Conflict. In *Culture and Politics in Northern Ireland, 1960–1990*, edited by E. Hughes. Philadelphia, Open University Press.

Russell, George. (AE). 1904. *New Songs: A Lyric Selection Made by A.E.* Dublin: O'Donoghue; London: A. H. Bullen.

———. 1915. *The Gods of War*. Dublin: n.p.

———. 1917. Letter to the *Irish Times*, 19 December.

———. 1935. *Collected Poems*. 4th ed. London: Macmillan.

Russell, Jane. 1987. *James Starkey/Seumas O'Sullivan*. Rutherford, N.J.: Fairleigh Dickinson University Press.

Rutherford, Andrew. 1989. *The Literature of War: Studies in Heroic Virtue*. London: Macmillan.

Said, Edward. 1994. *Culture and Imperialism*. New York: Knopf.

Sawyer, Roger. 1993. *We Are but Women: Women in Ireland's History*. London: Routledge.

Schama, Simon. 1995. *Landscape and Memory*. New York: Knopf.

Schreibman, Susan. 1991. Introduction and notes to *Collected Poems of Thomas MacGreevy: An Annotated Edition*. Washington, D.C.: The Catholic University Press of America.

———. 1995a. The Unpublished Poems of Thomas MacGreevy: An Exploration. In *Modernism and Ireland: The Poetry of the 1930s*, edited by P. Coughlan and A. Davis.

———. 1995b. "When We Come Back from First Death": Thomas MacGreevy and the Great War. *Stand To! The Journal of the Western Front Association* 42: 15–18.

Shaw, George Bernard. 1962. *Bernard Shaw: Complete Plays with Prefaces*. Vol. 5. New York: Dodd and Mead.

Sheridan, Kathy. President and Queen to Remember Irish War Dead. *Irish Times* (Dublin), 7 November 1998 <http://irish-times.ie/>.

Simmons, James. 1968. Remembrance Day. *The Honest Ulsterman* (October).

———. 1969. *In the Wilderness and Other Poems*. Oxford: The Bodley Head, 1969.

———. 1986. *Poems, 1956–1986*. Dublin: Gallery.

———. 1992. The Trouble with Seamus. In *Seamus Heaney: A Collection of Critical Essays*, edited by E. Andrews. New York: Macmillan.

Smith, Michael. 1975. The Contemporary Situation in Irish Poetry. In *Two Decades of Irish Writing: A Critical Survey*, edited by D. Dunn. Chester Springs, Pa.: Dufour.

Smyth, Alastair J. 1980. Introduction to *My Lady of the Chimney Corner*, by Alexander Irvine. Dublin: Eveleigh Nash, 1913. Reprint, Belfast: Appletree Press.

The Somme Heritage Centre. 1996. Newtownards, N. Ireland: The Somme Association.

Southern, Neil. 1998. God or Ulster. *Fortnight* (Belfast) 374: 13–14.

Spear, Hilda D. 1979. *Remembering, We Forget: A Background Study to the Poetry of the First World War*. London: Poynter-Davis.

Stallworthy, Jon. 1969. W. B. Yeats and Wilfred Owen. *Critical Quarterly* 11: 199–214.

———. 1995. *Louis MacNeice*. London: Faber and Faber.

Stedman, Michael. 1995. *Battleground Europe: Thiepval, Somme*. London: Leo Cooper.

Stephen, Martin. 1996. *The Price of Pity: Poetry, History, And Myth*. London: Leo Cooper.

Summerfield, Henry. 1975. *That Myriad-Minded Man: A Biography of George William Russell "A. E.," 1867–1935*. Totowa, N.J.: Rowan and Littlefield.

Tamplin, Ronald. 1989. *Seamus Heaney*. Milton Keynes, England, and Philadelphia: Open University Press.

Tierney, Mark, Paul Bowen, and David Fitzpatrick. 1988. Recruiting Posters. In *Ireland and the First World War*, edited by D. Fitzpatrick.

Tinley, Bill. 1999. Two in Chapbooks. *Irish Literary Supplement* 19: 18.

Tylee, Claire M. 1990. *The Great War and Women's Consciousness: Images of Militarism and Feminism in Women's Writings, 1914–64*. Iowa City: University of Iowa Press.

Tynan, Katharine. 1915. *Flower of Youth: Poems in War Time*. London: Sidgwick and Jackson.

———. 1916. *The Holy War*. London: Sidgwick and Jackson.

———. 1918. Francis Ledwidge. *The English Review* 26 (February): 127–37.

———. 1919. *The Years of the Shadow*. London: Constable.

———. 1930. *Collected Poems*, with a foreword by George Russell. London: Macmillan.

Unterecker, John. 1959. *A Reader's Guide to William Butler Yeats*. New York: Noonday Press.

Walsh, Michael. 1929. *Brown Earth and Green*. Dublin: Talbot.

———. 1931. *The Heart Remembers Morning*. Dublin: Talbot.

Ward, Alan J. 1974. Lloyd George and the 1918 Irish Conscription Crisis. *Historical Journal* 17: 107–27.

Waterman, Andrew. 1992. "The Best Way Out Is Always Through." In *Seamus Heaney: A Collection of Critical Essays*, edited by E. Andrews. New York: Macmillan.

Weaving, Willoughby. 1916. *The Star Fields and Other Poems*. Oxford: Blackwell.

———. 1917. *The Bubble and Other Poems*. Oxford: Blackwell.

A Wee British Tommy. 1915. *Armagh Guardian*, 12 February.

Weekes, Ann Owens. 1990. *Irish Women Writers: An Uncharted Tradition*. Lexington: University Press of Kentucky.

———. 1993. *Unveiling Treasures: The Attic Guide to the Published Works of Irish Women Literary Writers*. Dublin: Attic.

Westendorp, Tjebbe. 1991. The Great War in Irish Memory: The Case of Poetry. In *The Crows Behind the Plough: History and Violence in Anglo-Irish Poetry and Drama*, edited by G. Lernout. Amsterdam: Rodopi.

White, R. S. 1995. Frederick S. Boas. In *The Dictionary of Literary Biography*. Vol. 149, edited by Steven Seraflin, Detroit: Gale.

Whyte, John. 1990. *Interpreting Northern Ireland*. Oxford: Clarendon.

Wills, Clair. 1993. *Improprieties: Politics and Sexuality in Northern Irish Poetry*. Oxford: Clarendon.

Wilson, Judith C. 1981. *Conor 1881–1968: The Life and Work of an Ulster Artist*. Belfast: Blackstaff.

Wilson, Robert McLiam. 1995. The Glittering Prize. *Fortnight* (Belfast) 344: 23–25.

Wiltsher, Anne. 1985. *Most Dangerous Women: Feminist Peace Campaigners of the Great War*. London: Pandora.

Wohl, Robert. 1979. *The Generation of 1914*. Cambridge, Mass.: Harvard University Press.

Woolf, Virginia. 1960. *Collected Essays*. Vol. 2. London: Hogarth Press.

Yeats, W. B. 1921. *Michael Robartes and the Dancer.* Dublin: Cuala Press.

————, ed. 1936. Introduction to *The Oxford Book of Modern Verse, 1892–1935*. New York: Oxford University Press.

————. 1955. *The Letters of W. B. Yeats*. Edited by Allan Wade. New York: Macmillan.

————. 1957. *The Variorum Edition of the Poems of W. B. Yeats*. Edited by Peter Allt and Russell K. Alspach. New York: Macmillan.

————. 1961. *Essays and Introductions*. New York: Macmillan.

————. 1983. *W. B. Yeats: The Poems*. Edited by Richard J. Finneran. New York: Macmillan.

————. 1989. *The Collected Works of W. B. Yeats. W. B. Yeats: The Poems*. Vol. 1. Edited by Richard J. Finneran. New York: Macmillan.

Index

303